THE
Naval
Officer's
Guide

THE
Naval
Officer's
Guide

ELEVENTH EDITION

VICE ADM. WILLIAM P. MACK, USN (RET.),
CAPT. HARRY A. SEYMOUR JR., USN (RET.),
and
CDR. LESA A. MCCOMAS, USN

Naval Institute Press
Annapolis, Maryland

First edition published in 1943

ISBN-13 978-1-55750-645-0

Library of Congress Cataloging-in-Publication Data

Mack, William P., 1915–
    The naval officer's guide / William P. Mack, Harry A. Seymour, Jr., and Lesa A. McComas. — 11th ed.
    p.   cm.
    Includes bibliographical references and index.
    ISBN 1-55750-645-0
    1. United States. Navy—Officers' handbooks.   I. Semour, Harry A., 1942–   II. McComas, Lesa A., 1958–   III. Title.
V133.M28   1998
359'.00973—dc21   98-29988

Printed in the United States of America on acid-free paper ∞

15 14 13 12 11 10 09   20 19 18 17 16

Unless otherwise noted, all photos are from official U.S. Navy sources.

CONTENTS

CONTENTS

PREFACE

The Naval Officer's Guide is a collection of information and advice for officers in the U.S. Navy, intended to serve primarily as a resource from their preparation for commissioning through their years as junior officers.

To reflect recent modifications to the Navy's organization and policies, sweeping changes in the global balance of power, and the natural growth and evolution of traditions and social norms, the eleventh edition has been completely revised and updated. Every attempt has been made to retain the original inspiration of the first author, Rear Admiral Arthur Ageton, as well as the accumulated wisdom of the other authors who have shared in the development of this book over the years.

A debt of gratitude is owed to all of the officers who helped research, review, and "sanity-check" this edition, including Lieutenant Commander Scott Armacost, USNR; Commander Tom Goodall, USN; Commander Darlene Iskra, USN; Commander Jim O'Keefe, USN; Lieutenant Colonel Norman Parlier, USA; Captain Tom Reynolds, USN; and Captain Rick Schuknecht, USN (ret.).

THE
Naval
Officer's
Guide

1

THE UNITED
STATES NAVY

SEAPOWER IS OUR HERITAGE. . . . SEAPOWER IS NOT MERELY A FLEET OF SHIPS AND
PLANES. SEAPOWER REACHES INTO EVERY PHASE OF OUR NATIONAL LIFE. IT MEANS
DOMINATION OF THE SEA AND THE AIR ABOVE IT. IN ORDER TO MAINTAIN SUCH
POWER THE FRUITS OF OUR FARMS, THE MINERALS OF OUR LAND AND THE PRODUCTS
OF OUR FACTORIES MUST FLOW INTO THE SINEWS OF MARITIME STRENGTH.

—Fleet Admiral Chester W. Nimitz

THE WIDEST USE OF THE SEA, INTEGRATED FULLY INTO OUR NATIONAL STRENGTH, IS
AS IMPORTANT TO AMERICA IN THE AGE OF NUCLEAR POWER AND SPACE TRAVEL AS IN
THOSE STIRRING DAYS OF THE BIRTH OF THE REPUBLIC.

—President John F. Kennedy

The United States Navy has served the American people with distinction and pride for more than two hundred years, in times of peace and war. The United States is fundamentally a maritime nation and has always maintained an active role in keeping open the sea lines of communication that connect us to our allies and trading partners. The recent change in the strategic landscape brought about by the fall of the Berlin Wall and the end of the Cold War marked a fundamental shift in the Navy's mission. No longer primarily focused on the open-ocean, "blue water" role in which the Navy had so successfully served as a counter to the Soviet Union since the end of World War II, today the Navy's primary role is to deter and control conflicts among smaller regional powers, and to protect vital U.S. interests and the interests of our allies around the world.

Far from creating the world peace that many had hoped for, the fall of the Soviet Union and dissolution of the Warsaw Pact have resulted in new missions and high demand for naval forces. Recent conflicts in Somalia, Haiti, and Bosnia as well as continuing hostilities amid the instabilities of the Persian Gulf region have demanded the flexibility, mobility, and rapid-response capability of U.S. naval forces.

The recent Department of Defense document *Joint Forces 2020*, the Navy publications *From the Sea* (1992), *Forward . . . from the Sea* (1994), and subsequent updates and refinements have articulated the strategic concepts designed to carry the DoD and the naval service into the twenty-first century.

Sea Power

Although sea power has been understood and exploited since the time of the ancient Greeks, who used navies and merchant shipping, the first real analyst of sea power was Admiral Alfred Thayer Mahan. Every naval officer should know something of his achievements and a lot about his philosophy. One of his most notable works was the trilogy composed of *The Influence of Sea Power upon History, 1660–1783* (1890) and *The Influence of Sea Power upon the French Revolution and Empire, 1793–1812*, 2 vols. (1892). He wrote *The Interest of America in Sea Power, Present and Future* (1897) and about thirty other volumes as well, including a biography of Nelson.

Admiral Mahan summarized what was known of sea power up to his time and did his best to predict the trends of the future. Since Mahan, many more experts have written about sea power, but none has emerged as preeminent. You will find the best of current literature on modern sea power listed in appendix 2. As a young naval officer, you may well become one of the new experts if you excel at your profession, observe well, and learn the art of written expression. The study of sea power is not a static discipline, even though certain general principles remain unchanged since Mahan's time. New theories about, and additions to, the basic principles of the functioning of sea power may provide us with the insights we need to gain the margin of victory in future years.

Definition of Sea Power. Sea power is the sum of all physical, demographic, geographic, economic, and military resources of a nation that are derived from or related to the sea and that are used by that nation to advance its political, economic, and security interests. As you study the subject, your research will reveal a dozen other definitions by as many experts. However, all agree that sea power cannot survive without the following:

1. A strong, ready navy, capable of projecting its power across the sea and ashore with combinations of surface, submarine, and

amphibious forces and carrier- and shore-based air forces, and capable of maintaining a sea-based strategic deterrent system.

2. A merchant marine that can carry overseas trade, enable the import of strategic materials, and promote the balance of trade. The ships of the merchant marine should be capable of assisting the navy in time of war, and some should be capable of rapid conversion to navy auxiliary vessels.

3. A shipbuilding industry capable of producing superior naval vessels and merchant ships in peacetime and of being expanded in wartime to meet the nation's naval and maritime needs.

4. Ports, harbors, and bases to serve and support a navy and merchant marine in peace and in war.

5. Adequate inland transportation systems linking manufacturing centers to ports and harbors.

6. A population with the seagoing temperament, fighting ability, and patriotism to man a navy and merchant marine.

7. Surrounding seas that provide both protection from possible enemies and avenues of access to those enemies and to allies and areas where strategic materials may be obtained.

The Sea Power of the United States.   The previous section set forth the essentials of sea power. How does the United States meet these criteria?

1. The United States has a strong, ready Navy. Opinions differ as to whether it is adequate in size or in readiness. It does have the ability to project power across the sea and ashore by virtue of its surface and subsurface forces, carrier air power, and Navy–Marine Corps amphibious teams, and to protect the sea lanes with its air, surface, and submarine forces. Further, its missile-equipped submarine strategic deterrent force is adequate, capable, and virtually invulnerable.

2. Our merchant marine is sadly deficient in size, capability, and readiness. We have a few good ships, but not enough to meet even the minimum export or import requirements. This is a glaring weakness in our sea power.

3. Our shipbuilding industry is inadequate. In order to build and maintain a navy large enough to project our presence to the far reaches of the world, honor our commitments to friends and allies, and protect our own strategic interests, we must have a corresponding industrial-shipyard capacity. We do not have enough shipyards qualified to build nuclear-powered ships and

submarines, or even enough shipyards to build the numbers of conventional warships and merchant ships we require.

4. Even though several important naval bases have recently closed as a result of downsizing, we are still blessed with natural harbors and have several well-developed and well-equipped ports, of adequate size and location.

5. We do have an excellent internal transportation system made up of superb highways and trucking systems, railways and railroad systems, and airports and airlines.

6. We have a population capable of manning almost any size navy and merchant marine. Our countrymen have lived by the sea, sailed and fought on it, and understood it. We love it, we use it, and we excel on it. We are truly a seagoing nation.

7. We are protected by adjacent seas from potential enemies. In order to reach our shores, any enemy must pass through large ocean areas dotted with shore and air bases. Conversely, we can approach and reach potential enemies under the protection of these same bases.

In summary, we are the greatest sea power on earth, as we were during World War II, but we must guard against deficiencies in naval forces and in shipbuilding and merchant marine capabilities.

The Navy and National Security: Prospects for the Future

Since the beginning of our history as a nation, our Navy has been a leading contributor to our national security and our military victories. More important, since World War II our Navy has been devoted to preventing wars and keeping the peace. The Navy has always been the first force to be called upon in times of crisis and the quickest to respond. We must preserve and strengthen this vital service.

Our Present Naval Posture. The readiness and mission of our military and the ability of our Navy to help maintain national security are described in posture statements by civilian and military leaders of the armed forces. One such statement is the Navy Department paper *Forward . . . from the Sea* (1994), which describes our current naval posture ("forward-deployed, ready for combat, and engaged to preserve the peace") and is reprinted at the end of this chapter.

The USS *Barry* under way in the Persian Gulf. JO2 Craig P. Strawser

Naval Operations

Operations in War.   During wartime, the Navy's primary mission is to establish control of the sea. This does not mean total control but rather control of specific regions during specific times as necessary to project power ashore and to insert and resupply forces along an adversary's coast while denying the adversary the ability to do the same. The United States accomplishes control of the sea through the following operations:

• Destroying or neutralizing enemy combatants, including ships, aircraft, submarines, and mines
• Disrupting enemy command-and-control capabilities
• Destroying or neutralizing the enemy's land-based infrastructure that supports naval forces
• Seizing choke points, islands, and other key areas in the littorals and conducting barrier operations in choke points to impair enemy mobility

Operations Other Than War. The U.S. Navy is prepared to defend the nation's interests by maintaining a credible presence abroad. Nations have the right, under international law, to provide for individual and collective self-defense. In peacetime, Navy operations in support of this right can include the following:

- Contingency operations
- Evacuation of noncombatant personnel from a hostile area
- Combatting terrorism
- Providing security assistance to other nations
- Enforcement of U.N. sanctions
- Participation in peace-support operations
- Law enforcement operations
- Participation in humanitarian assistance, disaster relief, public health, and civil support operations

The Officer's Role

Some junior officers join the Navy out of a sense of patriotism and duty; some join with the goal of obtaining education and skills to prepare themselves for civilian careers after their initial obligations are over; some enter the Navy out of the necessity of finding jobs or as a means of financing their college educations; some simply want to "see the world" before settling down into more mundane careers. If you count yourself among these latter categories, you are far from alone; few senior officers can look back on their first days in the Navy and say that they always knew they would stay for twenty or thirty years.

The Navy offers a unique opportunity to the young men and women who become commissioned officers. Regardless of your designator, within your first few years you will receive training and hands-on experience to become qualified in some technical specialty, and you will learn to lead the men and women in your charge to accomplish a mission that is of vital importance to your country. You may find yourself surprised at the magnitude of the sense of accomplishment you feel when you achieve a new milestone or are entrusted with a new responsibility, be it qualification as engineering officer of the watch, landing on the deck of an aircraft carrier for the first time, or conning your submarine out of a crowded harbor. Many of the experiences you will have over the next few years have no counterpart in the civilian world.

The opportunity for you to succeed is there, but you will have to earn your success every step of the way. When you report to your first duty station after completing your initial schooling, you may feel that your education as an officer is complete, but in fact it has only begun. From then on it will be largely up to you to find out what you need to know and set about learning it. You will be guided to some extent by the Navy's formal watch-qualification programs, and there will be many people willing to help you learn, including senior petty officers and more experienced officers, but no one will push you. You must push yourself—set goals for yourself and work at achieving them, and then set higher goals.

Some officers, as soon as they earn their initial warfare qualifications, want to slack off and relax for the remainder of their tours. If you choose to do this, you will not only be letting down your superiors and shipmates who are depending on you to take the next step in your development, but you will also be robbing yourself of the opportunity to learn something you may never have another opportunity to learn. If you find yourself in a rut, look for new opportunities; ask to be rotated to a new department, volunteer to take on a demanding collateral duty, work on a new watch qualification. This kind of initiative is the way in which outstanding senior officers begin to establish their service reputations early in their careers. As you become more senior, you should constantly have an eye on your next career milestone: selection for department head, executive officer, commanding officer, major command. For each step, find out what you need to do to be competitive for selection, and make sure you do it and do it well. Chapter 17 offers additional information on career planning. The ultimate goal of any unrestricted line officer is command at sea; as you become more senior, the Naval Institute publication *Command at Sea* will provide valuable guidance to help you work toward this goal.

From the time you receive your commission, your education and professional development are largely up to you and represent the keys to success in a very complicated and technical profession. Contrary to what you might expect, extra effort on your part will not have a negative effect on your ability to perform your regular duties; you will find, over and over, that the more you do, the more you can do. That is what this profession is all about.

Appendix: *Forward . . . from the Sea*

The following description of current U.S. naval posture is reprinted from the Navy Department paper *Forward . . . from the Sea* (1994).

Introduction

With the publication of *From the Sea* in September 1992, the Navy and Marine Corps announced a landmark shift in operational focus and a reordering of coordinated priorities of the Naval Service. This fundamental shift was a direct result of the changing strategic landscape—away from having to deal with a global maritime threat and toward projecting power and influence across the seas in response to regional challenges.

In the two years since *From the Sea* became our strategic concept, the administration has provided expanded guidance on the role of the military in national defense. A major review of strategy and force requirements resulted in a shift in the Department of Defense's focus to new dangers—chief among which is aggression by regional powers—and the necessity for our military forces to be able to rapidly project decisive military power to protect vital U.S. interests and defend friends and allies. In defining our national strategy for responding to these new dangers, the review emphasized the importance of maintaining forward-deployed naval forces and recognized the impact of peacetime operational tempo on the size of Navy and Marine Corps force structure. In addition to recognizing the unique contributions of the Navy and Marine Corps in the areas of power projection and forward presence, it restated the need for the Navy to support the national strategic objectives through our enduring contributions in strategic deterrence, sea control and maritime supremacy, and strategic sealift.

Forward . . . from the Sea addresses these naval contributions to our national security. Most fundamentally, our naval forces are designed to fight and win wars. Our most recent experiences, however, underscore the premise that the most important role of naval forces in situations short of war is to be engaged in forward areas, with the objectives of preventing conflicts and controlling crises.

Naval forces thus are the foundation of peacetime forward-presence operations and overseas response to crisis. They contribute heavily during the transitions from crisis to conflict and to ensuring compliance with terms of peace. At the same time, the unique capabilities inherent in naval expeditionary forces have never been in higher demand from U.S. theater commanders—the regional commanders in chief—as evidenced by operations in Somalia, Haiti, Cuba, and Bosnia, as well as our continuing contribution to the enforcement of United Nations sanctions against Iraq.

The Strategic Imperative

The vital economic, political, and military interests of the United States are truly global in nature and scope. In many respects these interests are located across broad oceans, and to a great extent they intersect those of current and emergent regional powers. It is in the world's littorals [that] the Naval Service, operating from sea bases in international waters, can influence events ashore in support of our interests.

Because we are a maritime nation, our security strategy is necessarily a transoceanic one. Our vital interests—those interests for which the United States is willing to fight—are at the endpoint of "highways of the seas" or lines of strategic approach that stretch from the United States to the farthest point on the globe. Not surprisingly, these strategic lines and their endpoints coincide with the places to which we routinely deploy naval expeditionary forces: the Atlantic, Mediterranean, Pacific, Indian Ocean, Red Sea, Persian Gulf, and Caribbean Sea. Reductions in fiscal resources, however, dictate that we must refocus our more limited naval assets on the highest priorities and the most immediate challenges, even within these areas of historic and vital interest to the United States.

Naval forces are particularly well suited to the entire range of military operations in support of our national strategies. They continue the historic role of naval forces engaged in preventive diplomacy and otherwise supporting our policies overseas. Moreover, forward-deployed naval forces—manned, equipped, and trained for combat—play a significant role in demonstrating both the intention and the capability to join our NATO and other allies, as well as other friendly powers, in defending shared interests. Finally, if deterrence fails during a crisis and conflict erupts, naval forces provide the means for immediate sea-based reaction. This could include forcible entry and providing the protective cover essential to enabling the flow of follow-on forces which will be deployed, supported, and sustained from the continental United States.

In short, forward-deployed naval forces will provide the critical operational linkages between peacetime operations and the initial requirements of a developing crisis or major regional contingency.

Peacetime Forward-Presence Operations

Naval forces are an indispensable and exceptional instrument of American foreign policy. From conducting routine port visits to nations and regions that are of special interest, to sustaining larger demonstrations of support to long-standing regional security interests, such as with UNITAS exercises in South America, U.S. naval forces underscore U.S. diplomatic initiatives overseas. Indeed, the critical importance of a credible overseas presence is emphasized in the President's 1994 National Security Strategy: "Presence demonstrates our commitment to allies and friends, underwrites regional stability, gains U.S. familiarity with overseas operating environments, promotes combined training among the forces of friendly countries, and provides timely initial response capabilities."

In peacetime U.S. naval forces build "interoperability"—the ability to operate in concert with friendly and allied forces—so that in the future we can easily participate fully as part of a formal multinational response or as part of "ad hoc" coalitions forged to react to short-notice crisis situations. Participation both in NATO Standing Naval Forces and in a variety of exercises with the navies, air forces, and land forces of coalition partners around the Pacific rim, Norwegian Sea, Arabian Gulf, and Mediterranean basin provides solid foundations for sustaining interoperability with our friends and allies.

Additionally, the outreach to the former Warsaw Pact countries in the NATO Partnership for Peace program will further build solidarity and interoperability. We have already made solid progress in expanding and intensifying our cooperation with the navies in Eastern Europe with exercises such as BALTOPS 94 and BREEZE 94, which included units from Bulgaria, Estonia, Latvia, Lithuania, Poland, Romania, Russia, and Ukraine.

U.S. forward-deployed naval forces have also contributed to humanitarian assistance and disaster-relief efforts—from the Philippines to Bangladesh to Rwanda—with similar, very positive, results.

Officers and crew members man the bridge aboard the USS *Josephus Daniels* as the ship prepares to depart from a port during UNITAᴗ XXXI, an annual, joint exercise between the U.S. Navy and the naval forces of nine South American countries. PH1 Michael D. P. Flynn

Although naval presence includes a wide range of forward-deployed Navy and Marine Corps units afloat and ashore in friendly nations, our basic-presence "building blocks" remain aircraft carrier battle groups (with versatile, multipurpose naval tactical aviation wings) and amphibious ready groups (with special-operations-capable Marine expeditionary units). These highly flexible naval formations are valued by the theater commanders precisely because they provide the necessary capabilities forward: ready and positioned to respond to the wide range of contingencies and available to participate in allied exercises, which are the bedrock of interoperability.

We have also turned our attention to examining the naval capabilities that could contribute to extending conventional deterrence. In this regard, forward-deployed surface warships—cruisers and destroyers—with theater ballistic missile defense capabilities will play an increasingly important role in discouraging the proliferation of ballistic missiles by extending credible defenses to friendly and allied countries. By maintaining the means to enhance their security and safety, we may reduce the likelihood that some of these nations will develop their own offensive capabilities. Our efforts will thereby slow weapons proliferation and enhance regional stability.

In addition, even as we have shifted our emphasis to forward presence and power projection from sea to land, the Navy continues to provide a robust strategic nuclear deterrent by maintaining strategic ballistic missile submarines at sea. As long as it is U.S. policy to ensure an adequate and ready strategic nuclear deterrent, our highly survivable strategic ballistic missile submarines will remain critical to national security.

Crisis Response

U.S. naval forces are designed to fight and win wars, as are all elements of our military arsenal. To successfully deter aggressors, we must be capable of responding quickly and successfully in support of U.S. theater commanders. Forces deployed for routine exercises and activities undergirding forward presence are also the forces most likely to be called upon to respond rapidly to an emerging crisis. The potential for escalation dictates that presence forces must be shaped for missions they may encounter. This provides theater commanders with credible crisis-response capabilities in the event normal conditions or outcomes do not turn out as we expect.

Building on normally deployed forces, we can mass, if the situation requires, multiple aircraft carrier battle groups into carrier battle forces, amphibious ready groups with embarked Marine expeditionary units [into amphibious task forces], and as needed project our naval expeditionary forces ashore using the afloat maritime prepositioning force. Such a massing of naval units can be complemented by the deployment of Army and Air Force complements to provide a joint force capable of the full range of combat operations that may be required.

A U.S. warship is sovereign U.S. territory, whether in a port of a friendly country or transiting international straits and the high seas. U.S. naval forces, operating from highly mobile "sea bases" in forward areas, are therefore free of the political encumbrances that may inhibit and otherwise limit the scope of land-based operations in forward theaters. The latter consideration is a unique characteristic and advantage of forward-deployed naval forces. In many critical situations, U.S. naval forces alone provide theater commanders with a variety of flexible options—including precise measures to control escalation—to respond quickly and appropriately to fast-breaking developments at the operational and tactical levels.

Whether surging from adjacent theaters or from continental U.S. deployment bases, naval forces are uniquely positioned, configured, and trained to provide a variety of responses in the event of an unexpected international crisis. Their operational flexibility and responsiveness are a matter of record.

Regional Conflict

Naval forces make a critical contribution in a major regional contingency during the transition from crisis to conflict. Forward naval forces deployed for presence and reinforced in response to an emerging crisis can serve as the transition force as land-based forces are brought forward into the theater.

Using a building-block approach, U.S. naval forces can be "tailored" with specific capabilities. The resulting naval expeditionary force—conceptually built around fleet operational forces and a forward-deployed Marine expeditionary force—can provide a highly flexible force for a wide range of missions, including long-range strike operations and early forcible entry to facilitate or enable the arrival of follow-on forces.

Focusing on the littoral area, Navy and Marine Corps forces can seize and defend advanced bases—ports and airfields—to enable the flow of land-based air and ground forces, while providing the necessary command and control for all joint and allied forces. The power-projection capabilities of specifically tailored naval expeditionary forces can contribute to blunting an initial attack and, ultimately, assuring victory. The keys to our enabling mission are effective means in place to dominate and exploit littoral battle space during the earliest phases of hostilities.

Moreover, the unique capabilities inherent in naval tactical aviation operating from our sea bases or expeditionary airfields, as well as the capability to contribute to sustained land combat operations, provide theater commanders with flexibility in the conduct of littoral operations. Throughout the twentieth century,

Marine air-ground task forces, placed ashore initially as an enabling force, have fought and contributed decisively in every major ground conflict. Similarly, naval tactical aviation has made pivotal contributions when the nation's air power was needed in combat.

In the event of a future regional conflict, U.S. naval forces will assume critical roles in the protection of vital sealift along the strategic lines of approach to the theater of conflict including the air- and sea-ports of debarkation. Our success in a major regional contingency will depend upon the delivery of heavy equipment and the resupply of major ground and air elements engaged forward. Sealift is the key to force sustainment for joint operations, and we are committed to a strong national capability.

Joint and Combined Operations

No single military service embodies all of the capabilities needed to respond to every situation and threat. Our national strategy calls for the individual services to operate jointly to ensure both that we can operate successfully in all warfare areas and that we can apply our military power across the spectrum of foreseeable situations—in peace, crisis, regional conflict, and the subsequent restoration of peace.

The enhanced combat power produced by the integration of all supporting arms that we seek to attain through joint operations is inherent in naval expeditionary forces. For example, the aircraft carrier battle group integrates and focuses diverse technologies and combat capabilities to assure the dominance of the air, surface, and sub-surface battle space necessary for the prosecution of subsequent campaigns. Further, Marine expeditionary forces, employing Marine air-ground task force (MAGTF) combined-arms doctrine, are the most versatile expeditionary force in existence. Established by law to be "forces of combined arms, together with supporting air components," MAGTFs are expeditionary, rapidly expandable air-ground formations, capable of operating from sea bases, ashore, or both, simultaneously. They are the model for the joint air-ground task forces evolving as conflicts grow smaller and the forces available grow fewer.

Naval expeditionary forces have long operated as integral elements of joint forces acting with other joint or allied sea, land, air, and space forces. Just as the complementary capabilities of Navy and Marine Corps forces add to our overall strength, combining the capabilities and resources of other services and those of our allies will yield decisive military power.

Maintaining Our New Direction

The new direction for the Naval Service remains focused on our ability to project power from the sea in the critical littoral regions of the world. We remain committed to structuring our naval expeditionary forces so that they are inherently shaped for joint operations, with the emphasis on operations forward from the sea, tailored for national needs. Recent Department of the Navy budget decisions, which resulted in a real increase in spending on littoral warfare and the means for power projection, are illustrative of the shift in priorities we have undertaken since the publication of *From the Sea*. As we continue to improve our readiness to project power in the littorals, we need to proceed cautiously so as not to jeopardize our readiness for the full spectrum of missions and functions for which we are responsible.

In the two years since *From the Sea* was published, we have expanded on and capitalized upon its traditional expeditionary focus. "Expeditionary" implies a mind set, a culture, and a commitment to forces that are designed to be deployed forward and to respond swiftly. Our new direction provides the nation:

— Naval expeditionary forces
— Shaped for joint operations
— Tailored for national needs
— Operating forward—from the sea

Conclusion

From the Sea was the initial step in demonstrating how the Navy and Marine Corps responded to the challenges of a new security environment. Our strategy and policies continue to evolve as we learn from our recent experiences and prepare for the new challenges and opportunities of this highly dynamic world. Naval forces have five fundamental and enduring roles in support of the National Security Strategy: projection of power from sea to land, sea control and maritime supremacy, strategic deterrence, strategic sealift, and forward naval presence. We will continue to carry out these roles to protect vital U.S. global interests, citizens, allies, and friends, wherever they may be at risk.

The Cold War may be over, but the need for American leadership and commensurate military capability endures. Many of our most vital interests remain overseas where the Navy and the Marine Corps are prepared for new challenges—forward-deployed, ready for combat, and engaged to preserve the peace.

2

CORE VALUES, ETHICS, AND CONDUCT

NEARLY ALL MEN CAN STAND ADVERSITY, BUT IF YOU WANT TO TEST A MAN'S CHARACTER, GIVE HIM POWER.

—President Abraham Lincoln

I AM A UNITED STATES SAILOR.

I WILL SUPPORT AND DEFEND THE CONSTITUTION OF THE UNITED STATES OF AMERICA AND I WILL OBEY THE ORDERS OF THOSE APPOINTED OVER ME.

I REPRESENT THE FIGHTING SPIRIT OF THE NAVY AND THOSE WHO HAVE GONE BEFORE ME TO DEFEND FREEDOM AND DEMOCRACY AROUND THE WORLD.

I PROUDLY SERVE MY COUNTRY'S NAVY COMBAT TEAM WITH HONOR, COURAGE, AND COMMITMENT.

I AM COMMITTED TO EXCELLENCE AND THE FAIR TREATMENT OF ALL.

—The "Sailor's Creed"

The above creed applies equally to all sailors, from seaman recruit to admiral. Although recently drafted, these words embody the traditions and values that have guided our Navy and the men and women who have served in it since its inception. As an officer, you will be expected not only to uphold the standards that apply to all members of the Navy but, in view of the "special trust and confidence" placed in you, to exceed them.

Honor Concept

Whatever your commissioning source, you have probably already been exposed to some form of honor concept or code. The "Honor Concept" used by the Brigade of Midshipmen at the U.S. Naval Academy reads as follows:

Midshipmen are persons of integrity: They stand for that which is right. They tell the truth and ensure that the full truth is known. They do not lie. They embrace fairness in all actions. They ensure that work submitted as their own is their own, and that assistance received from any source is authorized and properly documented. They do not cheat. They respect the property of others and ensure that others are able to benefit from the use of their own property. They do not steal.

The "Concept of Honor" for Naval ROTC midshipmen reads, in part, as follows:

Never before has the individual character of the American Sailor and Marine weighed so heavily on the calculus of potential conflict. For all the intrinsic excellence of our technology, experience demonstrates that its successful employment in battle continues to depend upon the integrity, courage, commitment and professional excellence of those called to bring it to bear in defense of freedom. With ruthless efficiency and finality, the awesome violence of modern warfare distinguishes forces filled with these attributes from those rendered hollow by their absence. Unlike previous conflicts in our history, technology no longer permits us the luxury of awaiting the first battle to determine whether our forces are ready. The pace of conflict will afford us little, if any, chance to profit from our mistakes.

Military systems, which often operate under extreme duress, are built on a foundation of absolute trust and fidelity. You don't learn that when you get to the fleet; you take it to the fleet. This may seem to be a harsh standard, but it's not that difficult to understand what your obligations are.

For the Naval Reserve Officers Training Corps midshipman, those obligations are succinctly stated in the following honor code:

A midshipman does not lie, cheat or steal.

These ideals were intended to serve as a foundation upon which to begin your training as a naval officer. Once you become a commissioned officer you do not become exempt from these standards but will continue to build on them throughout your career.

Core Values of the United States Navy

The U.S. Navy has established its core values of honor, courage, and commitment. These values guide both the institution and the men and women who serve.

Honor: "I will bear true faith and allegiance . . . " Accordingly, we will: Conduct ourselves in the highest ethical manner in all relationships with peers, superiors and subordinates; Be honest and truthful in our dealings with each other, and with those outside the Navy; Be willing to make honest recommendations and accept those of junior personnel; Encourage new ideas and deliver the bad news, even when it is unpopular; Abide by an uncompromising code of integrity, taking responsibility for our actions and keeping our word; Fulfill or exceed our legal and ethical responsibilities in our public and personal lives twenty-four hours a day. Illegal or improper behavior or even the appearance of such behavior will not be tolerated. We are accountable for our professional and personal behavior. We will be mindful of the privilege to serve our fellow Americans.

Courage: "I will support and defend . . . " Accordingly, we will: Have courage to meet the demands of our profession and the mission when it is hazardous, demanding, or otherwise difficult; Make decisions in the best interest of the Navy and the nation, without regard to personal consequences; Meet these challenges while adhering to a higher standard of personal conduct and decency; Be loyal to our nation, ensuring the resources entrusted to us are used in an honest, careful, and efficient way. Courage is the value that gives us the moral and mental strength to do what is right, even in the face of personal or professional adversity.

Commitment: "I will obey the orders . . . " Accordingly, we will: Demand respect up and down the chain of command; Care for the safety, professional, personal and spiritual well-being of our people; Show respect toward all people without regard to race, religion, or gender; Treat each individual with human dignity; Be committed to positive change and constant improvement; Exhibit the highest degree of moral character, technical excellence, quality and competence in what we have been trained to do. The day-to-day duty of every Navy man and woman is to work together as a team to improve the quality of our work, our people and ourselves.

Code of Conduct for Members of the Armed Forces of the United States

From the experiences of U.S. prisoners of war during past conflicts, it became apparent that the armed forces needed to provide a clear but realistic moral compass to guide the action of service members taken prisoner by hostile forces. This code applies not only to prisoners of war but also to members of the armed forces detained during peacetime by terrorists or a hostile government. The code reads as follows:

ART I. I am an American, fighting in the forces which guard my country and our way of life. I am prepared to give my life in their defense.

ART II. I will never surrender of my own free will. If I am in command I will never surrender the members of my command while they still have the means to resist.

ART III. If I am captured I will continue to resist by all means available. I will make every effort to escape and to aid others in escape. I will accept neither parole nor pardon nor special favors from the enemy.

ART IV. If I become a prisoner of war, I will keep faith with my fellow prisoners. I will give no information or take part in any action which might be harmful to my comrades. If I am senior, I will take command. If not I will obey the lawful orders of those appointed over me and will back them up in every way.

ART V. When questioned, should I become a prisoner of war, I am required to give name, rank, service and date of birth. I will evade answering further questions to the utmost of my ability. I will make no oral or written statements disloyal to my country and its allies or harmful to their cause.

ART VI. I will never forget that I am an American, fighting for freedom, responsible for my actions, and dedicated to the principles which made my country free. I will trust in my God and in the United States of America.

This code provides faith, sustenance, and inspiration, as well as guidance, to those whose service leads them into the most extreme circumstances imaginable. It is well worth your while to contemplate the code under less arduous circumstances as well, as a reminder of your responsibilities to uphold the faith that your country has placed in you.

Standards of Conduct

The following Standards of Conduct for Department of Defense employees (DoD 5500.7-R) cover the circumstances peculiar to those placed in a position of fiduciary trust:

Each employee has a responsibility to the United States Government and its citizens to place loyalty to the Constitution, laws and ethical principles above private gain. To ensure that every citizen can have complete confidence in the integrity of the Federal Government, each employee shall respect and adhere to the principles of ethical conduct as set forth in this section, as well as the implementing standards contained in this part and in supplemental agency regulations.

Navy members' duties, as well as the duties of other DoD military and civilian employees, frequently require them to safeguard the taxpayers' money, and the taxpayers deserve no less from public employees than their unwavering honesty and integrity. The following general principles apply to all DoD employees:

(1) Public service is a public trust, requiring employees to place loyalty to the Constitution, the laws and ethical principles above private gain.

(2) Employees shall not hold financial interests that conflict with the conscientious performance of duty.

(3) Employees shall not engage in financial transactions using nonpublic Government information or allow the improper use of such information to further any private interest.

(4) An employee shall not . . . solicit or accept any gift or other item of monetary value from any person or entity seeking official action from, doing business with, or conducting activities regulated by the employee's agency, or whose interests may be substantially affected by the performance or nonperformance of the employee's duties.

(5) Employees shall put forth honest effort in the performance of their duties.

(6) Employees shall not knowingly make unauthorized commitments or promises of any kind purporting to bind the Government.

(7) Employees shall not use public office for private gain.

(8) Employees shall act impartially and not give preferential treatment to any private organization or individual.

(9) Employees shall protect and conserve Federal property and shall not use it for other than authorized activities.

(10) Employees shall not engage in outside employment or activities, including seeking or negotiating for employment, that conflict with official Government duties and responsibilities.

(11) Employees shall disclose waste, fraud, abuse, and corruption to appropriate authorities.

(12) Employees shall satisfy in good faith their obligations as citizens, including all just financial obligations, especially those—such as Federal, State, or local taxes—that are imposed by law.

(13) Employees shall adhere to all laws and regulations that provide equal opportunity for all Americans regardless of race, color, religion, sex, national origin, age, or handicap.

(14) Employees shall endeavor to avoid any actions creating the appearance that they are violating the law or the ethical standards

set forth in this part. Whether particular circumstances create an appearance that the law or these standards have been violated shall be determined from the perspective of a reasonable person with knowledge of the relevant facts.

Regardless of your designator, at some point in your career it is likely that you will be placed in a position in which these standards will come into play. The circumstance may be as simple as purchasing office supplies from a civilian vendor or as complex as managing contract negotiations for a new weapon system. Regardless of the amount of money involved, your duty to place the public trust above any personal gain is paramount.

Conflicts of Interest. Navy members are prohibited from participating personally and substantially in an official capacity in any matter in which they have a financial interest, if that particular matter will have a direct and predictable effect on that interest. This prohibition also covers the interests of a spouse, child, general partner, organization in which a member serves (i.e., as a director or trustee), or anyone with whom the member is seeking or negotiating future employment.

If you find yourself in a situation in which a conflict either exists or could be perceived to exist, you are required to seek the opinion of an ethics counselor (normally a JAG officer), disqualify yourself from taking action on the matter, and provide written notice of the conflict to your superior requesting to be excused from any responsibility for decisions affecting the situation.

Outside Employment. Commanding officers generally require subordinates to obtain permission prior to seeking outside employment, and Navy members' outside employment may not interfere or conflict with their military duties. Employment by a defense contractor or any other employer doing business with the military could result in a conflict-of-interest situation (see above).

General Conduct Issues

Alcohol-Abuse Prevention. In 1996 the Department of the Navy announced the "Right Spirit" campaign, designed to deglamorize and prevent alcohol abuse in the Navy and Marine Corps. This campaign requires all leaders to set the right personal example and to establish a command climate in which the same leadership, personal responsibility, and accountability applied to other readiness areas are brought to bear to prevent the misuse of alcohol.

When the Secretary of the Navy announced this campaign, he also canceled the Navy's earlier policy, which had allowed under-age drinking at certain installations located within fifty miles of a foreign country (such as Mexico) having a lower drinking age. Under new policy, all Navy and Marine Corps installations are required to conform to the drinking age of the state or country in which they are located, but in no case may they permit drinking under age eighteen.

There may have been a perception in the past that alcohol is somehow central to some of the traditions of the Navy, or that Navy members were encouraged under certain circumstances to drink to excess. This perception is wrong. Nonalcoholic beverages must always be provided as an alternative whenever alcoholic beverages are served at a command-sponsored function, and for those who drink, moderation is expected. Any alcohol-related incident, such as a conviction for driving while intoxicated, is likely to have career-ending consequences, particularly for an officer.

Drug-Abuse Detection and Prevention.   The Navy's "zero-tolerance" policy toward illicit drug use has resulted in a 91 percent reduction in drug use during the decade 1985–95, and a Navy that today is virtually drug-free. From the time new recruits enter the Navy, they are given the message that drug use is incompatible with the Navy's high standards of performance, military discipline, and readiness. "Zero tolerance" means harsh and immediate consequences for those found to be in violation of drug-abuse policies.

The Navy's success in drug-abuse prevention is demonstrated by the fact that, despite the heavy skewing of the Navy's population toward the high-risk group of young, unmarried males, the incidence of drug use among sailors is notably lower than in the general population. Less than two-thirds of 1 percent of random drug samples test positive for any form of drugs.

The cornerstone of the Navy's success lies in the frequent, random urinalysis testing required of everyone, regardless of pay grade. You may be tasked with acting as a witness during such a test at your command, and you will certainly be tapped on a regular basis to provide samples for testing. It is your responsibility as a leader to set the example by demonstrating your whole-hearted support, regardless of whatever short-term personal inconvenience such testing may cause.

Regulations Prohibiting Fraternization.   The Office of the Chief of Naval Operations has issued an instruction, OP-

NAVINST 5370.2, *Navy Fraternization Policy,* that lays out the Navy's regulations concerning personal relationships between Navy members of different pay grades or within the same chain of command. The following is an excerpt from that instruction:

> Personal relationships between officers and enlisted members that are unduly familiar and that do not respect differences in rank and grade are prohibited and violate longstanding custom and tradition of the naval service. Similar relationships that are unduly familiar between officers or between enlisted members of different rank or grade may also be prejudicial to good order and discipline or of a nature to bring discredit on the naval service and are prohibited.

The instruction clarifies that fraternization does not pertain strictly to dating relationships between personnel of disparate pay grades. The regulation prohibits any relationship between a senior and a junior that results in, or gives the appearance of, favoritism, preferential treatment, personal gain, or loss of objectivity, or that otherwise undermines the morale and discipline of a command. This can include business relationships as well as social relationships. The responsibility for preventing inappropriate relationships rests primarily with the senior, although both members involved in such a relationship can be held accountable for their conduct.

Although marriage does not forgive any previous fraternization that may have preceded the marriage, there are legitimate circumstances under which an officer may be married to an enlisted member, as when the officer was promoted from the enlisted ranks following the marriage. Navy members who are married or have other familial relationships with personnel of different ranks or grades must maintain the requisite respect and decorum while on duty or in uniform in public.

Fraternization policy is not meant to preclude all social interaction between seniors and juniors. Command-sponsored functions, such as division or command picnics, can foster morale and esprit de corps, and it is not considered inappropriate for a senior to join a group of subordinates for an occasional celebration of an achievement or other notable event. Seniors must take care, however, to maintain the proper level of professional demeanor in all such interactions, and to ensure that their participation does not cross the line into routine socializing.

Gambling. Small wagers (e.g., card games, pools on sporting events) based on personal relationships, transacted entirely within assigned government quarters, and not in violation of local law are permissible. However, gambling is prohibited on board ship and whenever it would violate *Navy Regulations* or the Navy's policies prohibiting fraternization between seniors and subordinates.

Sexual-Harassment Prevention. Sexual harassment is defined as a form of sex discrimination that involves unwelcome sexual advances, requests for sexual favors, and other verbal or physical conduct of a sexual nature when: (a) submission to or rejection of such conduct is made either explicitly or implicitly a term or condition of a person's job, pay, or career; or (b) submission to or rejection of such conduct by a person is used as a basis for career or employment decisions affecting that person; or (c) such conduct interferes with an individual's performance or creates an intimidating, hostile, or offensive environment.

Any person in a supervisory or command position who uses or condones implicit or explicit sexual behavior to control, influence, or affect the career, pay, or job of a military member or civilian employee is engaging in sexual harassment. Similarly, any military member or civilian employee who makes deliberate or repeated unwelcome verbal comments, gestures, or physical contact of a sexual nature is also engaging in sexual harassment.

To combat sexual harassment as well as other forms of inappropriate behavior, the Navy has developed a three-tiered zone approach to classify behavior:

- Red-zone behavior is always unacceptable. This behavior includes asking for sexual favors in return for favorable supervisory decisions (termed "quid pro quo," Latin for "this for that"), making supervisory decisions based on a person's race or gender, sending "hate" mail or explicit unwanted messages of a sexual nature, and, as the most extreme example, assault.
- Yellow-zone behavior is that which would be regarded as inappropriate by most people and includes making racial, ethnic, or sexual comments or "jokes," violating personal space, or touching someone in a sexually suggestive way.
- Green-zone behavior is that which is always acceptable and includes performance counseling, normal social interaction, polite compliments, and touching **that** could not reasonably be perceived in a sexual way.

Minor infractions of a "yellow-zone" nature, particularly between peers, should normally be dealt with under the Navy's informal resolution system. Under this system, individuals have three options and may use any or all as necessary to resolve the conflict:

• Under the direct approach, the individual would approach the person whose conduct is of concern and, politely and respectfully, explain the situation and request that the individual refrain from further such conduct.

• Alternatively, a member may choose to send a letter to the offender, placing the same information in writing.

• A third alternative is for the individual to ask a third party, usually a friend or co-worker, for assistance.

When a subordinate feels threatened or intimidated by a senior's conduct, the subordinate may request redress through the chain of command. When the senior is the subordinate's immediate superior, a request chit to see the next senior member in the chain of command is appropriate.

The informal resolution system is not meant to replace disciplinary action against serious offenders. Red-zone behavior, which often represents a violation of the Uniform Code of Military Justice, should always be immediately reported to the chain of command.

To maintain a working environment free from sexual harassment, commanding officers are required to:

• Publish a command policy statement outlining the command's stance on sexual harassment

• Publish notes in the plan of the day (POD) or plan of the week (POW) to promote the Navy's zero-tolerance sexual-harassment policy

• Periodically publish and place on command bulletin boards information concerning command equal-opportunity counselors, a member's right to submit a formal or informal grievance, and the availability of legal advice

• Conduct annual sexual-harassment prevention training

Hazing Prevention.   Hazing is the mistreatment of trainees or juniors by those entrusted to oversee their training and development. It is defined as any action taken without chain-of-command approval that subjects a Navy member to physical, mental, or verbal abuse; any act, including horseplay, that could even remotely subject a member to injury, ridicule, or degradation; or any situation in which a person assumes the authority to coerce a sailor into participating in cruel, humiliating, unsafe, or meaningless conduct. Whether an individual consents or volunteers is immaterial and does not render an incident of hazing any more acceptable.

Specific actions that are clearly prohibited include "tacking on" promotions or warfare pins by pounding them into an individual's arm or chest; initiations that have not been approved and are unsupervised by the chain of command; handcuffing members to fixed or movable objects; taping or tying member's arms or legs; forced or nonconsensual cutting or shaving of hair; forced or nonconsensual removal of clothing; placing or pouring a liquid or foreign substance (e.g., grease or shoe polish) on a person or their property; requiring a person to consume substances or food not normally prepared or suitable for consumption; sabotaging the personal property of another to cause even minor injury or damage; any horseplay or minor assault upon the person of another; or any other similar act.

In short, any behavior that causes or has potential to cause an individual or group to be embarrassed, humiliated, or injured represents a serious breach of the trust the Navy has placed in the trainer or supervisor. Those in the Navy who are engaged in the indoctrination, training, or supervision of more junior members are expected to use the power of their positions wisely and compassionately, for the good of the Navy and the individuals entrusted to them.

There is a common misperception that a certain degree of hazing is an essential element of effective military training; such a perception represents a serious misunderstanding of the concept of hazing. Rigorous training and stern discipline, when used to improve the performance of trainees or junior members, remain legitimate and beneficial training tools; harassment or humiliation of trainees or juniors for the amusement and personal gratification of their instructors or seniors does not now have, and indeed has never had, a legitimate place in any training or indoctrination program.

Initiation Ceremonies. Any form of initiation ceremony must be approved by the chain of command. Two commonly authorized initiation ceremonies are crossing-the-line, for crossing the equator, and chiefs' initiations for new chief petty officer selectees. Some general rules for the conduct of such ceremonies include the following:

- The CO or his or her direct representative must personally be involved in the planning and execution of the ceremony.
- Glamorization of alcohol and alcohol abuse by participants and guests must not be tolerated.
- Sexually suggestive activities, props, costumes, skits, gags, or gifts are prohibited.
- Personal, ethnic, and religious beliefs of those in attendance shall be respected.
- There will be no coercion of Navy members to participate. Any participation by principals or guests must be strictly voluntary.
- Proper medical screening of participants is required (when appropriate for the type of event), and compliance with applicable health, safety, and environmental regulations must be part of the event planning.

3

FIRST STATION

THE DISTANCE IS NOTHING, IT IS ONLY THE FIRST STEP WHICH COUNTS.

—*The Marquise du Deffand*

WHEN YOU JOIN YOUR FIRST SHIP YOU MUST NOT LET ANYTHING DETRACT FROM YOUR DETERMINATION TO GIVE IT YOUR FULL EFFORT AND ATTENTION, BUT IF YOU ARE WORTH YOUR SALT THERE WILL ALWAYS BE IN THE BACK OF YOUR MIND THE UN-VOICED THOUGHT THAT YOU WILL COMMAND SUCH A SHIP SOMEDAY.

—*Vice Admiral Alexander Sharp*

Receipt of Orders

Receipt and Delivery of Orders.   Once in receipt of your first set of orders as a naval officer, you will want to begin to make preparations for the challenges of your new assignment. Under most circumstances, you can expect to have orders in hand at least three months before you are commissioned. Your first duty station may be the command at which you are commissioned, although you may remain there only for a matter of days or even hours after commissioning. Your first assignment after you detach from that command will likely be to a training command. Some officer communities (such as surface warfare) designate officers' ultimate duty stations on their initial orders in addition to any intermediate training commands. Other communities (such as aviation) determine an officer's ultimate duty station during the training period.

Letter to the Commanding Officer. Your first task upon receipt of your orders will be to introduce yourself in writing to your commanding officer. It is not necessary to write a letter to the CO of a training command, but it is an expected courtesy to write to the CO of your first ship, squadron, or submarine as soon as you receive your orders. Do your research before writing your letter so that you can address the CO by name. The only thing that could make a worse first impression than addressing your letter to a generic "Dear Sir or Ma'am" would be not making the effort to write at all.

In your letter you should briefly describe your background and interests and provide your planned itinerary, addresses and phone numbers where you can be reached until reporting to the command, a brief statement of your family situation, and any other relevant information. It is always a good idea to express at least a moderately appropriate level of enthusiasm for your new assignment. Even though this will likely happen without your having to ask, you should request that a sponsor be assigned to you. A sponsor is someone of a similar pay grade and community who will help you make plans to prepare for your new assignment by providing information and answering questions about the command and geographic area.

A formal but unofficial letter might read as follows:

Dear Captain Goodall,

I am in receipt of orders to USS THACH, to report in January of next year following my completion of Surface Warfare Officers School. I anticipate reporting aboard during the week of January 5.

I graduated from the University of California at Berkeley in May, with a B.S. in electrical engineering, and I hope eventually to be able to put my degree to use in the engineering department. I am currently single but plan to be married in December upon graduation from SWOS. My fiancée, Mary Beth Monroe, also a spring U.C. Berkeley graduate, plans to seek employment in the telecommunications industry. Through December 20, you may reach me at Room 213, Bachelor Officers' Quarters, Naval Education and Training Center, Newport, RI 02841, (401) 555-1000. After my graduation from SWOS, I can be reached at my parents' address, 5120 Court Rd., Ocean View, CA 94609, (408) 555-2000. I would very much appreciate being assigned a sponsor to help answer my questions about the ship and the San Diego area.

The recent article on USS THACH in "Surface Warfare" magazine was very interesting, and I consider myself fortunate to have orders to a ship with such an outstanding reputation. I look forward with great anticipation to reporting aboard.

Very respectfully,
John P. Jones
Ensign, U.S. Navy

After sending such a letter, you will normally receive a reply within a few weeks. The CO may advise you of your first assignment and may offer a few details on the command's upcoming employment schedule. In addition to providing you with a sponsor to help answer your questions, your new command should send you a packet of information to acclimate you with the command and the area. If your orders are to a ship, squadron, or other mobile command, and if the CO anticipates that the command will be away from home port at the time you are scheduled to report, you may be directed to report instead to the CO's immediate superior in command (ISIC) or to the nearest personnel support detachment (PSD) to make follow-on transportation arrangements.

Once you are in touch with your sponsor, you will have a valuable resource to help you prepare for your new assignment. Your sponsor can provide you with information on the local housing market as well as frequent updates on the command's schedule as your reporting date approaches. Your sponsor can also help you determine what uniforms you will need to obtain for your assignment.

Uniforms

Initial Uniform Requirements. Well before your date of departure you must give some thought to the uniforms you will need at your next command. The number and types of uniforms you will need depend on a variety of factors, including the command's mission, the climate, the normal working uniform and more formal uniform of the day, the availability of laundry facilities, and how easy it will be to augment your uniform wardrobe after you report. Find out as much of this information as you can from your sponsor, or from the student liaison desk at a training command; this knowledge will help you plan your purchases and packing wisely.

All major ports and training sites have uniform stores located inside Navy Exchange stores where you can purchase additional uniforms. If you are not fortunate enough to be located near a uniform store, uniforms are also readily available for mail-order purchase (Uniform Support Center Mail Order Program, 1545 Crossways Drive, Suite 200, Chesapeake, VA 23320, [800] 368-4088).

If you are not yet completely familiar with the different designations of uniforms and how they are worn, you should consult a copy of *Navy Uniform Regulations,* which is available at any command.

If you will be meeting your command on deployment, you will need to limit your initial stock of uniforms to what will fit in your baggage. You should attempt to find out in advance the climate the command will be operating in and whether there are any ceremonial or formal social events planned that would require you to bring a larger array of uniforms. Officers below the rank of lieutenant commander are not required to own either dinner dress jackets or swords, so you can easily leave these items behind without potential for embarrassment.

Officers on board surface ships normally wear working khaki; for safety reasons, this uniform is generally worn with a long-sleeved shirt. Submarine crews normally wear coveralls when under way. Both uniforms are normally worn with black socks and black leather safety shoes. Officers assigned to aviation squadrons that are not embarked aboard ship normally wear summer khaki, made from "certified Navy twill" (CNT) fabric (vice the wash-and-wear blend fabric used in working khaki), with khaki socks and brown shoes. Flight suits are worn when actually engaged in flying. Although traditionally only aviators have worn brown shoes and khaki socks, these wardrobe items are optional for all officers regardless of designator.

At a shore-based training command, you may wear some combination of service dress blue, summer white, winter blue, working khaki, and summer khaki. At a school or other shore command with ready access to laundry facilities, you may be able to get by with two sets of the normal working uniform; on board a ship you may find four sets of uniforms sufficient. In either case, you will probably find that you eventually want more than the bare minimum number of uniform changes so that you have an extra set for emergencies, and an "inspection-ready" set for personnel inspections and other special occasions.

In addition to your normal working uniform, you will probably also need two sets of summer white uniforms, one service dress blue uniform with two white shirts, one service dress white uniform, black and white dress shoes, a combination cover with white and khaki cap covers, a khaki garrison cap, and sufficient belts, ties, appropriate insignia, ribbons, and medals, black and white socks, and undergarments. (The latter should always be plain white or flesh-toned to prevent them from being visible under white uniforms.) Depending on the climate, you may also desire to bring a V-neck blue "woolly pulley" sweater, a khaki windbreaker or black jacket, and an overcoat or reefer.

Both men and women are required to wear crew-neck T-shirts with all shipboard uniforms, and for reasons of safety, CNT uniforms and shoes made of man-made materials (e.g., Corfam) are not generally worn aboard ship. Women do not wear skirts or pumps aboard ship unless prescribed for special occasions.

When reporting for duty, you should wear the uniform of the day rather than the working uniform. This is likely to be summer white in warm weather and service dress blue in cool weather, but you should consult your sponsor for the best information.

Uniform Care. Most of the uniforms you will wear on a regular basis are relatively easy to care for. If you are aboard ship, the ship's laundry will wash and press your working uniforms. Dress blues and whites must be dry-cleaned and should be stored on a wooden hanger in a plastic bag or other protective cover to preserve their appearance. When at sea, secure your hanging uniforms with the clothes clamps provided in your closet to prevent them from sliding back and forth and abrading. White plastic cap covers, which can be easily wiped clean, are normally permissible for use aboard ship and are much easier to care for than fabric covers, which must be laundered.

You will need to polish all of your shoes regularly, even your safety boots, to maintain a sharp appearance. Apply edge dressing to the edges of the soles. Shoes made of man-made materials need not be polished but can be simply wiped clean; however, this type of material is easily scratched and marred, does not stand up as well as leather to heavy use, and will need to be replaced more often.

Uniform Recognition. Prior to your commissioning, you may have come into regular contact only with members of the Navy and Marine Corps, and so you may not be familiar with the uniforms worn by other branches of the service. When determining who to salute, bear in mind that the collar devices worn in the various branches of the service are equivalent. For example, a Navy lieutenant wears the same double silver bars as an Army captain. Other rank or rate insignia may be worn on the shoulder or sleeve. Figure 3.1 shows the comparative insignia of the different services.

A distinctive feature of any uniform is the headgear. Headgear insignia and ornamentation vary according to pay grade. Figure

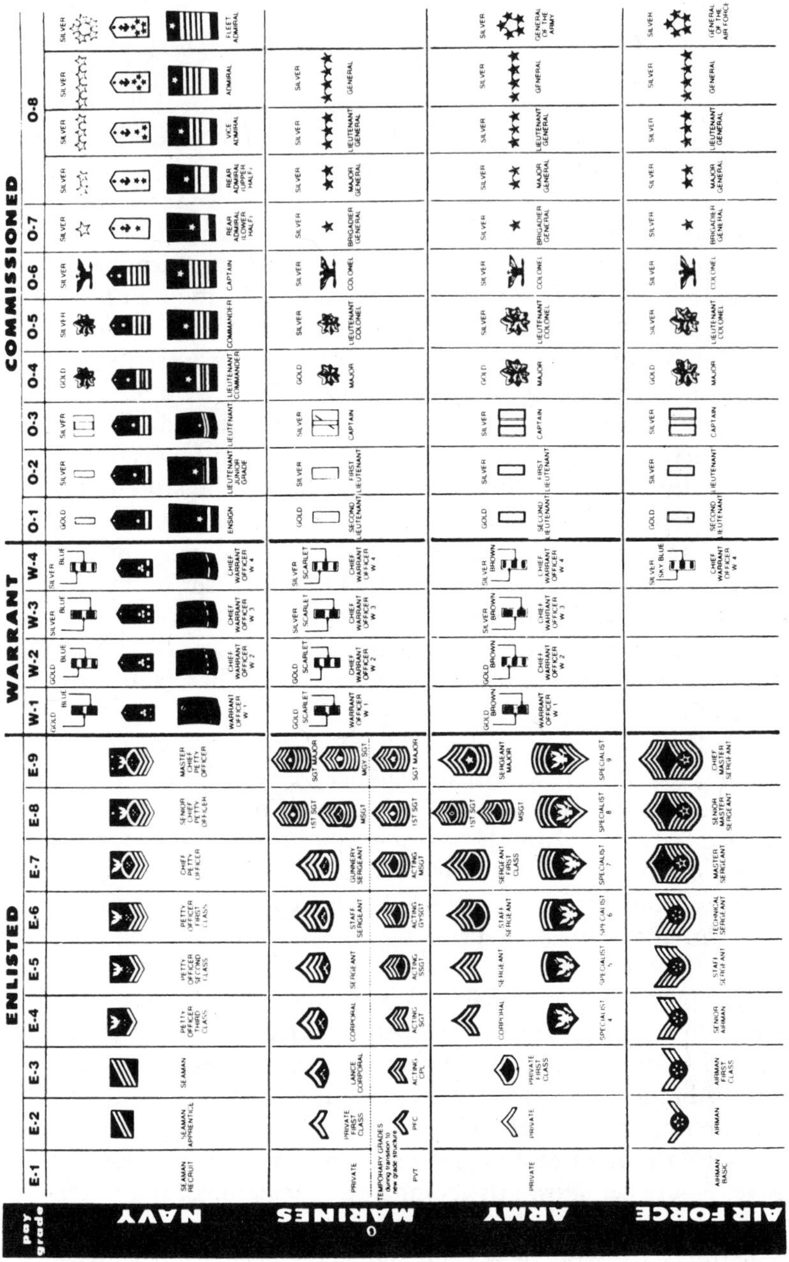

Fig. 3.1. Comparative insignia of the U.S. armed forces by pay grade.

FLAG OFFICERS   COMMANDER CAPTAIN   OTHER COMMISSIONED OFFICERS   WARRANT OFFICER NON-COMMISSIONED

HATS-ALL WOMEN

FLAG OFFICER   COMMANDER CAPTAIN   OFFICER 0-5 AND ABOVE   OFFICER BELOW 0-5

WARRANT OFFICER NON-COMMISSIONED   CPO   ENLISTED E1-E6

CAPS-MIDSHIPMEN, CPOS

MIDSHIPMEN OC AOC NAOC   CPO

CAP DEVICES-ALL OFFICERS AND CPOS

COMMISSIONED OFFICER   WARRANT   CPO   ENLISTED WOMEN E1-E6

Fig. 3.2. Headgear for men and women officers. Cap devices are the same for men and women in the same ranks. A midshipman's cap is also worn by all officer candidates. For the chief petty officer device, one, two, or three stars are added above the stock to indicate senior chief, master chief, or master chief petty officer of the Navy.

3.2 shows the variations in headgear for Navy officers and enlisted members.

In addition to the rank insignia with which you are familiar, naval officers wear different insignia on their sleeves and shoul-

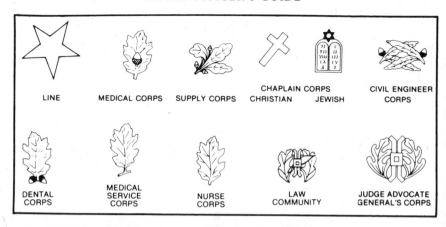

LINE   MEDICAL CORPS   SUPPLY CORPS   CHAPLAIN CORPS   CIVIL ENGINEER
                                           CHRISTIAN   JEWISH   CORPS

DENTAL   MEDICAL   NURSE   LAW   JUDGE ADVOCATE
CORPS   SERVICE   CORPS   COMMUNITY   GENERAL'S CORPS
          CORPS

Fig. 3.3. Distinguishing marks of the different officer corps.

derboards to indicate their specialties. Unrestricted and restricted
line officers wear stars, and staff corps officers display the distinguishing marks of their communities. These marks are shown in
figure 3.3. Staff corps officers also wear these marks on the right
collar instead of a rank insignia. Warrant officers and limited duty
officers display a variety of insignia depicting their designators;
figure 3.4 shows some of the more common ones.

Breast insignia, shown in figure 3.5, are used to indicate warfare designations and other specialties.

Figure 3.6 illustrates the identification badges that indicate
that a member is serving or has served in various organizations.

Permanent Change of Station (PCS) Orders

Interpretation of Orders. The Bureau of Naval Personnel (BU-
PERS), located in Memphis, Tennessee, will normally transmit
your orders by Navy message unless restrictions on sending routine message traffic (termed "minimize") are in effect. BUPERS
sends a copy of your orders to your current command, your
prospective command, the PSDs servicing each command, and
any intermediate duty stations or other commands that have an
interest in your orders. At the top of your orders are a BUPERS order number, your name, social security number, and designator,
and an indication of the BUPERS detailing code (PERS-4XXX) that
wrote the orders.

Fig. 3.4. Warrant officers' devices.

Immediately upon receipt of your orders, you should read them in their entirety to ensure that they seem correct and that you understand them. Pay particular attention to any dates listed in the message; you are expected to arrange your travel plans to ensure that you arrive at the designated locations on the dates indicated. You should promptly resolve any apparent errors or problems by bringing them to the attention of your administration officer or your detailer, as appropriate.

As previously mentioned, your first set of orders as a commissioned officer will likely direct you to report immediately for duty to the command from which you received your commission. There may be a notation to indicate your "home of record" (HOR), if your orders authorize you to ship household goods from that location rather than the location of your commissioning source. Your orders will indicate the dates or range of dates on which you are to report to any intermediate duty stations and your ultimate duty station. Your orders may also direct you to report to additional locations, such as your new command's PSD,

Fig. 3.5. Breast insignia for officers.

NAVAL PARACHUTIST

BASIC PARACHUTIST

DIVING OFFICER

FIRST CLASS DIVER

SECOND CLASS DIVER

SCUBA DIVER

COMMAND ASHORE /
PROJECT MANAGER

EXPLOSIVE
ORDNANCE DISPOSAL

Fig. 3.5. Breast insignia for officers. (continued)

for accounting purposes. Make sure you read through the entire text, as more specific reporting dates and times may be indicated farther down in the body of the message.

Your orders may advise your present command to initiate a special background security investigation. If so, and if you have not already initiated this investigation, you should report promptly to the administration or security office, as appropriate, to begin this sometimes lengthy process. If you are ordered to an overseas location, your command will be directed to complete an overseas screening process on you, as well as on any family members who will be accompanying you, to ensure that there are no medical issues or other special circumstances that would be of particular concern in an overseas location. If you plan to be married before reporting to your overseas duty station, your fiancée or fiancé will also need to be screened. In addition, depending on the laws of the country in which you will be stationed, you and your family members may need to obtain passports and/or visas.

Information on housing availability in the locations of your intermediate and ultimate duty stations may be included in your orders. You will likely be directed to report to the base housing of-

Fig. 3.6. Organization badges.

fice prior to negotiating arrangements for off-base housing. If so, you must check with this office first to determine whether there are any off-base housing facilities or landlords with whom you are prohibited from doing business. The housing office will probably also be able to provide you with listings for rental housing in the area, some of which may not be advertised to the general public. In areas in which critical housing shortages are known to exist, you may be advised to finalize your housing arrangements before moving your family.

Your orders may direct you to report "no later than" a particular date and time. If this is the case, you have the option of checking in earlier than this date, but you should do so only if you are prepared to go to work. It is usually a good idea to check in at least one day prior to the "no later than" date, particularly at a school, so that you have some time to find out what will be expected of you on the first day of class and prepare accordingly. If you are on temporary duty orders in which per diem is authorized and your orders specify a "not earlier than" date, you may check in earlier but will not be entitled to draw per diem prior to the "not earlier than" date.

Once you have established your reporting date at your next command, you should consult with your administration officer or PSD to determine the amount of travel time you will be authorized, and then count backward that number of days from your report date to determine the date you will need to check out of your present command to begin your travel. If your detaching command allows you to check out earlier than this date, any additional time you take above your authorized travel time will be charged as leave. Ordinarily new officers are permitted to take ten days of leave on their first set of orders; subsequent orders normally allow for thirty days of leave. Once you have determined the date you desire to check out, your administration office or PSD will give you some paperwork to fill out and have signed by your superiors indicating their concurrence with your plan. This paperwork will be used to draft the detaching endorsement to your orders.

When executing a set of PCS orders subsequent to your initial PCS move, you may be entitled to additional benefits. Subject to your command's authorization, you will normally be entitled to up to ten days of temporary duty, at your own expense, to househunt in the location of your new duty station. If you are reporting to or from overseas or sea duty you will also be authorized four days of additional delay in reporting not chargeable as leave, called "proceed time."

Travel

Travel Allowances.   Table 3.1, taken from NAVEDTRA 12967, lists the usual travel and transportation allowances for new commissionees. These examples cover most cases; if you have a complicated case, you should consult with your administration office or servicing PSD for assistance. You may desire to consult a copy of the *Joint Federal Travel Regulations (JFTR),* available at any

Table 3.1. Travel and transportation allowance upon first orders to a permanent station

	Naval Academy	OIS AOCS OCS	NROTC Graduates (Reserves and Regulars) and Officers Appointed from Civil Life
Personal Expenses: A predetermined rate per mile or transportation request(s) plus a daily per diem rate	May receive reimbursement either from Annapolis or from home to duty station. That is, an academy graduate who lives in San Francisco and who is ordered to New York can go (at own expense) to San Francisco and then at end of leave go to New York at government expense. This privilege is given only to Annapolis graduates on the occasion of their first orders to duty as ensigns, and then only if so specified in orders.	Entitled to travel expenses from place stated in orders to first permanent duty station; that is, an OIS graduate ordered from Newport to New York will be entitled to claim only expenses from Newport to New York—any other travel will be at own expense.	NROTC graduates appointed USN officers are entitled to travel expenses from place stated in orders (usually NROTC unit where appointed) to first permanent duty station.

NROTC graduates appointed USNR officers and officers appointed from civil life are entitled to travel expenses from place stated in orders (usually home) to first permanent duty station. |
| TRs, government vehicle, and so forth may be substituted for above without regard to the number of dependents | Entitled to travel expenses for travel actually performed not exceeding the distance from Annapolis or home (irrespective of point designated in orders) to first duty station, and dependency must exist on or before effective date of orders. | Entitled to travel expenses for travel actually performed not exceeding the distance from home address in orders to place of first permanent duty. Dependency must exist on or before effective date of orders. | Entitled to travel expenses for travel actually performed not exceeding distance from place of first permanent duty. Dependency must exist on or before effective date of orders. |

Naval Academy	OIS AOCS OCS	NROTC Graduates (Reserves and Regulars) and Officers Appointed from Civil Life
NOTE: LACK OF SPACE PREVENTS MORE THAN A LIMITED TREATMENT HERE. CONSULT JFTR AND YOUR DISBURSING OFFICER IN ALL CASES.	If marriage takes place after detachment but before the effective date of orders, entitlement will be from the place where the dependent is acquired (place of marriage) to the new duty station, not to exceed the distance from the old to the new duty station.	
	From last permanent duty station or from home to new duty station.	From last permanent duty station or from home to new duty station.
Household Goods: Entitled to shipment of 10,000 lb household goods. Does not include automobiles, baggage carried free on tickets, liquors, or articles for sale.	May elect to ship from Annapolis to home or from Annapolis and/or home to first permanent duty station. That is a privilege permitted only to Academy graduates and only upon the occasion of their first orders to a permanent station as ensigns.	

Source: NAVEDTRA 12967, table 2-2.

command as well as on the Internet (see Sources, under Internet Sites, "Per Diem, Travel, and Transportation Allowance Committee"), in order to understand the sometimes complex rules for travel entitlements as they pertain to your situation.

If your ship or squadron will be deployed away from home port when you are due to arrive, you should double-check the schedule with your sponsor or, if that is not possible, with the command's ISIC or type commander (e.g., SURFPAC, SUBLANT) before finalizing your travel arrangements.

The Navy will either furnish you with transportation or reimburse you for travel that you furnish yourself, or some combination of the two (e.g., if you drive your own car to your ship's home port, then fly to meet the ship in its deployed location). For those portions of travel in which you drive your own vehicle, you will be reimbursed 15 cents per mile and $50 per day to pay for lodging and meals. Your allowable mileage is based on the official distance between your old and new duty stations, not the number of miles you actually travel. You will be authorized one day of travel for every 350 miles and a day for any remainder greater than 50 miles. If your dependent family members travel with you to your new duty station, you will receive additional allowances of 2 to 5 cents per mile (depending on the number of dependents) plus $37.50 per day for dependents over the age of twelve and $25 per day for younger children. Normally, unless unusual circumstances require you to travel separately from your dependents, you will be entitled to mileage for only one vehicle. If you and your family own more than one car, you will probably be required to move the second vehicle at your own expense.

If you travel on a government aircraft or on a commercial aircraft with a government-purchased ticket, you will normally be allowed one day of travel time (or longer, if the trip actually takes longer) to reach your destination and will be allowed per diem as appropriate.

In addition to the above travel allowances, in most cases members executing PCS moves are entitled to a dislocation allowance. Members executing their first set of active-duty orders are not entitled to a dislocation allowance; nor are members executing retirement or separation orders.

Travel Claims.   You will normally be entitled to draw an advance in the amount of 75 percent of your anticipated travel and per diem allowances prior to commencing travel. Once you and

Table 3.2 Joint Federal Travel Regulations weight allowances (in pounds)

Paygrade	PCS without Dependents	PCS with Dependents	Temporary Weight Allowance
O-10	18,000	18,000	2,000
O-9	18,000	18,000	1,500
O-8	18,000	18,000	1,000
O-7	18,000	18,000	1,000
O-6	18,000	18,000	800
O-5	16,000	17,500	800
O-4/W-4	14,000	17,000	800
O-3/W-3	13,000	14,500	600
O-2/W-2	12,500	13,500	600
O-1/W-1	10,000	12,000	600

your family have arrived at your duty station, you must promptly file a travel claim form with your administration office or servicing PSD. Failure to document your travel properly by filing this form will not only prevent you from receiving the balance of any travel entitlements but will also eventually result in the Defense Finance and Accounting Service taking action to recoup your advance payment. You may file a supplemental claim if your family travels at a later date.

Moving Your Household Goods

As soon as you receive your orders you should contact your closest personal-property transportation office to make arrangements for shipping your household goods and other personal property. When you go to the office for your appointment, bring ten copies of your orders (and any modifications) with you.

Weight Allowances. The maximum weight that can be moved at government expense for each pay grade and dependency status is indicated in table 3.2. The allowance includes the weight of household goods shipped, placed in storage, or sent as unaccompanied baggage. If you exceed your maximum weight allowances, you will be held responsible for the additional costs. For this reason it's a good idea to estimate the weight of your household-goods shipment well in advance of the move, and to sell or give away any excessively heavy items (such as older appliances) that you can replace more inexpensively than you can move. An easy and fairly dependable estimating method is to figure one thousand pounds per room (not including bathrooms), then add the estimated weight of large appliances and items in the garage, storage rooms, and the basement. If you have a large library of books, weight-training equipment, or other heavy items, you should also take this additional weight into account.

Authorized Items.   You may move your household furnishings, appliances, equipment, clothing, personal effects, professional books, papers, and spare parts for a privately owned vehicle including a motorcycle. Some items are not authorized to be moved at government expense, including vehicles, hot tubs, and other unusually heavy or bulky items. In addition to your household goods, you will generally be authorized to ship one automobile to an overseas duty station.

Storage.   The government provides two types of storage: temporary and nontemporary. Temporary storage can run for up to ninety days. It can be used at point of origin, en route, or at your destination. You can obtain an additional ninety-day emergency extension by submitting a formal request in writing. Service members are expected to pay for any temporary storage time exceeding the 180-day period. Nontemporary storage is long-term storage authorized in specific cases, such as an overseas assignment.

Overseas Shipments.   Your entitlement is limited to two thousand pounds, or 25 percent of your household-goods weight allowance, whichever is greater, when the shipment is to or from an overseas station where public quarters or private housing is furnished with government-owned furnishings.

Do-It-Yourself (DITY) Moves.   Instead of having your household goods shipped by a commercial moving company, you may elect to move some or all of your household goods yourself. If you perform a DITY move, you will be reimbursed for 80 percent of the amount the government would have paid a moving company to do the same job, based on the weight of your shipment and the distance it is moved. A DITY move can be an attractive alternative for several reasons: you won't have to wait for delivery at your new duty station, you will be able personally to safeguard and protect your valuable and fragile items, and you can pick up a little extra money. Bear in mind, however, that any amount you earn on a DITY move in excess of your actual expenses (van rental, mileage, etc.) is considered taxable income.

Housing

Whether you are single or have a spouse or other family members, you will have to make a decision whether to seek government quarters or to find your own housing in the civilian market. As an officer, even when you are provided with government quarters (such as your stateroom aboard ship), you have the right to decline such quarters and elect to live elsewhere. If you do so, it is expected that you will "live" (i.e., sleep) in your government-provided quarters only as necessary to the performance of your duties.

Government Quarters. For single officers, government quarters ashore normally consist of a room or suite in the bachelor officers' quarters (BOQ). These quarters may be spartan or luxurious, depending upon your rank as well as the age and design of the building. In most cases a BOQ room will include a private bath and small kitchenette with compact refrigerator and microwave, but no extensive cooking facilities. BOQs also normally provide laundry facilities to residents free of charge. The advantages of living in a BOQ are that it is probably closer to your duty station than you would otherwise be able to live (in many cases you may be able to walk or bicycle to work), and living in the BOQ is uncomplicated. A resident of the BOQ doesn't need to purchase a large assortment of furniture, appliances, and household goods, or to pay utility bills (except for telephone charges). The primary disadvantage of such quarters is that your room in the BOQ will almost certainly be smaller, more austere, and less homelike than an apartment or home you would choose and furnish according to your own tastes and preferences.

Officers who are married or have other dependent family members are entitled to live in government family housing. In some areas where such housing is scarce, there can be a lengthy wait, perhaps up to a year or more, making it an impractical alternative for a relatively short tour. If you are considering the option of residing in government family housing, ask your sponsor to help you determine in advance if there is a waiting list and what the procedure is to get on it. Junior officer family housing generally consists of a small house, duplex, or townhouse on base or in a nearby housing area. In some areas the Navy leases housing from private owners for the use of members. As in the BOQ, utilities (except for telephone) are provided with the quarters.

Civilian Housing. If you elect to seek civilian housing, before beginning your search check first with the base housing office to find out if there is any prohibited housing. In lieu of government quarters, you will be authorized basic allowance for housing (BAH), the amount of which is based on your pay grade, local housing costs, and whether or not you have dependents. It is a good idea to find out how much housing allowance you will be entitled to before beginning your housing search. Bear in mind that in addition to your rent or mortgage payment you will also have to keep room in your budget for utilities, insurance, and commuting expenses. If you are considering living in an outlying suburb, you may want to test-drive your commute during rush hour before committing yourself to a lease or purchase.

If you decide to rent a house or apartment, make sure your lease includes a "military clause" allowing you to terminate the lease with no penalty if you receive orders out of the area. This is not a guaranteed protection for military members unless it is explicitly stated in the lease, but most landlords are more than happy to agree to this clause if asked.

If you are considering the purchase of a home, carefully weigh such variables as the strength of the local market, the length of your tour, and the likelihood that you will be able to remain in the area or return to it on a subsequent tour. In most cases, even in a rising market, if you sell a home you have owned for only two or three years, you will see a loss due to all of the one-time fees, taxes, commissions, and other expenses associated with purchasing and selling real estate. If you do purchase a home you intend to live in over the span of several tours, make sure you take into account the possibility that the size of your family will increase in the interim.

Spouse Employment

If you are married and your spouse plans to work outside the home, you will have the added task of helping him or her find suitable employment in your new area. The family service center at your new base may be able to provide your spouse with advance information on the local job markets, and in many areas spouses' clubs provide a valuable additional networking resource.

Necessary Paperwork

Before detaching from your commissioning source, you should have in your possession a copy of your orders, any modifications to them, and a detaching endorsement from the command indicating the date you checked out. You should have an active-duty identification card for yourself as well as dependent identification cards for your spouse and family members. You will need to provide marriage, birth, and adoption records to the PSD issuing ID cards to your family so that they can validate their eligibility. At the time ID cards are issued, your family will automatically be registered in the Defense Enrollment Eligibility Reporting System (DEERS) so that they will be eligible to receive military healthcare services. Chapter 4 discusses health-care options for dependents in more detail.

Reporting Aboard

Advance Preparations.   Whenever possible, it is a good idea to arrive in your new home port, or other port where your ship is located, at least one day in advance. This will allow you to confirm the ship's location and schedule, get your uniforms in order, and be sure that you are ready to report aboard in the morning. It is always a good idea to try to report aboard prior to 0900, as checking in after 0900 will result in your being charged an additional day of leave. If meeting your ship in a foreign port with limited pier facilities, you may need to make arrangements to take a small boat out to where the ship is anchored.

When reporting for the first time, it is best to avoid bringing unnecessary baggage. If the ship's schedule permits, you will find it much easier to leave large bags in the BOQ or at your new home and bring them aboard at a later time when you will have more opportunity to unpack. If you must bring your bags aboard right away, and it appears safe and convenient to do so, you may leave them on the pier or in the ship's boat while you check aboard. If the officer of the deck (OOD) is expecting you, he or she may be alert to your arrival and send a messenger to help carry your bags. In any case, you should have with you your orders and endorsements and your service, medical, dental, and physical-readiness records. Carry these in your left hand so that your right hand is free for saluting.

Procedure. As you approach the quarterdeck, stop at the head of the brow and if the ensign is flying, turn to face the stern of the ship, stand at attention, and salute. Then, turn to face the OOD, salute, and say, "Sir (or Ma'am), I request permission to come aboard." The OOD will not always be an officer; frequently it will be a chief or senior petty officer. Nevertheless, you always salute and say "Sir" (or "Ma'am")—the courtesy is to the position, not to the individual. After the OOD returns your salute and grants permission to come aboard, you will say, "Ensign (name) reporting for duty, sir (ma'am)." You will need to furnish your ID card and orders to the OOD so that he or she may properly note your arrival in the deck log. The OOD will then likely have the messenger of the watch show you to the XO's office, administration office, or other designated location to complete the remainder of your check-in process.

The procedures for checking in at a shore command vary widely. Shore commands without a formal quarterdeck and watch officer may direct you to the administration office to check aboard. If in doubt as to the procedure, query your sponsor prior to your arrival.

4

PERSONAL ADMINISTRATION

YOUR PERSONAL RECORDS ARE YOU, AS FAR AS THE NAVY IS CONCERNED, UNTIL YOU HAVE HAD TIME TO CREATE A SERVICE REPUTATION. THEREFORE, MAKE SURE YOUR RECORDS ARE COMPLETE, ACCURATE AND INCLUDE ALL OF YOUR QUALIFICATIONS AND ACHIEVEMENTS.

—Admiral Chester Nimitz

A FEW MOMENTS SPENT TAKING CARE OF YOUR DEPENDENTS' AFFAIRS WILL GIVE YOU PEACE OF MIND AND YOUR LOVED ONES A SETTLED FUTURE.

—Vice Admiral Charles Melson

Officer Records

Of all the responsibilities you will hold in your career, none will be more uniquely important to you than the proper maintenance of your personal records and those of your family members. These records will play a key role in your personal and professional success.

Service Record. This is a paper record that you will be responsible for hand-carrying with you to your command. Your command's administrative office, or designated personnel support detachment (PSD), will maintain your service record. Your service record contains information on your assignment history, personal awards, family data and Servicemen's Group Life Insurance beneficiary information, and other key data. Unlike enlisted service records, it does not contain copies of your fitness reports. Individuals in your administration office or chain of command may review your record if they have a need to do so as part of their official duties.

Medical and Dental Records. The medical department on board your ship, or the nearest Navy medical and dental clinics, will normally maintain your medical and dental records. Before checking out of your command, you will need to pick up these records so that you can hand-carry them to your next duty station. Each time a medical or dental clinic provides you with treatment, the health-care provider will make an appropriate notation in your record. If the clinic refers you to another facility for specialty care, you must check out your medical record and take it with you to your appointment so that the specialist can review your record of treatment. Your medical record will also include a separate shot record to enable your medical department or clinic to determine quickly when you are due for new immunizations.

Because your health record is government property, you must surrender it to the appropriate office rather than maintain it yourself. For this reason, whenever you are treated for anything significant, it is a good idea to make copies of the appropriate pages of your medical record and retain them in a safe place for future reference in the event that your record is ever misplaced.

In addition to these hard-copy medical and dental records, the Bureau of Medicine and Surgery (BUMED) maintains a master record. This record generally includes only the results of your required physical exams.

Your Microfiche Record. The Bureau of Naval Personnel (BUPERS) maintains a microfiche personnel record for every active-duty Navy member and reservist. An officer's personnel record is a compilation of up to five separate microfiche pages designated fiche 1 through fiche 5, although not everyone has a fiche 5. Officers who had prior service as enlisted members have an additional record consisting of fiche 1E through fiche 3E, reflecting information on the period of their enlisted service. Each fiche is designated with the officer's name, social security number (SSN), and fiche number.

One to three months before the convening date for a board, the selection board office at BUPERS begins reviewing records of officers who will be considered by that board. At least six months prior to your consideration by any selection board you should review your microfiche record for accuracy and completeness. You may do this in person at the Bureau of Naval Personnel (PERS-313C1), or you may request that a copy be sent to you by mail, using NAVPERS form 1070/879. When ordering a copy of your fiche, ensure that you include a correct return address, telephone number, name, rank, SSN, and signature. You may not order your microfiche record by phone, e-mail, or the Internet because your signature is required for its release.

The following is a description of each of the fiche files. Active-duty promotion boards screen fiches 1, 2, and 5, while reserve boards screen fiches 1, 2, 4, and 5.

- Fiche 1: Photo, five rows of fitness reports, and two rows of awards. Trailer fiches contain any additional fitness reports or awards (which are numbered T1, T2, etc.). Letters of commendation are not retained in the microfiche record. If you have such letters and your fitness reports did not make note of them, you may forward copies to the selection board as enclosures to a letter to the board president.

- Fiche 2: Education (transcripts, diplomas, military correspondence courses); qualifications (designator qualifications—not command qualifications such as OOD, CDO, etc., which should be noted in fitness reports); appointments and promotions; reserve status (USNR appointment, reserve officer performance record); service determination (statements of service, discharge documentation, separation letters); miscellaneous professional history.

- Fiche 3: Security/personal history; record of emergency data; record changes (such as SSN or name changes); personal background data (such as home of record, casualty data); miscellaneous personal data (medical forms, physicals, Servicemen's Group Life Insurance beneficiary form).

- Fiche 4: Orders (new appointment, first duty, inactive duty, active duty for training, recalls to active duty, separation).

- Fiche 5: Privileged information (medical board cover letters, POW data, adverse data—nonjudicial punishment letters, administrative or punitive letters, detachment for cause). Not everyone will have a fiche 5. Almost any adverse entry in fiche 5 can negatively affect an officer's chances for promotion.

Duty-Preference Card.   Two officers at BUPERS are directly involved in every set of orders you receive: your detailer and the placement officer who represents your next command. Your detailer is your representative in the negotiating process with the placement officer. Well in advance of the date you expect to transfer, you should establish communications with your detailer to make sure he or she is aware of your particular desires for your next set of orders, and that you are aware of the billets that are likely to be available, taking into consideration your qualifications, experience, and career progression needs. Chapter 17 discusses this process in greater detail.

Prior to discussing your preferences with your detailer, you should file a preference card, listing your preferred billets, geographic areas, and commands, to allow your detailer to research the options available to you. The duty-preference card can be an actual card that you fill in and mail, or you may submit the same information electronically via e-mail.

Officer Data Card (ODC). BUPERS produces the officer data card from the active-duty naval officer automated record. The ODC provides up-to-date information in an easy-to-use format that detailers and placement officers use in the distribution process. Additionally, BUPERS uses the ODC to provide information for the cover sheet of the performance summary record (PSR).

The ODC, which used to be printed on a long green card, is now printed on plain white paper. BUPERS forwards an ODC once each year to every officer on active duty. When you receive your ODC, review it carefully for accuracy and determine whether any updates or changes are necessary. Circle items requiring correction in red and indicate the correct information on the back of the form. To make corrections, you must return the ODC to the appropriate BUPERS code along with substantiating documentation (certified copies of appropriate documents). If no corrections are required, your administration office will place the ODC in your service record with a signed annotation that it has been verified as correct.

Full-Length Photograph. Within three months of your acceptance of each promotion, you must submit a full-length photograph to BUPERS attached to NAVPERS form 1070/10. This photograph must be taken in khakis, three-quarter face, with your name, designator, and social security number and the date of the photograph displayed on a board in the foreground.

The purpose of this photograph is to allow a selection board to evaluate your general level of physical fitness and military bearing. When having your photograph taken, it pays to take extra care, making sure that your uniform is clean, neatly pressed, and properly aligned. If you are in doubt about your appearance in a photograph, before mailing it in you may find it worthwhile to have it honestly evaluated by another officer whose judgment you trust.

Fitness Reports (FITREPs).   The Navy requires that all officers and enlisted personnel be regularly and formally counseled on their performance. For officers and senior enlisted personnel, these evaluations are called fitness reports.

BUPERS changed the fitness report format in 1996 in an effort to combat the "grade creep" that led to the perception that the only acceptable report was one with greatly inflated performance marks. A "perfect" fitness report is no longer a common occurrence, and in fact few officers are likely ever to receive one under the new system. The fitness report system evaluates every officer in each of the following areas:

- Professional expertise
- Equal opportunity
- Military bearing/character
- Teamwork
- Mission accomplishment/initiative
- Leadership

Performance traits are measured on a five-point scale, from 1.0 ("below standards") to 5.0 ("greatly exceeds standards"). A grade of 3.0 ("meets standards") represents performance to full Navy standards, with higher grades reserved for performance that significantly exceeds those standards. Reporting seniors must justify all grades of either 1.0 or 5.0 with explicit comments.

The FITREP form also provides a five-step promotion recommendation scale: "significant problems," "progressing," "promotable," "must promote," and "early promote." A recommendation of "early promote" does not require the officer receiving it actually to be eligible for early promotion, nor does it guarantee such promotion. Officers of the same pay grade and designator in a single command are ranked against each other in the same competitive group. There are strict limits on the number of officers within a competitive group who can be ranked in the top two promotion categories: a maximum of 20 percent of any group may be categorized as "early promote," and for pay grades above O-2, a maximum of 40–50 percent (depending on pay grade) may be in the combined categories of "early promote" and "must promote."

Because of space constraints, comments on a fitness report must be brief and succinct. A well-written fitness report contains comments, written in bullet form, that are fact-based and specific, and that reflect quantifiable or documented achievements.

To enable a promotion board to evaluate fairly an officer's fitness report grades, the reporting senior's average fitness report grade is provided to the board. This practice also helps to prevent grade inflation; a 4.0, "above standards" grade from a CO whose average grade is 3.3 will carry much more weight with a selection board than one from a CO whose average grade is 4.5.

Pay and Allowances

Types of Compensation. The two broad categories of regular compensation are pay and allowances. In general, pay is taxable and is intended to compensate members for the performance of duty. Allowances are generally not taxable and are intended to reimburse members for certain costs, such as for meals, lodging, or travel.

Pay. The primary component of the pay for most military members is basic pay. The amount of basic pay, which is set in law, is based on pay grade or rank and years of service, and the same pay table is used for all of the uniformed services. Basic pay is augmented by special pays for certain types of duty, such as sea pay, submarine pay, flight pay, hazardous duty pay, command responsibility pay, and special duty assignment pay. Additional types of pay, such as medical and dental pay, aviation and nuclear retention bonuses, and reenlistment bonuses, act as an incentive to help retain officers and enlisted personnel who have specialized skills.

Allowances. Basic allowance for subsistence (BAS) compensates members for the costs of food when a government mess is not provided.

In lieu of government quarters, you will be authorized basic allowance for housing (BAH), based on your pay grade, dependency status, and actual local housing costs. It is a good idea to find out what the local BAH rate is before beginning your housing search so that you know what kind of quarters you can afford. In principle, BAH should reimburse a typical officer or enlisted member for 85 percent of out-of-pocket housing costs (including utilities) in a given geographic area.

Another common type of allowance is the cost-of-living allowance (COLA). These allowances compensate military members for the cost-of-living differential (exclusive of housing expenses) in high-cost areas either overseas (COLA) or in the continental United States (CONUS COLA).

When Paid.   Payday for all members falls on the first and fifteenth of each month. When the first or fifteenth falls on a Sunday or holiday, payday is held the day before.

Pay Increases.   The basic pay tables are designed to provide periodic pay raises (often called "fogeys"), normally every two years. Your pay raise dates are based on the anniversary date of your entry into active duty, called the pay entry base date (PEBD), or simply pay date. You will also receive significant increases in pay each time you are promoted to a higher rank. In addition, Congress normally authorizes an annual cost-of-living increase, which takes effect on January 1. Housing allowances are also adjusted annually, based on the housing costs in each geographic area.

Direct Deposit.   Rather than receiving an actual check on payday, you will be required to have your pay deposited directly into your bank account. This saves the government the effort and expense of drafting and distributing paychecks. Because pay is always deposited one day before payday, it allows you and your spouse rapid access to your funds even when you are on deployment.

Allotments.   You may withhold set amounts from your pay for charitable contributions to the Navy and Marine Corps Relief Society or Combined Federal Campaign, to make loan or insurance payments, or for deposits to bank accounts or other investments. Amounts withheld for these purposes are automatically transferred to the designated recipients.

Pay Record.   The Defense Finance and Accounting Service maintains all pay records electronically. Each month (normally on the midmonth payday) you will receive a leave and earnings statement (LES) that reflects your compensation and leave activity over the previous month. After reviewing your LES, store it in a safe place for at least several years in case any later question concerning your pay should arise. As of early 1998, the Navy converted to a new pay system called the Defense Joint Management System (DJMS), the same pay system shared by the Army and Air Force.

Figure 4.1 shows a sample LES. The information on the statement is organized as follows:

DEFENSE FINANCE AND ACCOUNTING SERVICE MILITARY LEAVE AND EARNINGS STATEMENT

ID	|Name (Last, First, MI)	|SSN	|Grade| PyDate |Yrs| ETS	|Branch|ASDN OSSN|Period Covered
			|930921| 04|970920| Navy|	1-30 SEP 97

	ENTITLEMENTS		DEDUCTIONS		ALLOTMENTS		SUMMARY	
	TYPE	AMOUNT	TYPE	AMOUNT	TYPE	AMOUNT	*Amt Fwd	.00
A	BASE PAY	1245.60	FEDERAL TAXES	120.57				
B	BAQ	285.00	FICA SOC SECURITY	77.23			*Tot Ent	
C	BAS	220.80	FICA MEDICARE	18.06				
D	VHA	178.00	STATE TAXES	21.67			*Tot Ded	
E	ADVANCE PAY	5000.00	SGLI FOR 100,000	8.50				
F			REPAY ADVANCE	70.83				
G			ADVANCE PAY					
H			STATUS DET					
I			MID MONTH PAY					
J								
K								
L								
M								
N								
O								
		Total						

	BfBal	Ernd	Used	CrBal	ETS Bal	Lost	Paid	UseLose	Fed	WagePeriod	WageYTD	MS	EX	Addl Tax	Tax YTD
Leave	19.0	30.0	36	13.0	12.5	.0	.0	.0	Taxes	1245.60	12218.23	S	01	.00	1236.81

FICA	WagePeriod	WageYTD	Tax YTD	Med Wg YTD	Md Tx YTD	STATE	St	Wg Period	Wage YTD	MS	EX	Tax YTD
Taxes	1245.60	11210.40	695.05	11210.40	162.55	TAX	OH	1245.60	11210.40	S	01	233.30

PAY DATA	BAQ Type	BAQ Depn	VHA Zip	Rent Amt	Share	Sto	JFTR	Depns	2d JFTR	BAS Type	Charity	Tpc	Pacidn

Remarks:

YTD ENTITLE	6929.40	YTD DEDUCT	316.86

STATUS DETERMIN XLDPAY BAL	1441.25	|REPAY ADVANCE DEBT BAL	566.68
TOTAL INDEBTEDNESS	5000.0 (262)	|RATE CHG BASIC PAY	970901 (244)
ADVANCE PAY	970910 (256)	|STOP DISCRETIONARY ALLOTMENT	9708 (266)
STOP BANK ACCOUNT ALLOTMENT	9708 (266)	|STOP BANK ACCOUNT ALLOTMENT	9708 (266)
HELD PAST ETS	970921 (266)	|START HELD PAY-STATUS	970923 (266)
BAH BASED ON W/O DEP, ZIP		|ACCT #	

Fig. 4.1. Sample leave and earnings statement.

• The top section includes your name, social security number, pay grade, pay date (date of entry into active service), years of active service, and the period covered (normally one month).

• The entitlements section includes the types of entitlements you are receiving (e.g., base pay, BAS, etc.), their amounts, and the total amount of entitlements.

• The deductions section includes the types of deductions taken from your pay (state and federal taxes, etc.), their amounts, and the total amount of deductions.

- The allotments section includes the types of allotments withheld from your pay (e.g., withholdings to make loan payments), their amounts, and the total amount of allotments.

- The summary section adds the amount carried over from previous unpaid pay and allowances to the current month's entitlements and subtracts the total deductions and allotments to arrive at the net pay amount. This amount, less any amount to be carried forward to the next month, represents your net pay.

- The leave section includes the leave balance brought forward from the beginning of the fiscal year or your first day of active duty, whichever was later; the amount of leave earned during the reporting period (2.5 days per month); the amount used during the reporting period; any leave lost during the period (under most circumstances, any unused leave in excess of sixty days is lost at the end of the fiscal year); leave paid to date (military members may not be paid for more than sixty days of accrued leave during a military career; officers may sell back leave only at retirement or separation); and leave projected to be lost if not taken in the current fiscal year.

- The federal tax section includes wages earned during the current reporting period that are subject to federal income tax withholding (FITW); FITW wages earned to date; marital status; number of exemptions; additional taxes withheld in excess of the calculated amount from the appropriate tax tables; and cumulative total of FITW withheld throughout the calendar year.

- The FICA tax and state tax sections contain similar information for these taxes.

- The pay data section includes the type of BAH entitlement (with dependents/without dependents/partial, etc.); a letter code indicating the type of dependents for which BAH is paid; the zip code used to compute BAH; the amount of your monthly rent or mortgage payment; the number of individuals (exclusive of dependents) sharing the housing cost; the number of your dependents; the type of BAS (left blank for officers); cumulative charitable contributions for the calendar year; and the unit identification code used to represent your command.

- The remarks section contains additional information, including the cumulative total of all entitlements for the calendar year, cumulative total of all deductions for the calendar year, and other pertinent facts and announcements.

It is your responsibility to review your LES carefully and to report any errors or questionable entries to your disbursing officer or PSD promptly. Whenever an error in an officer's pay account occurs and the officer had received an LES for that period, the Navy assumes that the officer had sufficient understanding of the pay system to have been aware that the error occurred. (The same assumption is not always made for enlisted personnel.)

Travel Expenses. Whenever you are ordered to travel, either in conjunction with a permanent change of station (PCS) or for a brief period as temporary additional duty (TAD), you will be authorized certain travel entitlements, including mileage (if you are authorized to use your own vehicle), lodging and meal costs (per diem), and incidental expenses. If you are required to fly on a commercial airline, the government will normally provide you with a plane ticket directly.

Although you may be authorized to receive some portion of your anticipated expenses in advance, this is becoming a less common practice. Frequent travelers are provided with credit cards to use for their travel expenses. All travelers must file detailed travel claims, including certain receipts, upon completion of travel in order to receive compensation.

Medical Benefits

Although all active-duty members are eligible to receive treatment at military clinics and hospitals, dependents and retirees may have limited access to these facilities, depending on the demand in the local area. The TRICARE system was designed to ensure that adequate health care would be available to all dependents and retirees. Beneficiaries have three options for seeking care under the TRICARE program, each with a different cost-sharing feature and level of flexibility.

The Defense Enrollment Eligibility Reporting System (DEERS) provides a means of rapidly verifying a dependent's eligibility for health care. Dependents are automatically enrolled in DEERS when they receive their military dependent identification cards.

TRICARE Prime. This option is similar to most civilian health maintenance organizations. There is no annual fee for dependents of active-duty members (although there is a small fee for retirees), no annual deductible, and minimal co-payments, making it the least expensive option. However, it is also the least flexible option. All TRICARE Prime users must utilize a single primary care manager, which may be either a network civilian provider or, if available, a military treatment facility. This provider treats routine ailments and authorizes any additional tests, treatments, and referrals that may be necessary. Enrollment in TRICARE Prime is not automatic and must be initiated by the member or dependents.

TRICARE Standard. Under TRICARE Standard, also known as CHAMPUS, beneficiaries have almost complete freedom to choose their own health-care providers. However, this option has a significant annual deductible as well as an annual benefits cap, and the beneficiary bears 20–25 percent of all outpatient costs.

TRICARE Extra. This option is very similar to TRICARE Standard, with the exception that beneficiaries who receive health care from a TRICARE network physician pay a smaller co-payment.

All dependents and retirees are automatically eligible to participate in TRICARE Standard and TRICARE Extra.

Emergency Treatment. Although under normal circumstances active-duty members receive all of their health care from military treatment facilities, you may always seek emergency treatment from the closest emergency room. After seeking such care, contact your local health-benefits adviser (who is normally attached to a military hospital or medical center) as soon as possible to arrange for payment of the bills.

Dental Care. Active-duty members receive free dental care from military dentists, although such care is rarely available to dependents and retirees. Active-duty members may enroll their dependents in the TRICARE dental plan, which provides some benefits for a minimal annual cost.

Death and Burial

Servicemen's Group Life Insurance (SGLI). Every member on active duty is entitled to purchase term life insurance coverage in amounts up to $200,000 under the SGLI program. The cost for this insurance is 8 cents per month per $1,000 coverage, or $16 per month for the maximum amount. The cost of SGLI compares very favorably with that of most commercial life insurance policies, and unlike many such policies SGLI includes coverage for deaths resulting from aviation accidents or combat action.

Notification and Arrangements. Whenever an active-duty member dies, the Navy assigns a casualty assistance calls officer (CACO), who is frequently accompanied by a Navy chaplain, to notify in person the member's primary next of kin (usually the spouse or, in the case of a single member, a parent). Officers and senior enlisted members serving in a particular geographic area may be assigned as collateral duty CACOs for that area. These individuals receive training to enable them to assist the families with paperwork, funeral arrangements, and receipt of benefits. Once assigned to a member's family, the CACO remains available to assist them full-time for as long as is required. When a secondary next of kin, such as a parent or adult child, is located in a different geographic area, another CACO may be assigned to notify and assist him or her.

Dependency and Indemnity Compensation. Dependency and Indemnity Compensation (DIC) provides continuing financial support to a deceased member's surviving spouse and dependent children. Entitlements for spouses of deceased officers range from approximately $900 per month to approximately $1,800 per month, depending on the officer's rank at time of death, and $210 per month for each dependent minor child. Spouses who later remarry lose their entitlement to DIC, although such remarriage does not affect the children's entitlements.

Burial. Members who die on active duty are entitled to burial in a national cemetery (or burial at sea), a grave marker, and a flag. The military pays all funeral expenses, including the cost of the casket, transportation to the place of disposition, interment (if in a national cemetery), and marker. If the member is buried in a private cemetery, the family is also entitled to a grave marker and flag, as well as an allowance of up to $3,100 to help defray interment costs. The deceased's next of kin is also entitled to a "death gratuity" of $6,000.

Miscellaneous Benefits

Legal Assistance. Legal services offices on most installations provide free legal advice and counseling for active-duty members, although they cannot represent members in court. Legal services offices also draft wills for service members free of charge.

DoD Military Spouse Preference Program. This program provides priority in the employment selection process for individuals who are relocating as a result of their military spouse's permanent change of station. Spouse preference may be used for most vacant civil service positions in DoD and applies only within the commuting area of the spouse's permanent duty station. It is not limited to the branch of the military in which the spouse is serving or to those who have previously worked for the federal government. The preference program does not obligate the government to create jobs or make jobs available especially for military spouses, and it does not guarantee employment.

Educational Benefits. The Navy offers service members a wide variety of opportunities to further their academic studies. These programs are discussed in detail in chapter 17.

Personal Financial Management

Budgeting. The simplest way to establish a budget is to list all of your income, including pay, allowances, and investment income. Then list your expenses, including your rent or mortgage, commuting costs, mess bill and other food expenses, utilities, insurance, taxes, and loan payments. The difference is your discretionary income, some of which you will probably need to pay for uniforms and other work-related expenses. If you find you are spending more than this on a regular basis and are beginning to accumulate credit-card and other debt, you may be headed for trouble.

Savings and Investment. As soon as you receive your commission, you should plan to implement a savings and investment strategy. You should establish a short-term savings account, equal to several months' pay, to take care of unexpected bills and emergency expenditures. This account should be very accessible and safe, such as a bank or credit union savings account. In addition, you should establish a long-term investment program to enable you to buy a house, continue your education, or pursue other long-term goals. This type of account does not need to be as liquid as your short-term savings, and if you are willing to accept a higher risk, over the long run you can obtain a higher rate of return with mutual funds or individual stocks and bonds than you can with savings accounts or other insured vehicles. Early establishment of an individual retirement account (IRA) is a smart move for any officer. Although current law does not permit deposits to IRAs to be deductible for military personnel, who are considered to be covered under a pension plan, the interest and capital gains you earn on such an account are always tax-exempt until you actually withdraw the funds after retirement. You may want to consider consulting with a professional investment counselor to assist you in developing your investment strategy.

Insurance. Servicemen's Group Life Insurance was discussed earlier in this chapter. Taking into account the size of your family and the amount of your outstanding debts and expenses (e.g., house payments), you may determine that you need to obtain additional insurance. A number of associations, such as the Armed Forces Relief and Benefit Association (AFRBA) and United Services Automobile Association (USAA), specialize in insurance policies for military members. Before purchasing any life insurance, ensure that it does not exclude from coverage deaths due to combat action or aviation accidents.

Wills. No Navy member should be without a will. Navy legal services offices will prepare wills free of charge and frequently arrange visits aboard soon-to-deploy ships to ensure that all crew members on board have the opportunity to have their wills drawn.

Loans and Credit. It is advisable to have a general-purpose credit card, which is safe and convenient and can provide a ready source of cash in an emergency. It is good practice to pay off your credit-card bills in full every month to avoid piling up debt and paying the generally high interest rates associated with these cards. You may eventually desire to obtain additional credit, such as for a car loan or mortgage. Be sure to pay your bills promptly to help build a good credit rating.

5

MILITARY COURTESY, HONORS, AND CEREMONIES

A NAVAL CEREMONY SHOULD FOLLOW THE LONG-ESTABLISHED RULES FOR ITS EXECUTION CAREFULLY AND EXACTLY. SUCH ATTENTION TO DETAIL HONORS THOSE WHO, LONG BEFORE US, ESTABLISHED THE RITUAL, AND ALL THOSE WHO, PAST, PRESENT, AND FUTURE, TAKE PART IN THAT SAME CEREMONY.

—*Fleet Admiral Chester Nimitz*

A COMPLIANCE WITH THE MINUTIAE OF MILITARY COURTESY IS THE MARK OF WELL-DISPOSED TROOPS.

—*John A. Lejeune*

Any profession has its standards of appropriate courtesy and decorum, but this is particularly true in the Navy. As an officer you will be expected to be familiar with the fundamentals of military honors, ceremonies, customs, and traditions. Not only must you be comfortable with these procedures yourself, but you must also be prepared to instruct and supervise your subordinates in this matter. Military "smartness" is a much valued trait in the Navy. You will find your mastery of the subject tested daily, starting when you step aboard the quarterdeck of your first command.

Fortunately, the information you will need on a day-to-day basis is relatively easy to master, and you will normally have time to research and rehearse for major ceremonial events, such as changes of command and official visits from dignitaries. *Navy Regulations* (available in every command), *Naval Ceremonies, Customs, and Traditions,* and *Watch Officer's Guide* are several publications that might prove useful to you in preparing for such events.

Courtesy

Honors and ceremonies are based on the societal principle of courtesy, which implies politeness and considerate behavior toward others.

Military Courtesy. Military courtesy is a more codified extension of the system of civilian courtesy, and strict adherence to it is important to the maintenance of discipline. Military courtesy and mutual respect and consideration operate from senior to junior as well as from junior to senior. Seniors must treat juniors with fairness and compassion just as juniors must treat seniors with respect and obedience.

The Salute. The hand salute, performed at the meeting of a junior and a senior who is an officer, is the most basic act of military courtesy. The salute has been handed down through the ages and is an integral part of military life. The senior is as much obliged to return it as the junior is to render it. You should learn to execute a sharp salute, for a sloppy salute is nearly as discourteous as a failure to salute. Figure 5.1 illustrates the proper procedure. You must also understand the circumstances under which salutes are required, as well as those in which salutes are not appropriate. Figure 5.2 illustrates some of the more common situations.

Fig. 5.1. The hand salute.

IN GENERAL

ENLISTED MEN SALUTE OFFICERS AND JUNIOR OFFICERS
SALUTE SENIOR WHEN MEETING, PASSING NEAR, WHEN ADDRESSING
OR BEING ADDRESSED

WHEN SEVERAL OFFICERS ARE
SALUTED, ALL SHALL RETURN IT

WHEN OVERTAKING A SENIOR,
THE SALUTE SHALL BE GIVEN WHEN
ABREAST, WITH "BY YOUR LEAVE, SIR."

OFFICERS AND ALL ENLISTED MEN NOT IN FORMATION SALUTE
DURING HONORS TO THE FLAG OR PLAYING OF NATIONAL ANTHEM

WHEN REPORTING (COVERED)

GUARDS SALUTE ALL OFFICERS
PASSING CLOSE ABOARD

(Courtesy of All Hands Magazine)

Fig. 5.2a. When to salute.

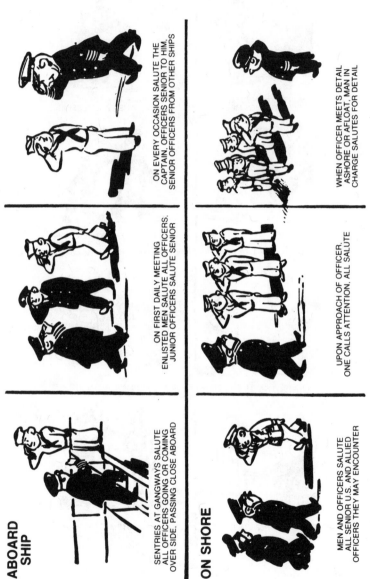

(Courtesy of All Hands Magazine)

ABOARD SHIP

SENTRIES AT GANGWAYS SALUTE ALL OFFICERS GOING OR COMING OVER SIDE, PASSING CLOSE ABOARD

ON FIRST DAILY MEETING ENLISTED MEN SALUTE ALL OFFICERS. JUNIOR OFFICERS SALUTE SENIOR

ON EVERY OCCASION SALUTE THE CAPTAIN, OFFICERS SENIOR TO HIM, SENIOR OFFICERS FROM OTHER SHIPS

ON SHORE

MEN AND OFFICERS SALUTE ALL SENIOR U.S. AND ALLIED OFFICERS THEY MAY ENCOUNTER

UPON APPROACH OF OFFICER, ONE CALLS ATTENTION, ALL SALUTE

WHEN OFFICER MEETS DETAIL ASHORE OR AFLOAT, MAN IN CHARGE SALUTES FOR DETAIL

Fig. 5.2b. When to salute.

IN BOATS

WHEN OFFICER PASSES NEAR, OFFICER OR PETTY OFFICER IN CHARGE SALUTES, IF NONE PRESENT, MEN DO

OFFICERS RISE AND SALUTE WHEN A SENIOR ENTERS OR LEAVES

ENLISTED MEN RISE AND SALUTE WHEN AN OFFICER ENTERS OR LEAVES

VEHICLES

PASSENGERS IN CARS RENDER AND RETURN SALUTE (DRIVER: NO, IF SAFETY IS INVOLVED)

WHEN COLORS ARE SOUNDED MAN IN CHARGE OF DETAIL SALUTES; OTHERS AT ATTENTION

RENDER SALUTES DUE THEM TO ALL OFFICERS IN VEHICLES (IF SAFETY PERMITS)

Fig. 5.2c. When to salute.

Fig. 5.2d. When not to salute.

Enlisted members do not exchange salutes except under special circumstances, as when one of the members is standing watch as officer of the deck (OOD). You will normally salute with your right hand, unless an injury or other reason makes this impracticable, in which case you should salute with your left hand. The custom of offering left-handed salutes under such circumstances is unique to the Navy and Marine Corps; Army and Air Force personnel never salute with their left hands. When under arms, Navy members render the appropriate salute for the type of arm.

Juniors salute first. Seniors in uniform and covered (wearing a hat) must return all salutes; at other times seniors must appropriately acknowledge salutes, such as with a nod or verbal greeting. Uncovered members do not salute, except when failure to do so would cause embarrassment or misunderstanding. This is another circumstance in which the custom followed by members of the Navy and Marine Corps differs from the custom followed by Army and Air Force members, who may render salutes when uncovered.

Navy Regulations sets forth the occasions on which salutes must be rendered. Members of the naval service render salutes to senior officers of the armed forces of the United States, the National Oceanic and Atmospheric Administration, the Public Health Service, and foreign armed services.

All persons in the naval service must salute all officers senior to themselves on each occasion of meeting or passing near, or when addressed by or addressing such officers, with the following exceptions:

- On board ship, salutes may be dispensed with after the first daily meeting, except for those rendered to the CO and those senior to him or her, to visiting officers, to officers making inspections, and to those officers when addressed or being addressed by them.
- At crowded gatherings, or in congested areas when normal procedures for saluting are impracticable, salutes must be rendered only when addressing, or being addressed by, a more senior officer.
- Members at work or engaged in games must salute only when addressed by a more senior officer, and then only if covered.
- Members in formation must salute only on specific command to the formation. Normally only the person in charge of a formation will salute.
- When boats pass each other with embarked officers or officials in view, the senior officer or boat officer and coxswain in

each boat exchange salutes. More information on boat etiquette is included later in this chapter.

Wearing of Covers. Navy personnel in uniform normally wear headgear at all times when outdoors, except when at sea (at the discretion of the CO), when doing so could create a safety hazard (as during flight operations), or at religious or funeral services. You should always uncover when entering any mess or berthing area or sick bay, unless you are conducting an inspection. As a general rule, you should normally uncover when indoors unless you are attending an official military function at which headgear is prescribed or are under arms or on watch.

General Notes on Salutes and Other Military Courtesies. Salutes are normally exchanged at a distance of no less than six paces, although twenty-five paces is not considered excessive. The junior remains at the salute until the senior returns the salute or the senior is well past. Conversely, seniors must always be alert to salutes rendered from farther away than the minimum distance. Juniors should always accompany their salutes with greetings such as "Good morning, Lieutenant," or "Good evening, ma'am," which should be returned by the senior.

When you are overtaking a senior, approach to the senior's left, salute when abreast, and say, "By your leave, sir (ma'am)." You may pass the senior after he or she returns your salute and responds with "Very well" or "Permission granted."

If you are seated when approached by a more senior officer, you should rise and salute. When your hands are full so as to prevent a salute, or when you are uncovered, you should greet the senior with a verbal salutation such as "Good morning, sir (ma'am)." When you are covered, you should salute whenever you recognize a senior officer, regardless of whether the senior is covered or in uniform. Under such circumstances, the senior should nod or speak to you to acknowledge the salute.

When formally addressing, or being addressed by, a senior, stand at attention. If covered, salute when first addressed and again upon the conclusion of the instruction or conversation, and stand at attention throughout the conversation unless otherwise directed by the senior. You should rise, uncover, and stand at attention whenever a senior visits your stateroom or office.

If anyone observes an officer or high-ranking civilian approaching an area where his or her passage would otherwise be blocked, he or she should give the command "Gangway." Enlisted personnel should not use this word to clear a passage for themselves or for other enlisted persons but should say, "Coming through," or something to that effect. When the command "Gangway" is given, the senior petty officer in the vicinity is responsible for seeing that it is carried out.

Always use "sir" or "ma'am" after "yes" or "no" when conversing with senior officers. Many senior officers use these terms as a matter of courtesy when conversing with junior officers. Also add "sir" or "ma'am" to any routine statement, request, or report to a more senior officer, such as "The watch is relieved, ma'am," or "I request permission to leave the ship, sir."

A junior never initiates a handshake but waits for the senior to do so. Juniors walk, ride, or sit on the left of seniors they are accompanying. Juniors also open doors for seniors, passing through last when practicable.

Officers enter boats and automobiles in inverse order of seniority, unless the senior indicates that he or she desires other arrangements. Juniors always allow seniors the most desirable seats. Although the traditional seat of honor is in the rear of a vehicle, in practice many seniors prefer to ride in the front passenger seat.

Small-Boat Etiquette

Figure 5.3 illustrates some of the more common rules of boat etiquette. You should master them thoroughly prior to riding in a boat or being assigned to serve as a boat officer. The following general rules apply:

- Juniors normally board first and leave last, unless given an order to the contrary. Juniors must ensure that there is sufficient room left in the boat for seniors; if there is not, juniors should leave the boat without being asked and wait for the next one.
- The most desirable seats in any boat are in the stern. Juniors must move forward as necessary to give seniors more room astern.
- Juniors rise when seniors embark, unless it is unsafe to do so.
- For safety reasons, all personnel must keep their hands and arms inside the boat. All officers and petty officers are responsible for ensuring that junior personnel on the boat do not become loud or unruly or otherwise cause a hazard or distract the coxswain and boat crew from the safe operation of the boat.

ENTERING BOAT, JUNIORS GO FIRST
LEAVING BOAT, SENIORS GO FIRST

ALWAYS STAND WHEN A SENIOR
ENTERS OR LEAVES A BOAT

SENIORS ARE ACCORDED THE
MOST DESIRABLE SEATS

ALWAYS OFFER A
SEAT TO A SENIOR

IF BOAT IS TOO CROWDED AND YOU
ARE JUNIOR, CATCH NEXT BOAT

WHEN A SENIOR OFFICER IS
PRESENT, DO NOT SIT IN STERN
SHEETS UNLESS ASKED TO DO SO

DON'T CROSS BOWS, CROWD, OR IGNORE
PRESENCE OF A SENIOR

DON'T MAKE LAST-MINUTE DASH
GET INTO BOATS BEFORE
LAST BOAT GONG

(*Courtesy of* All Hands *Magazine*)

Fig. 5.3. Boat etiquette.

- All personnel on a boat should step carefully and avoid walking on varnished areas.
- The senior unrestricted line officer in a boat should identify himself or herself to the boat officer and coxswain. This officer is responsible for the safe and proper operation of the boat but should leave the normal operation to the boat officer and coxswain unless it is necessary to intervene in an emergency.

Responsibilities of Boat Officers. Boat officers are normally assigned to each boat operating in an unfamiliar port, in periods of poor visibility or bad weather, at night, when senior officers or other dignitaries are embarked, or at other times as prescribed by the CO or higher authority. When you are assigned as a boat officer you are responsible for the safe operation and navigation of the boat and must ensure that the coxswain is aware of and ready to execute the appropriate rules of etiquette. Just as military courtesy must be observed between individual juniors and seniors, similar courtesies must be observed between "junior" boats and boats carrying more senior officers or dignitaries. These rules include the following:

- No junior should overtake and pass a senior without permission.
- The senior officer or boat officer and the coxswain in the junior boat salute passing seniors; the senior officer or boat officer and the coxswain in the senior boat return the salute. Other passengers do not salute but, if practicable, sit in a position of attention facing the direction of the boat being saluted. The coxswain and saluting officer rise to salute unless doing so would be hazardous.
- When approaching a ship or landing, a junior boat gives way to a senior boat.
- The coxswain must haul clear of the ship or boat landing while waiting for passengers and must not allow the crew to leave the boat.
- The crew must not lounge in the boat while it is running.
- A boat crew should be outfitted in the same uniform, which must be clean and properly worn. For safety, tennis shoes may be authorized for boat crews in place of uniform shoes.
- During colors, the boat stops and disengages the clutch, and the senior officer or boat officer and the coxswain stand at attention and salute. Other passengers remain seated at attention. Dur-

ing gun salutes, the procedures are similar, although only the person being honored rises.

Boat Appearance.　The reputation of a ship is based in part on the smartness and appearance of its boats and boat crews. An alert, well-uniformed crew is the first step in this direction, as a sharp crew will take pride in their boat. Chrome and fancywork may further enhance an already sharp boat but are not substitutes for cleanliness, preservation, and neatness. Boats should have a full complement of safety devices and life jackets, as well as flags and flagstaff devices, and coxswains should understand their use.

Boat Hails.　In the days prior to World War II, large ships normally anchored or moored to buoys, even when in home port. Under such circumstances, boat operations were far more common than they are today, and the system of boat hails developed to allow the OOD to determine the seniority of passengers in approaching boats. Although today it is normal for ships to be moored to piers and the use of hand-held radio communications between a ship and its boats has become common, the system of boat hails is still in use.

All boats approaching a ship at night should be hailed as soon as they are within hearing distance. The proper hail is "Boat ahoy!" The coxswain should answer as appropriate to indicate the rank of the senior passenger, as follows:

Senior Passenger	*Hail*
President or Vice President of the United States	"United States"
Secretary of Defense	"Defense"
Secretary of the Navy	"Navy"
Commander in Chief of the Fleet	"Fleet"
CO of a ship	"(ship name)"
Other commissioned officer	"Aye, aye"
Midshipman	"No, no"
Enlisted person	"Hello"
Passenger of any status in a boat not intending to come alongside	"Passing"

Boat Flags and Pennants.　In addition to the national ensign, a boat should display the personal flag or pennant of an officer en-

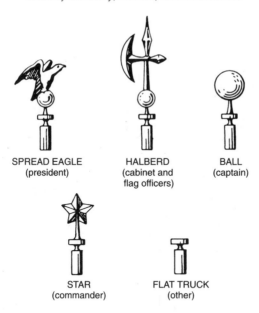

SPREAD EAGLE
(president)

HALBERD
(cabinet and
flag officers)

BALL
(captain)

STAR
(commander)

FLAT TRUCK
(other)

Fig. 5.4. Boat staff insignia.

titled to the boat, or when the officer is embarked for some other reason.

Boat Staff Insignia.   Boats should display, on both staffs, insignia appropriate to the rank and position of the senior passenger. Figure 5.4 illustrates these insignia.

Boat Gongs.   Boat gongs are used to announce the impending departure of a scheduled boat. Three gongs indicate ten minutes to departure, two gongs five minutes, and one gong one minute.

Display of the National Ensign

Marks of Respect.   Title 36, United States Code, chap. 10, describes the conduct required with respect to the national ensign. The following excerpt outlines the appropriate actions during the hoisting, lowering, or passing of the ensign:

> During the ceremony of hoisting or lowering the flag or when the flag is passing in a parade or in review, all present except those in uniform should face the flag and stand at attention with the right hand over the heart. Those present in uniform should render the

military salute. When not in uniform, men should remove their headdress with their right hand and hold it at the left shoulder, the hand being over the heart.

Display of the National Ensign and Union Jack Afloat. When not under way, ships display the national ensign and union jack from 0800 until sunset, the national ensign from the flagstaff (at the stern of the ship) and the union jack from the jackstaff (at the bow). The union jack must be the size of the union (the blue star-studded field) in the national ensign.

Ships under way must display the national ensign during daylight hours from the gaff under the following circumstances, unless otherwise directed by the senior officer present:

- Getting under way and coming to anchor
- Falling in with other ships
- Cruising near land
- During battle

Display of the National Ensign Ashore. Shore commands display the national ensign from 0800 until sunset near the headquarters building, or at the headquarters of the senior commander when the proximity of headquarters for two or more commands makes the display of separate ensigns inappropriate.

Half-Masting the National Ensign and the Union Jack. The ensign is half-masted at the direction of higher authority to recognize the death of a senior officer or official. In half-masting the national ensign, it must, if not previously hoisted, first be hoisted to the truck or peak and then be lowered to half-mast. Before lowering from half-mast, the ensign is hoisted to the truck or peak and then lowered.

When the national ensign is half-masted, the union jack is likewise half-masted.

Dipping the National Ensign. When any vessel under U.S. registry, or under the registry of a nation formally recognized by the government of the United States, salutes a ship of the Navy by dipping its ensign, the Navy ship answers dip for dip. If not already being displayed, the national ensign must be hoisted for the purpose of answering a dip. An ensign being displayed at half-mast is hoisted to the truck or peak before a dip is answered. No ship of the Navy should dip the national ensign unless in return for such compliment.

Morning and Evening Colors. All ships and shore commands follow the movements of the senior officer present afloat (SOPA) upon all occasions of hoisting, lowering, or half-masting the national ensign. The ship in which SOPA is embarked displays the "starboard" pennant from the inboard halyard of the starboard main yardarm for easy identification.

Ships in port observe certain ceremonies at colors. Each day, members of the duty section are detailed in the watch bill as the color guard. At 0755, in preparation for morning colors, a designated member of the duty section, who is in a position to observe the actions of SOPA, follows SOPA's lead and plays a recorded bugle call or announces "First call to colors." As first call is sounded, another member of the duty section (normally the duty signalman) hoists the "prep" pennant. At 0800, still following the movements of SOPA, the bugle call "Attention," or one blast on a whistle, is sounded, and the duty signalman dips the "prep" pennant. This is followed by the playing of the national anthem, if music is available. At the beginning of the national anthem, members of the color guard simultaneously hoist the ensign and the jack smartly to the peak or truck. All Navy personnel face the ensign and render an appropriate salute as the ensign is hoisted. The salutes terminate, and the signalman hauls down the "prep" pennant, when the bugle call "Carry on" is played or three whistle blasts are sounded.

Ships observe the same ceremony during evening colors, beginning with first call at five minutes prior to sunset and ending at sunset when the ensign is lowered.

Ships do not hold colors when under way. The procedure is similar on shore, except that the "prep" pennant is not hoisted, and bugle calls, music, and whistles are not always used.

During colors, a boat within sight or hearing of the ceremony must lie to (take all way off) or proceed at the minimum safe speed for navigation. The boat officer (or, in his or her absence, the coxswain) must stand and salute, except when it is dangerous to do so. Other passengers remain seated and do not salute. Automobiles in the vicinity also stop, and the individuals riding in them do not salute but remain seated at attention during the ceremony.

The National Anthem. The same conduct prescribed for when the ensign is being hoisted, being lowered, or passing is also followed when the national anthem is played, except that when

Morning colors on a large ship.

the flag is not displayed, those present should face toward the music and act in the same manner they would if the flag were displayed there.

The national anthem of the United States, when played by a naval band, is played through without repetition of any part, except for those measures repeated to accommodate the words when the anthem is sung. It is prohibited to play the national anthem of the United States or of any other country as a part of a medley.

Commission Pennants and Other Distinctive Marks. Except when another distinctive mark is displayed as described in this section, commissioned ships display a commission pennant that is continuously flown from the after masthead. Commissioned hospital ships display a Red Cross flag in lieu of a commission pennant.

When a flag officer eligible for command at sea is embarked, the ship hauls down the commission pennant and displays the flag officer's personal flag in the same manner. The personal flags of Navy officers are blue flags with white stars; Marine Corps officers have red flags with gold stars. A small boat displays a similar, smaller flag when a flag officer is aboard. A non-flag officer who is in command of a force, group, or squadron of ships or an aircraft wing is similarly entitled to display a broad command pennant. A burgee command pennant is displayed by officers in command of a division of ships or craft or a major subdivision of an aircraft wing. A ship may display only one distinctive mark at any one time.

Dress Ship/Full Dress Ship. Dress ship is prescribed for ships in port on all national holidays except Presidents' Day and the Fourth of July, and when directed by higher authority. For dress ship, the "holiday" ensign (the largest ensign with which the ship is furnished) is flown from the flagstaff and an appropriately sized jack from the jackstaff. In addition, except when as prescribed for a ship displaying a personal flag or command pennant, a national ensign is displayed from each masthead.

Full dress ship is prescribed for Presidents' Day, the Fourth of July, and special occasions when directed by higher authority. Full dress ship entails the same flag arrangements as in dress ship, with the addition of a rainbow of signal flags running from the foot of the jackstaff to the mastheads to the foot of the flagstaff. These signal flags are arranged in a specific prescribed order.

Dress ship and full dress ship are not displayed when under way.

Honors, Visits, and Calls

Honors, visits, and calls are important to military courtesy, and you must learn to carry them out meticulously. When acting as an OOD or otherwise involved in the preparations, you should carefully review all regulations concerning the events to take place. The CO, XO, and command duty officer (CDO) will all be concerned with planning and preparing for these events and should be consulted if you have any questions, but the OOD is responsible for executing the required honors and must master all the details. Because advance notice is not always possible, you must always be prepared to render honors without the opportunity for extensive preparation.

The OOD is responsible for instructing the watchstanders in their responsibilities and for assembling, inspecting, and rehearsing the boatswain's mate and sideboys.

Quarterdeck Honors. Gongs are routinely used to announce the arrival and departure of the CO and embarked officers senior to the CO, as well as visiting officers in the pay grade of O-5 and senior; in special circumstances (such as to mark a retirement ceremony) gongs may be sounded for officers junior to pay grade O-5. The number of gongs corresponds to the number of sideboys appropriate to the officer's rank, although gongs are sounded even for informal visits when sideboys are not employed. Gongs are always sounded in pairs; the appropriate number of gongs for each pay grade is as follows:

Officers in pay grades O-4 and below	2
Officers in pay grades O-5 and O-6	4
Officers in pay grades O-7 and O-8	6
Officers in pay grades O-9 and above	8

Immediately following the gongs, if the officer is in command, his or her organization is announced followed by the word *arriving* or *departing*. The chief of staff of an embarked commander is announced as "Staff," and all other officers are announced by their rank, as in "Commander, United States Navy." For the CO, or embarked chief of staff or flag officer, one final gong is sounded as the officer actually steps aboard or off the ship. Although several minutes or more may elapse between the announcement of the officer's imminent arrival or departure and the final gong, no intervening announcements may be made except in an emergency.

Sideboys are enlisted personnel paraded to render honors to a visiting senior officer or other dignitary. A dignitary rates the same number of sideboys as the number of gongs as listed above. Under the supervision and tutelage of a boatswain's mate, who pipes the side with a boatswain's pipe as the dignitary comes aboard, the sideboys line either side of the quarterdeck or other ceremonial area and render a salute to the visitor. Officers appropriate to the occasion must attend the side on the arrival and departure of officials and officers.

Ships do not normally parade sideboys on Sunday, or on other days between sunset and 0800, or during meal hours of the crew, general drills, or overhaul; and sideboys are paraded only for scheduled visits.

Passing Honors. Passing honors are honors other than gun salutes that are rendered when ships (or boats with embarked officials or officers) pass, or are passed, close aboard. "Close aboard" is defined as within six hundred yards for ships, or four hundred yards for boats, although these rules are interpreted liberally to ensure that passing honors are always rendered when appropriate. The "senior" ship or vessel is defined as the ship with the more senior CO or embarked officer. The signalmen maintain a publication issued by the applicable fleet commander containing a list of all of the ships and the relative seniority of their commanding officers.

Passing honors between ships of the Navy and Coast Guard consist of the following sequence of events:

• When the bows of the two ships cross (or the bow and stern, if in an overtaking situation), the junior vessel sounds "Attention" to starboard/port using one/two short blasts on a whistle, respectively. All personnel on the appropriate side of the junior vessel come to attention. The senior follows the action of the junior, calling "Attention" on its own port or starboard side, as appropriate.

• The junior vessel sounds one short whistle blast for "Hand salute." All personnel on the appropriate side of the ship render a salute to the senior vessel. The senior vessel returns the salute by sounding one whistle blast, and all personnel on the appropriate side of the senior vessel return the salute.

- The senior vessel sounds two short blasts on the whistle, signifying "Ready, two," and all personnel on the senior vessel drop their salutes. The junior vessel follows suit.
- The senior vessel sounds three short blasts on the whistle for "Carry on," and the junior vessel follows suit.

Ships do not exchange passing honors between sunset and 0800 except when required by international courtesy, nor are honors exchanged when ships are engaged in tactical evolutions outside port. The senior officer present may direct that passing honors be dispensed with in whole or in part.

Official Visits and Calls.   In the naval service, only officers in command pay official visits and calls, which are distinct from personal calls.

Unless dispensed with by the senior, calls must be made in the following situations:

- An officer assuming command must call on his or her immediate superior in command (ISIC) and on any successor of that senior.
- The commander of an arriving unit must call on his or her immediate superior in the chain of command, if present; and, when circumstances permit, on the senior officer present.
- An officer in command must call on an immediate superior in the chain of command upon the arrival of the latter.
- An officer who has been the senior officer present must call on his or her successor.
- The commander of a unit arriving at a naval base or station must call on the commander of that base or station, except that when the former is senior, the latter will call on the former.

When visiting a foreign port, the CO may be required to make additional calls on senior officers and local officials. A message sent to the ship prior to its arrival in port generally outlines specific requirements for these calls.

Entering and Leaving Port.   When a ship departs from or returns to its home port, when it pays a visit to a foreign port, and on other special occasions at the discretion of the CO, the crew is mustered topside. There are two different procedures for this:

- Manning the rail. The crew members, dressed in the uniform of the day, line the rail. This may be on both sides of the ship, or on the side of the ship closest to the pier.

• Parade at quarters. Under this procedure, the crew members muster at their normal topside locations for quarters, normally in the uniform of the day.

The CO may dispense with the above procedures in foul weather.

Ceremonies

A ceremony is a formal series of acts carried out in a manner prescribed by authority or custom. *Navy Regulations* provides the details of formal ceremonies afloat, and informal ceremonies are governed by custom and tradition. This section covers a few of the more common Navy ceremonies.

Commissioning a Ship and Assuming Command. The ceremony for commissioning a ship is not prescribed specifically in *Navy Regulations,* but custom has established a relatively uniform procedure. The crew assembles on the quarterdeck, stern, or other open area, usually in two ranks facing inboard. Officers assemble in two ranks facing the ceremonial area. A band and guard form in or near the ceremonial area. Distinguished guests and principal participants are seated in a position to observe but not to be between the ceremonial area and the crew. If space is limited, guests may be seated on an adjacent ship or on the pier. The first watch, including the OOD, assembles on the quarterdeck. Sailors are stationed near the national ensign, jack, and commission pennant or personal flag halyards.

The officer making the transfer opens the ceremony by reading his or her orders for delivery of the ship. "Attention" is then sounded on the bugle, the national anthem is played, and the ensign, jack, and commission pennant or personal flag are hoisted simultaneously. The ship is officially commissioned with this act.

The officer effecting the transfer delivers the ship to the CO by saying, "I hereby deliver USS STETHEM. The officer ordered to command the ship reads his or her orders, then states, "I hereby assume command of USS STETHEM," and orders the XO to set the watch. The XO in turn directs the OOD to set the watch, and the ship's boatswain or senior boatswain's mate pipes the watch. The OOD and the other members of the watch take their stations.

The CO customarily makes a short speech, touching on the work of the building yard, the name of the ship, the history of any

The USS *Harry S. Truman* is in full dress during commissioning ceremonies held at the Norfolk Naval Base, Virginia. PHCS Terry Cosgrove

previous ships of the same name, and other items of interest. If appropriate, the state, city, or sponsor presents silver or some other commemorative gift, and the CO makes an additional speech of appreciation. The ship's chaplain or a staff chaplain concludes the ceremony with a benediction.

It is customary, particularly in peacetime, for the CO to provide the officers and crew with formal invitations, which they may use to invite family and friends to the ceremony. Some COs prefer to have the officers and crew submit lists of guests and then have the ship's office do the addressing and mailing. After the ceremony, receptions are usually held simultaneously in the wardroom, chief petty officer mess, and crew's mess to entertain the guests.

Change of Command. *Navy Regulations* states that "a commanding officer about to be relieved will call all hands to muster, read the orders of detachment and turn over the command to his or her relief, who will read the orders of relief and assume command." This ceremony may be modified at shore commands.

A change-of-command ceremony is almost always quite formal, even though in smaller ships and shore commands it may be relatively simple. The turnover of command is the official passing of responsibility, authority, and accountability of command from one officer to another. The ceremony is rich in naval tradition and has no counterpart in the other services.

All hands are called to quarters for the ceremony, with the crew, officers, and guests in similar positions as for a commissioning ceremony. The main purpose of the ceremony is to turn over the responsibility from one officer to another, followed by a chance for the relieved CO to say goodbye to his or her officers and crew and for the new CO to greet the crew. The uniform is normally full dress with swords for principal participants and service dress for the crew and military guests.

When the XO reports that the crew is at quarters and the ceremony ready, the CO being relieved, the relieving CO, the chaplain, and any distinguished guests proceed to the ceremonial area. The XO normally acts as master of ceremonies. The chaplain delivers an invocation, and the CO being relieved delivers a speech, followed by the reading of his or her orders. If the CO has invited a guest to make brief remarks, he or she does so at this time. The CO being relieved then steps back and says to his or her relief, "Sir (Ma'am), I am ready to be relieved." The new CO steps forward, reads his or her orders, then faces the CO who is being relieved and says "Sir (Ma'am), I relieve you." If the immediate superior in command is present, the new CO salutes him or her and says, "I report for duty." The new CO then makes a few brief remarks, usually confined to wishing the departing CO well and stating that all orders of his or her predecessor remain in effect. At the time of relief, a new commission pennant is broken. The old one is lowered, and the command master chief presents it to the departing CO. After the chaplain offers a benediction, the new CO orders the XO to "pipe down." The ceremony is over, and the official party retires. Usually the ship holds receptions simultaneously in the wardroom, the CPO mess, and the crew's mess.

Presentation of Awards. For this ceremony the crew forms in approximately the same manner as for a change of command. Those receiving awards form in a single rank in front of the lectern. The XO calls each recipient forward by name, and the recipient then marches to a point one pace in front of the lectern and salutes the CO, who returns the salute. The CO reads the citation, makes a few personal remarks if he or she desires, and receives the medal from the XO or command master chief. The CO pins the medal on the recipient's uniform, shakes his or her hand, and steps back one pace. The recipient salutes, the CO returns the salute, and the recipient steps back one pace and reenters the ranks.

6

TRADITIONS AND CUSTOMS OF THE NAVAL SERVICE

THE VALUE OF TRADITION TO THE SOCIAL BODY IS IMMENSE. THE VENERATION FOR PRACTICES, OR FOR AUTHORITY, CONSECRATED BY LONG ACCEPTANCE, HAS A RESERVE OF STRENGTH WHICH CANNOT BE OBTAINED BY ANY NOVEL DEVICE. RESPECT FOR THE OLD CUSTOMS IS PLANTED DEEP IN THE HEARTS, AS WELL AS IN THE INTELLIGENCE, OF ALL INHERITORS OF THE ENGLISH-SPEAKING POLITY.

—Rear Admiral Alfred Thayer Mahan

TWO HUNDRED YEARS OF TRADITION UNINTERRUPTED BY PROGRESS

—Anonymous commentary on the U.S. Navy

Chapter 5 described courtesy, honors, and ceremonies. You should also become familiar with the many customs and traditions of the naval service. This chapter will cover some of the better-known and most frequently practiced customs. The best comprehensive reference on the subject is the Naval Institute publication *Naval Ceremonies, Customs, and Traditions.*

Naval Customs and Traditions

Contrary to the anonymous quotation that appears at the opening of this chapter, tradition is not a stale, meaningless ritual that takes the place of innovation and initiative. The body of naval tradition and customs has grown and evolved with modern circumstances yet still permits modern naval officers to honor the memories of those who served before them. A custom may be defined as a course of action characteristically repeated under like circumstances, or a whole body of usages, practices, or conventions regulating social life. Much of our daily life is regulated by force of custom, many of which customs are so fully entrenched as to have become established as law.

There are many customs unique to the naval service. The origin of some of these is obscure, but Navy members conscientiously observe them nonetheless. Those that have been incorporated into regulations have the force of law, and of those that have not, some are more stringently enforced than others. Nevertheless, the ability to recognize the unifying purpose behind even the most obscure of traditions, and the willingness to observe them with enthusiasm, will mark you as an officer who is likely to succeed.

Naval Customs Afloat

The Quarterdeck. The publication *Navy Regulations* states that the CO must "clearly define the limits of the quarterdeck." The sanctity of the quarterdeck should be firmly entrenched in the crew, and whether you are on watch or not, you should take pride in observing, and enforcing, proper decorum on the quarterdeck.

The following rules govern quarterdeck etiquette:

• Never appear on the quarterdeck unless in the uniform of the day, except when crossing to arrive or depart.

• Never stand around on the quarterdeck for any length of time unless conducting business there.

- • Salute the officer of the deck every time you come onto the quarterdeck.

• Never smoke, eat, drink, or engage in horseplay on the quarterdeck.

• Never walk in an area of the quarterdeck reserved for the flag officer or CO unless on official business or on invitation of those officers.

• Never stand on the quarterdeck with your hands in your pockets. This pose is unmilitary in any area, but especially so on the quarterdeck.

Gangways. The gangway is the aperture in the side of a ship through which personnel and material pass. The ladders leading up to the gangway from the grating at the waterline are called accommodation ladders.

Larger ships may have two gangways: one a working gangway for enlisted members and the passage of supplies and material, and a more formal gangway for the use of officers and VIPs. If these gangways lead to separate areas of the ship, the area in which the officers' gangway terminates is the quarterdeck and is manned by the officer of the deck; the area in which the working gangway terminates is manned by another watchstander who may be given the title junior officer of the deck.

Forms of Address and Introduction. You can find the proper form of address and introduction for very senior U.S. officials and foreign dignitaries in the *Department of the Navy Social Usage and Protocol Handbook* (OPNAVINST 1710.7).

Navy Regulations states that every officer in the naval service is designated and addressed in official communications by the title of grade preceding his or her last name. In official spoken communications, officers are addressed by their ranks. Although the usage is no longer specified in *Navy Regulations*, in less formal spoken communications it is still common to address officers below the rank of commander as "Mr." or "Ms." instead of by their ranks. You may address officers of the medical and dental corps as "doctor" and officers of the chaplain corps as "chaplain." When addressing an officer whose grade includes a modifier (e.g., the *lieutenant* in *lieutenant commander*), the modifier may be dropped. In written communication, indicate the name of the corps to which any staff officer belongs immediately after his or her name.

By custom, one person in any ship or organization is correctly addressed as "the captain," and that is the CO regardless of his or her actual rank. Likewise, the XO is referred to as "the commander." You should address other captains and commanders attached to the ship or station by their rank and name, for example, "Commander Jones."

Introduce officers using their rank, and always introduce the junior to the senior. When introducing military personnel to civilians, follow the civilian custom of introducing men to women and young people to their elders.

Address Marine Corps enlisted personnel by their titles, as in "Lance Corporal Smith." Introduce enlisted personnel, both Navy and Marine Corps, in the same manner as officers. A chief petty officer is customarily addressed and introduced as "Chief Smith" or "Master Chief Green." Introduce a petty officer as "Petty Officer Brown" rather than as "Radioman Second Class Brown," particularly when the introduction is to a civilian. Introduce a nonrated sailor as "Seaman (or Fireman, Airman, etc.) White" rather than "Seaman Apprentice White."

Relations with Seniors.   When reporting to the office of a senior, first attempt, discreetly, to determine whether the senior is on the telephone or otherwise occupied. If not, knock on the door (even if it is open), announce yourself by name ("Ensign Gray reporting as ordered, sir [ma'am]"), and wait for permission to enter. In some cases, such as a busy office on board ship, you may be expected to enter without being told. Upon entering, proceed directly to the senior and, upon being recognized, state your business.

When conducting business with a senior, maintain a military bearing. Do not lounge against the desk or otherwise relax unless invited to stand easy or be seated. Unless on watch or wearing sidearms, always uncover when entering a room in which a senior is present.

It is customary to supplement your salute to a senior on the first meeting of the day with a brief greeting, such as "Good morning, Commander." Don't be too obtrusive with this greeting, particularly if the senior is engaged in conversation or otherwise occupied. Although you always salute the CO at every meeting, on board ship other seniors are normally saluted only at the first meeting of the day.

Never keep a senior waiting. When you are told that a senior wants to see you, you should assume that this means right away. If the senior cannot see you immediately, he or she may tell you to return at a particular later time rather than keep you waiting. You should learn to use the same thoughtfulness when summoning your juniors.

When a senior says "I desire," "I wish," or "Would you please," remember that the expressed desires and wishes of a senior, however tactfully presented, by custom and tradition are equivalent to an order. Even such statements as "I think it would be a good idea to . . ." should be construed as orders unless you obtain clarification to the contrary.

A senior presents "compliments" to a junior when the former is transmitting a message to the latter by a third person such as a messenger. A junior sends or pays his or her "respects" to a senior. In written correspondence a senior may "call" attention to certain matters, but the junior should "invite" attention. Similarly, a senior "requests" action of a junior, but a junior "respectfully requests" action of a senior. As discussed in chapter 9, in memoranda it is common practice for a senior to close with "respectfully," but a junior closes with "very respectfully."

When a senior orders you to perform a task, report back promptly when the task is complete. If you cannot complete the task right away, it is a good idea to give periodic reports on your progress. If you cannot complete the task as directed, report this fact back to your senior as soon as you are aware of the problem; don't wait until your deadline is imminent or has passed to report your inability to comply.

Learn to give accurate and brief responses to questions. If you don't know the answer to a question, don't guess! If your seniors can't rely on you to give them correct information, your credibility and reputation will suffer. A frank "I don't know, sir (ma'am), but I will find out and let you know" (followed by your actually finding out the answer and letting your superior know) is far better than an evasive or possibly incorrect reply. Chapter 9 discusses oral communications in more detail.

Phraseology. Certain standards of speech and address are in common use. The forms "Captain, I report . . ." and "Sir (Ma'am), I request . . ." are correct. At the end of the workday, enlisted personnel go on "liberty," but officers go on "shore leave." When preparing to leave your own ship, it is customary to check out with your immediate senior if he or she is still aboard. If appropriate, first brief your senior on the status of your work, and then say, "Sir (Ma'am), request permission to leave the ship."

At the quarterdeck, say to the OOD, "Sir (Ma'am), I have permission to leave the ship." On your return, say, "Sir (Ma'am), I report my return aboard." When boarding a ship to which you are not attached, say to the OOD, "Sir (Ma'am), I request permission to come aboard," and show your identification. When departing, say, "Sir (Ma'am), I request permission to leave the ship."

When acknowledging an order, always respond with "Aye, aye, sir (ma'am)." The *only* proper use of the phrase "Very well" is by a senior to acknowledge a report by a junior.

Chain of Command. You will have a different chain of command under different circumstances. For routine division business you will report to your department head; for watch-qualification issues you will report to the senior watch officer; for watchstanding responsibilities you will report to the appropriate senior in the in-port duty section or underway watch; for some collateral duties you may report to the XO or a department head other than your own; and for certain operational matters it may be appropriate to report directly to the CO. It is important that you be clear on the rules governing each situation so that you do not inadvertently "go over the head" of someone in your chain of command. If it is necessary to report directly to an officer other than your department head, and time does not permit you to brief your department head ahead of time, it is important to back-brief him or her as soon as possible.

The Wardroom

Wardroom Mess.   The term *mess* is applied to those in the Navy who, for convenience and sociability, eat together. It comes from the Latin word *mensa,* meaning table. Generally there are three messes on board a Navy ship: the general mess for the crew, the chiefs' mess, and the wardroom or officers' mess.

Wardroom Etiquette.   In very large ships, the CO may have his or her own mess, and the XO is president of the wardroom mess. Normally, however, the CO dines in the wardroom with the other officers and is president of the mess. Wardroom seating arrangements are no longer prescribed in *Navy Regulations,* but it remains customary for the president to sit at the head of the table, with the other officers seated in decreasing order of seniority on alternating sides of the table, starting with the highest-ranking officer below the president sitting to the president's right. Traditionally the mess treasurer occupies the seat at the foot of the table opposite the president. During the evening meal in port when a large number of mess members are ashore, the command duty officer may sit at the head of the table, with other officers present seated in order of seniority on alternating sides.

Wardroom protocol requires all members to arrive early for meals so that they may be seated at once when the president arrives and the meal is served. If you must join the mess late because of a watch or other responsibilities, before being seated you must approach the president and request permission to join the mess. Similarly, if you must leave the mess before the president, you must request permission to be excused. Proper uniforms are as designated by the mess president; coveralls, other nonuniform work attire, and civilian clothing are generally not permitted in the mess.

Wardroom Mess Fund.   Every officers' mess has a fund from which it purchases food and other supplies. When reporting aboard ship for duty, you will be required to buy a share of the mess—that is, to pay the mess fund an amount equal to your proportional share of the funds and supplies already on hand. When you detach from the ship, you will be refunded the appropriate current amount of a share of the mess. In addition, each member of the mess is required to contribute a monthly amount to the mess, which may be based either on a flat per-person rate or on the number of meals actually consumed. The mess fund is administered by the mess treasurer, who calculates bills and collects payments. Failure to pay a mess bill promptly is considered a serious breach of wardroom etiquette, and the president will likely counsel any officer who pays the bill habitually or significantly late.

Conduct in the Wardroom.   Particularly while on deployment, the wardroom serves as the officers' home on board ship. Wardroom amenities may include a comfortable sofa and chairs, a television and VCR, stereo system, books, magazines, and games. You should feel comfortable spending time in the wardroom after working hours, relaxing and socializing with your fellow officers. During working hours, you may take brief breaks to have a cup of coffee in the wardroom, but it is not appropriate to "hang out" for long periods in the wardroom during the workday or to do your paperwork there. As a rule, it is not appropriate to spend time in the wardroom wearing civilian clothes, although this rule may be relaxed at the CO's discretion.

Traditionally, during peacetime no business is transacted in the wardroom, and conversations during meals should not revolve around ship's business. Because of space limitations in small ships, the wardroom may be used for meetings and training lectures during working hours. Enlisted members (other than the mess specialists and food service assistants who work there) should never enter the wardroom unless specifically invited. Enlisted personnel should not conduct routine ship's business in the wardroom; if you have a need to confer with an enlisted member, it is appropriate to step outside the wardroom to do so.

The wardroom may upon occasion host a formal meal including one or more "guests of the mess." If such guests are invited by the mess at large, all members share equally in the associated costs as well as in their responsibilities to serve as hosts. It is polite to introduce yourself to all guests of the mess, and to help make them feel at home. Meal costs for guests of individual mess members are normally borne by the appropriate wardroom member, although the same rules of hospitality apply.

Wardroom Organization. The position of mess treasurer has already been mentioned; this officer is elected from among the members of the mess. It is not uncommon for a junior officer who arrives late to a meeting of the mess to find that he or she has been elected to serve as mess treasurer. The specific duties of the mess treasurer include the following:

• Maintain the accounts of the mess using a standard form of double-entry bookkeeping; obtain receipts for all expenditures by the wardroom mess supervisor; make entries in the books as they occur; keep books balanced; check the purchases of store-bought supplies frequently to make sure that full amounts are delivered; and check issues on a random basis in cases where purchases from the general mess are made.

• Maintain an appropriate checking account, and ensure safekeeping of any cash accounts. Advise mess members of the amount of their monthly bills, and collect payments.

• Close the books promptly at the end of the month, take an accurate inventory, and complete a monthly summary report. Arrange for the auditing board to meet promptly, and ensure that the audit is in the hands of the XO by the tenth of the month.

Mess caterer is frequently a permanent collateral duty assigned to one of the ship's supply corps officers, although that duty may be assigned to any member of the mess. This officer's duties include the following:

• Supervise the preparation of the menu, providing variety and proper nutrition.

• Supervise the wardroom mess specialists and food service assistants in the performance of their duties, to include cleaning and maintenance of officer staterooms as well as their duties in the wardroom.

• Inspect the wardroom, pantry, galley, and mess personnel for cleanliness. Ensure that food preparation is conducted in a hygienic manner.

Mess specialists and food service assistants are not personal servants but have specific responsibilities to operate the wardroom. Like all enlisted personnel, they should be treated with appropriate courtesy and professionalism. If you have a complaint about the performance of one of the wardroom personnel, it is appropriate to discuss your concerns with the mess caterer.

Navy Social Life

The social requirements of Navy life are generally kept as simple and informal as possible. The days in which the off-duty schedules of officers and their spouses were overburdened with onerous "command performance" social functions are long past, particularly in the case of junior officers. However, at some point in your career you will likely be invited to, perhaps even be tasked with organizing, a variety of events ranging from the casual to the traditional. A brief description of some customary naval social functions follows.

Receptions and Cocktail Parties. These events may be given for a variety of reasons and may be held in a private home, at a command, or at an officers' club. A reception or cocktail party may be hosted by an organization. For example, if your command is sponsoring a visiting foreign navy ship, it is common practice to host a reception for the ship's officers on the first night of the visit. In turn, visiting ships often host cocktail parties on board to entertain local dignitaries and officers of the host ship and other area commands. Although alcohol is not normally permitted on board U.S. Navy ships, exceptions are occasionally granted for this purpose when a ship visits a foreign port.

When invited to a cocktail party or reception, your invitation may specify a particular period of time (e.g., 1800 to 2000). At very large gatherings there will frequently be more than one "shift," with other guests invited for different blocks of time, so you should not overstay your invitation even if the party remains in full swing at the time scheduled for your departure.

Cocktail parties differ from receptions in that they are less formal, there is no receiving line and usually no guest of honor, and the time limits are not as strict. Both types of functions generally feature a buffet of light or heavy hors d'oeuvres, depending on the budget of the host(s), and some sort of beverage service ranging from a full bar at the high end to wine and nonalcoholic punch at more economical gatherings.

When visiting another port, your command may be issued a number of invitations to a variety of different social functions sponsored by local groups. You may be tapped to go to one of these functions and represent your command. These events will be some of your best opportunities to meet and socialize with local residents and officers of other navies. When attending, remember that you are a representative of your command as well as of the U.S. Navy, and be a gracious and sociable guest.

Balls and Dances. If you are stationed in a major fleet concentration area, you will have many opportunities to participate in formal balls and dances. The largest of these are given on the occasion of the Navy Birthday and the Marine Corps Birthday, but many officer communities host their own events, such as the Supply Corps Ball and the Surface Warfare Ball. These events are usually quite formal, which may be reflected in the cost, but a sliding scale is frequently used to make tickets more affordable for junior officers and enlisted members. Attendance at these balls will give you and your spouse the opportunity to spend time with a large number of officers who share your professional interests, and it can prove both socially and professionally rewarding.

Dining In/Dining Out. These formal dinners represent a tradition dating back hundreds of years. These events, also sometimes referred to as Mess Nights, have their roots in the customs of eighteenth-century European army regiments, in which the officers would gather together for an evening of food, drink, and fellowship. The difference between a Dining In and a Dining Out is that only the members of the mess attend the former, whereas spouses and other guests are invited to the latter. (In the Marine Corps, the meaning of the two terms is reversed.) There are only two recognized officers of the mess, the president and vice president. "Mr. (or Ms.) Vice" is normally a junior officer selected for his or her engaging and entertaining personality as well as ability to hold the sometimes unruly members of the mess to some semblance of order.

The evening commences with a gathering for cocktails, during which members of the mess and any guests note their seat locations on the posted seating chart to avoid later embarrassment. After the cocktail hour, the president, assisted by Mr. or Ms. Vice, forms the members into the order in which they will be seated in the mess, normally in order of seniority. A bagpiper engaged for the occasion plays appropriate marching music and leads the president, members, and guests (if present) into the mess. The group parades around the mess in a full circle, coming to rest behind their assigned seats. When all members are in place, the music ceases, the president or designated member offers grace, and the president seats the mess with a rap of the gavel. Once the mess is seated, no one may join or be excused from the mess without first obtaining permission from the president. Mr./Ms. Vice will then signal to the bagpiper to play "Roast Beef of Olde England" and will lead the procession of food service personnel to the president's seat. The president will sample the beef and determine its quality. Once the president finds the beef acceptable, he or she will announce, "Ladies and gentlemen, I pronounce this beef fit for human consumption."

Mr./Ms. Vice sits alone at a small table opposite the president and head table. Prior to addressing the president, members of the mess must first obtain permission to do so from Mr./Ms. Vice. Mr./Ms. Vice may choose to deny a request in order to prevent frivolous business from interfering with the president's enjoyment of the meal. Failure to obtain prior permission to address the president is a serious breach of mess etiquette, which the president normally allows Mr./Ms. Vice to deal with as he or she sees fit. Other violations of the mess include:

- Untimely arrival at the proceedings
- Haggling over date of rank
- Leaving the dining area without permission from the president
- Loud and obtrusive remarks in a foreign language or in English
- Being caught with an uncharged glass
- Rising to applaud particularly witty, succinct, sarcastic, or irrelevant toasts unless following the example of the president
- Hog-calling and rebel yells
- An inverted cummerbund
- A clip-on bow tie worn at an obvious list
- Foul language
- Carrying cocktails into the dining room
- Any other breach of proper decorum or etiquette

During the course of the meal, members may observe breaches of etiquette by other members of the mess, or recall such breaches from previous occasions, and feel compelled to bring these offenses to the attention of the president. After the member obtains permission from Mr./Ms. Vice and relates the circumstances of the offense to the president, the president may choose to allow the accused offender the opportunity to present information in his or her defense. After this, the president will render judgment and, if necessary, determine a suitable penalty for the offender or allow Mr./Ms. Vice to do so. Typical penalties include singing a song, reciting a poem, paying a fine, performing a service to the mess, wearing an appropriate article of attire, or other similar measures befitting the offense.

Following the meal, the president may choose to excuse the members and guests briefly to refresh themselves. As with the first entry into the mess, it is a serious breach of etiquette to be late rejoining the mess following this recess. When the mess is reassembled, preparations for formal toasting commence with the passing of the port. A bottle of port wine is passed from right to left ("to port"), with each member and guest filling his or her own glass and not allowing the bottle to touch the table until the last glass is filled. Nonalcoholic wine or cider may be substituted for the port to accommodate those who choose not to drink alcoholic beverages, but toasts may never be drunk with water. When the last glass is filled, the president rises, raps the gavel three times to require the attention of the members, and proposes a toast to the Commander in Chief: "Mr. (Ms.) Vice, the Commander in Chief of the United States." Mr./Ms. Vice then rises and seconds the toast by repeating as follows: "Ladies and gentlemen, the Commander in Chief," following which all members and guests rise, repeat the toast ("The Commander in Chief") in unison, and sip from their glasses. If a band or recorded music is available, "Hail to the Chief" is played. The president then raps the gavel to seat the members and guests.

Members of the mess offer additional formal toasts in the following order:

- The United States Marine Corps
- Missing comrades
- The Chief of Naval Operations

Additional toasts may be offered to the United States Army, Air Force, and Coast Guard, and to other appropriate organizations and dignitaries. Each toast that is not offered by the president is conducted in the following manner: the member rises, obtains permission from Mr./Ms. Vice to offer a toast, and says, "Mr. (Madam) President, the United States Marine Corps" (or other toast as appropriate). The president rises and seconds the toast by saying, "Ladies and gentlemen, the United States Marine Corps," following which all members and guests rise, repeat the toast ("The United States Marine Corps"), and sip from their glasses. Mr./Ms. Vice seconds all toasts offered by the president. Do not empty your glass until the final toast. If appropriate music is available, it will be played after each toast, following which the president reseats the mess with one rap of the gavel.

Following the formal toasting, the president introduces the guest of honor, if one is present, who briefly addresses the mess. Following this, the president invites informal toasting from members and guests. The procedures for informal toasting are the same as those for formal toasting; however, if the president fails to rise and second the toast, it has not been accepted. Individuals are never toasted by name, only by title. Following the informal toasts, without rising the president raps the gavel three times and proposes a final toast to the United States Navy. The president rises as Mr./Ms. Vice seconds the toast, and all members and guests rise and repeat the toast, drain their glasses, and remain standing for the playing of "Anchors Aweigh." Following the final toast, the president invites the members and guests to join him or her at the bar. Attendees should remain at their places until the president and those seated at the head table have departed the mess, and they should not depart from the bar until the president and guest of honor have done so.

The smoking of cigars, long a traditional feature of such events, has recently been curtailed because of health concerns and regulations. If smoking is permitted in the mess, it will be indicated by the president lighting a ceremonial "smoking lamp" following the toast to the Commander in Chief.

Wetting Down. It is traditional for an officer newly selected for promotion to share his or her good fortune with friends and fellow wardroom members with a Wetting Down party. Customarily an officer is expected to spend the equivalent of his or her first month's pay increase on the event; it is not uncommon for two or more officers to share in hosting a Wetting Down.

Wetting Down parties are generally extremely informal and may consist of nothing more than modest beverages and finger foods. If a group of officers share expenses, the event may be considerably more lavish.

Hail and Farewell. When new members join a wardroom or when old members depart, the wardroom will generally mark the occasion with a party called a Hail and Farewell. These events may be held at the home of the president of the mess or another member, or at an officers' club or restaurant. In any case, the costs of the event are borne equally by all members except those for whom the event is a farewell.

Although a Hail and Farewell is a relatively informal event, all wardroom members who are not on duty are expected to attend. It is considered extremely rude to miss a Hail and Farewell without good reason. If exceptional circumstances exist that would prevent your attendance, you should explain the situation to the XO in advance and request permission to be absent. Whether or not you attend, you will still be expected to contribute to the costs.

A Hail and Farewell generally consists of an informal cocktail party, which may include a buffet line or hors d'oeuvres. A more formal Hail and Farewell, such as for the CO, may include a sit-down dinner. After all members and their guests have had the opportunity to socialize, the CO addresses the gathering. The CO generally begins with a formal introduction and welcome for each of the new members being hailed and their spouses. Such introductions are normally made beginning with the most junior new member and ending with the most senior. Following this, the CO calls forward each of the members being bid farewell, beginning with the most junior, and provides a brief synopsis of that officer's accomplishments and contributions to the command. The CO may open the floor to allow other mess members to make presentations or tell stories about the departing officer, after which the departing officer says a few words of farewell. Each farewell generally concludes with the presentation of some gift or memento from the mess, such as a plaque.

Calls. The practice of junior officers and their spouses paying formal at-home calls on the CO and other officers of the command has all but disappeared. Nevertheless, this practice still exists in some quarters, and upon reporting to a new command you should inquire of the XO whether this courtesy is expected of you. If you are advised that calls are expected, you should request a convenient time to call on the CO, the XO, and your department head, normally within two weeks of reporting aboard. If you are married, your spouse should accompany you if possible. Your calls should be brief (approximately twenty minutes), and you and your spouse should leave calling (not business) cards if the XO has so advised you.

You can expect your calls to be returned within two weeks. If you are a single officer, you may need to express a specific invitation to indicate your ability and willingness to host calls. When entertaining callers, you will not be expected to entertain lavishly. Simply offer your guests a choice of alcoholic or nonalcoholic beverages and simple snacks, and engage in pleasant, light conversation.

Officers' Clubs. Naval bases and other large shore stations normally have a Commissioned Officers' Mess (Open), commonly referred to as an officers' club. Such clubs in the Navy sometimes offer formal memberships or require dues but are generally open to all officers and their guests. Officers' clubs normally serve meals in a restaurant-type setting. Breakfasts and lunches may be informal, sometimes cafeteria-style, although the evening meal is usually somewhat more formal. Officers' clubs may also offer off-site catering and rooms for special events.

Never wear your cover inside an officers' club. By custom and tradition, any officer entering a club covered must buy a round of drinks for all those present. This is not an error you are likely to make twice.

7

MILITARY DUTIES OF THE NAVAL OFFICER

AN ARMY FORMED WITH GOOD OFFICERS MOVES LIKE CLOCKWORK.

—*George Washington*

ON THE CONDUCT OF THE OFFICERS ALONE DEPENDS THE RESTORATION OF GOOD ORDER, DISCIPLINE, AND SUBORDINATION IN THE NAVY.

—*Lord St. Vincent*

Military leaders have long been interested in the practice of fixing responsibility. One of the best discourses on the subject came from Admiral Hyman G. Rickover, who said that responsibility is a "unique concept":

> It can only reside and inhere in a single individual. You may share it with others, but your portion is not diminished. You may delegate it, but it is still with you. You may disdain it, but you cannot divest yourself of it. Even if you do not recognize it or admit its presence, you cannot escape it. If responsibility is rightfully yours, no evasion, or ignorance, no passing the blame, can shift the burden to someone else. Unless you can point your finger at the man who is responsible when something goes wrong, then you never really had anyone responsible.

These strong words suggest just how sacred the concept of responsibility is in the Navy.

Basic Authority and Responsibility

Your authority and responsibility as a naval officer began the day you accepted your commission and took the oath of office. The "special trust and confidence" placed in your "patriotism, fidelity, and abilities" should be an inspiration to you. You swore to "support and defend the Constitution of the United States against all enemies, foreign and domestic; to bear true faith and allegiance to the same." This oath represents a solemn promise that no officer should enter into lightly.

On the day you accepted your commission and took this oath, you assumed authority as well as certain basic responsibilities. *Navy Regulations* and other directives describe some of these; you should review these publications and become familiar with the extent and limits of your responsibilities and authority as a naval officer.

Authority and Responsibility under *Navy Regulations*

Navy Regulations sets forth regulations concerning officers in chapter 10, entitled "Precedence, Authority, and Command." Art. 1130 gives the duties of officers with regard to laws, orders, and regulations and requires that all officers in the naval service acquaint themselves with, obey, and, so far as their authority extends, perform these duties to the best of their ability in conformance with their solemn profession of the oath of office. In the absence of instructions, officers must act in conformity with policies and customs to protect the public interest.

Required Conduct. Art. 1110, "Standards of Conduct," states that all Navy personnel are expected to conduct themselves in accordance with the highest standards of personal and professional integrity and ethics. At a minimum, Navy personnel must comply with the standards of conduct and the ethics directives issued by the Secretary of Defense and the Secretary of the Navy. Chapter 2 of this book discusses these standards in greater detail.

Exercise of Authority. Art. 1020, "Exercise of Authority," states that everyone in the naval service is at all times subject to naval authority. This article is somewhat convoluted, but in essence it says that any naval officer, unless on the sick list, under custody or arrest, suspended from duty, under confinement, or otherwise incapable of discharging duties, *may* exercise authority.

Officers in the Navy not only *may* exercise authority when necessary—they *must* exercise it. Such action is not simply a right but also a duty under naval custom. If, for example, you observe misconduct by a member of the naval service, whether or not you are in that member's chain of command, you are bound by custom to exercise your authority as a naval officer and take corrective action.

Amplifying Directives Concerning the Authority and Responsibilities of Officers

Authority from Organizational Position. While the basic authority for all officers comes from *Navy Regulations*, your organizational position invests you with additional authority and responsibilities described in OPNAVINST 3120.32, the *Standard Organization and Regulations Manual (SORM)*. *SORM* art. 141 states that authority falls into two categories: the general authority necessary for all officers to carry out their duties and responsibilities, and the organizational authority necessary to fulfill the duties and responsibilities of specific billets. The command organizational structure is described in command, department, and division instructions, which set forth the positions, duties, and responsibilities of all persons in the command.

Limits on Authority: Lawful Orders

Injurious or Capricious Conduct. Their broad authority notwithstanding, there are limits to what officers can do. Subordinates are not obliged to obey unlawful orders, and *Navy Regulations* prohibits those in authority from mistreating their subordinates with tyrannical or capricious conduct or abusive language. There have been several recent incidents in which commanding officers were relieved of their commands for just such abuse.

Limits on Organizational Authority. *SORM* art. 141.7 points out that since authority is given only to fulfill duties and responsibilities, seniors may delegate only so much organizational authority as a subordinate requires to fulfill his or her responsibilities. This is limitation of authority by command.

Contradictory Orders. *Navy Regulations* art. 1024 covers the subject of contradictory and conflicting orders. If one superior officer contradicts the orders issued to you by another superior, he or she is required to report that fact immediately, preferably in writing, to the superior whose orders were contravened. If you receive such a contradictory order, you must explain the facts in writing to the officer who gave you the last order. If that officer insists upon the execution of his or her order, you must obey it; at the earliest opportunity you must then report the circumstances to the officer who issued you the original order.

Imposition of Nonjudicial Punishment. SORM art. 142.1 states that no one may impose punishment except under procedures outlined in the Uniform Code of Military Justice (UCMJ). It further states that UCMJ nonjudicial punishment is reserved for commanders, commanding officers, and officers in charge. Appendix 3 provides an overview of the military justice system.

Extra Military Instruction (EMI). Officers and petty officers may take nonpunitive measures to correct minor deficiencies not meriting punishment under UCMJ art. 15. These measures, called EMI, must be intended to correct deficiencies in a subordinate's performance of military duty, or to direct completion of work assignments that may extend beyond normal working hours.

SORM art. 142.2 establishes policy guidance for EMI. This article defines EMI as instruction in a phase of military duty in which an individual is deficient. This instruction, sanctioned by the *Manual for Courts-Martial (MCM)* para. v-1g (1995), is a training device to be used to improve the efficiency of a command or unit and must not be used for punitive action that should have been taken under the UCMJ. *SORM* art. 142.2 describes how to implement this form of instruction and states that it may not be assigned for more than two hours a day, may be assigned at a reasonable time outside of working hours, must be no longer than necessary to correct the deficiency, and may not be assigned on a person's Sabbath. Further, any Navy member otherwise entitled to liberty may commence liberty upon completion of EMI.

Any officer or petty officer may assign EMI during normal working hours. After working hours, EMI is assigned by the CO, whose authority may be delegated to other officers and petty officers in the chain of command. If the CO delegates authority to assign EMI, he or she must monitor the process to ensure that it is not misused.

Withholding Privileges. The chain of command has the authority to withhold certain privileges temporarily, an act sanctioned by *MCM* para. v-1g. This procedure may be used to correct minor infractions of military regulations or performance deficiencies when stronger action is not required. Examples of privileges that may be withheld are special liberty, exchange of duty, special pay, special command programs, movies, libraries, and off-ship events on military bases. The authority to withhold a privilege rests with the individual empowered to grant the privilege. Withholding privileges from personnel in a liberty status is the prerogative of the CO. The CO may delegate this authority, but such withholding of privileges may not result in a deprivation of liberty itself.

Additional Work Assignments. *SORM* art. 142.2c states that deprivation of liberty as a punishment, except under the UCMJ, is illegal; no officer or petty officer may deny liberty as a punishment for any offense or unsatisfactory performance of duty. However, the article states that it is not a punishment to require a member to remain on board and perform work assignments that should have been completed during the normal workday, to perform additional essential work, or to maintain the required level of operational readiness.

Extending working hours for all hands or for certain selected personnel should be done only when absolutely necessary. When you recommend to your seniors that they extend working hours for your division, you should make every effort to ensure that your personnel understand the necessity for such action. If they understand it, they will carry out their duty readily and well. It may also be legitimate to extend working hours when work was not performed satisfactorily the first time or when there is a short-notice operational or administrative commitment.

Ordering and Assignment of Officers

Officer Distribution. The Chief of Naval Personnel has responsibility for assigning qualified officers to authorized billets. In determining an officer's next assignment, the distribution system considers the needs of the Navy, the effect of the assignment on the professional growth and development of the officer, the officer's record and qualifications, and the officer's personal preferences.

The officer distribution system, described in greater detail in chapter 17, is organized so that one group of officers, called placement officers, has the responsibility for groups of similar commands, and another group, called detailers, takes care of officers in particular designators and pay grades. Nine to twelve months in advance of an expected vacancy, the placement officer representing a particular command posts the requirement for an officer to relieve or fill the billet with the appropriate detailer, giving the date of the incumbent's expected rotation and the qualifications for the billet. The detailer then attempts to find an officer of appropriate rank and qualifications who is due to rotate at the proper time. The placement officer and the detailer then get together to work out the details before issuing the orders. The placement officer normally informs the ship's CO or XO of the results, and the detailer provides the individual officer similar advance notice and information. It is not appropriate for you as an individual officer to contact the placement officer regarding your future assignment; this is the role of your detailer.

Assignment to Specific Billets. The Bureau of Naval Personnel generally assigns officers to specific billets. In the orders, the officer either may be assigned to a specific billet identified by sequence code, or he or she may be designated as a "numerical relief for" another officer identified by name. Once you have arrived on board—and this is especially true if you have been ordered as a numerical relief—the CO has broad latitude to reassign you on the basis of your individual qualifications and the needs of the command. Junior officers can generally expect to rotate between several different assignments during a single shipboard tour.

Duties of Specific Assignments

When you arrive at a ship, squadron, or station and take position in the organization of that unit, you assume the authority and responsibility assigned to the billet by the ship's organization and regulations. These are described in chapter 3 of the *SORM*.

The Executive Officer and Assistants

Executive Officer (XO). The XO is second in command of the unit and is the alter ego of the CO. The XO takes precedence over all other officers of the command and has responsibility for the organization, performance of duty, good order, and discipline of the command.

A number of administrative assistants report directly to the XO. Many of these positions are collateral duties. The title of "officer" notwithstanding, senior enlisted members frequently perform many of these duties.

Administration Officer. The administration officer or administrative assistant is an aide to the XO, observing and reporting on the effectiveness of the administrative policies, procedures, and regulations of the command. The administration officer carries out duties assigned by the XO, which may include the screening and routing of incoming correspondence, assignment of responsibility for replies, maintenance of the tickler file, review of outgoing correspondence, and preparation of the plan of the day (POD). He or she also exercises budgetary control over executive assistants and acts as division officer for X (administration) division.

Automatic Data Processing (ADP) Security Officer. The ADP security officer is responsible for ensuring adequate security for ADP systems in the command, including software and hardware features. He or she oversees administrative, physical, and personnel security controls and conducts risk assessment, security tests and evaluations, and contingency planning.

Chief Master-at-Arms (CMAA). The CMAA is responsible for the supervision, direction, and employment of the security department or division and for assisting the CO in maintaining the security, good order, and discipline of the ship.

Command Career Counselor. The command career counselor is responsible for establishing a program to disseminate career information and for providing career counseling to the crew.

Command Master Chief (CM/C). The CM/C is the senior enlisted adviser to the command on the formulation and implementation of policies pertinent to morale, welfare, job satisfaction, discipline, utilization, and training of all enlisted personnel. The CM/C has direct access to the CO and is senior in precedence to all other enlisted persons in the command.

Drug and Alcohol Program Adviser (DAPA). The DAPA advises the command on how to set up a drug- and alcohol-abuse prevention program and then establishes and administers the program.

Educational Services Officer (ESO). The ESO administers educational programs, acts as a member of the planning board for training, and assists the training officer. He or she may be assigned other duties in the areas of education and training and usually administers examinations and examining boards.

Equal-Opportunity Program Specialist. This individual serves as equal-opportunity adviser to the command, provides briefings on equal-opportunity matters, and facilitates formal command training team (CTT) and command assessment team (CAT) courses, seminars, and workshops.

Health-Benefits Adviser (HBA). The HBA provides information on health benefits to the crew and their dependents. Although not expected to be an expert in all aspects of health benefits, the HBA advises crew members and refers those requiring additional assistance.

Lay Reader. The CO may appoint one or more lay readers to meet the religious needs of the members of particular faiths. Although no civilian credential or approval corresponds to this appointment, the CO consults with the command chaplain or chaplain attached to a higher-echelon commander to select lay readers with high moral character, motivation, and religious interest.

Legal Officer. The legal officer is an adviser and staff assistant to the CO and XO on all matters concerning the interpretation and application of the UCMJ and other military laws and regulations. The legal officer may be a member of the staff judge advocate general (JAG) corps or may be a line officer serving in this capacity as a collateral duty. In larger ships, the legal officer may be a department head.

Naval Reserve Coordinator. The reserve coordinator assists the XO in the proper administration of naval reserve personnel assigned for training or to fill mobilization billets within the command. The reserve coordinator integrates naval reserve personnel into the command organization and develops programs to enhance their training and readiness.

Personnel Officer. The personnel officer is responsible for the placement of all enlisted personnel and for the administration and custody of all enlisted records.

Public Affairs Officer (PAO). The PAO carries out the command's public affairs program. In large commands the public affairs officer may be a member of the restricted line with a specialty in public affairs. In smaller commands a line officer serving in a collateral duty capacity normally fills this position.

Recreation Services Officer. The CO appoints this officer to exercise administrative control and accountability for the recreational services program.

Safety Officer. This officer carries out the command's safety program. The safety officer distributes safety information, conducts training, maintains safety records, and monitors the command's safety program. In some larger ships this is a department head billet filled by an officer of the medical service corps.

Security Manager. The security manager is responsible for all matters concerning the security of classified information and prepares destruction bills, security procedures, clearance requests, and security classification plans.

Shipboard Nontactical Automatic Data Processing Program (SNAP) System Coordinator. This individual coordinates the implementation, operation, and maintenance of the command SNAP system. He or she coordinates, monitors, and schedules SNAP system production requirements with functional area supervisors.

Ship's Secretary. The ship's secretary is responsible for administering ship's correspondence and directives, maintaining officer personnel records, preparing the CO's personal correspondence and officer fitness reports, and maintaining the ship's unclassified reference library.

3M Coordinator. This officer is responsible for administering the ship's maintenance, material, and management (3M) system.

Training Officer. This officer, who is normally a department head, is adviser and assistant to the XO for training matters. The training officer is a member of the planning board for training and prepares and monitors training plans and schedules.

Collateral Duties. Other collateral duties are assigned to officers and senior petty officers. In assigning these duties, the XO and CO take care to ensure that those assigned are qualified, that there is no conflict of interest, and that no individual is overburdened. These duties include:

- Athletic officer
- Brig officer
- Command fitness coordinator
- Communications security material (CMS) custodian
- Controlled substances bulk custodian
- Crypto security officer
- Custodian of cleaning alcohol
- Diving officer
- Electrical safety officer
- Library officer
- Mess caterer

- Mess treasurer
- Naval warfare publications custodian
- Nuclear weapons handling supervisor
- Nuclear weapons radiological controls officer
- Nuclear weapons safety officer
- Photographic officer
- Radiation health officer
- Recreation fund custodian
- Security officer
- Ship's maintenance management officer
- Top secret control officer
- Wartime information security program officer
- Witnessing official

Department Heads

SORM art. 310 contains a detailed description of the duties and responsibilities of officers assigned as department heads in a ship organization.

Department heads have the right to confer directly with the CO concerning matters within their departments, if they believe such action to be necessary. That right should be used carefully, and department heads should always bring the XO up to speed on any matter discussed directly with the CO.

A department head is responsible for organizing and training the department for battle, preparing and writing bills and orders for the department, and assigning, training, and handling administrative matters for all personnel of the department. A department head in a large ship may have an assistant department head and an administrative assistant, and all department heads normally have a department training assistant. Division officers, the most junior managerial positions, report to department heads. Division officer billets are normally filled by junior officers but may be filled by senior enlisted members.

Operations Officer. The operations officer is responsible for the collection, evaluation, and dissemination of combat and operational information required by the mission of the ship. This covers the areas of air, surface, and subsurface search; control of aircraft; collection, display, analysis, and dissemination of intelligence; preparation of operating plans and schedules; meteorological information; and repair of electronic equipment.

In smaller ships, the following officers, if assigned, report to the operations officer:

- Administrative and training assistant
- Air intelligence officer
- Carrier air traffic control officer
- Combat information center (CIC) officer
- Communications officer (when not a department head)
- Computer programmer
- Cryptologic officer
- Electronic-warfare (EW) officer
- Electronics material officer (EMO; except when the ship has a combat systems department)
- First lieutenant (when the ship does not have a deck department)
- Intelligence officer
- Meteorological officer
- Photographic officer
- Strike operations officer

In large ships some of these officers may be heads of separate departments.

Navigator. The navigator is head of the navigation department. He or she is responsible under the CO for the safe navigation and piloting of the ship. The navigator will normally be senior to all watch and division officers. In some ships the XO is the navigator; in such cases the assistant navigator is generally a division officer reporting administratively to one of the department heads.

Communications Officer. In ships with a communications department, the communications officer is head of that department. This officer is responsible for visual and electronic exterior communication systems and the administration of the interior systems supporting them. Assistants to the communications officer include the radio officer, signal officer, custodian of CMS distributed material, crypto-security officer, and communications watch officers. In ships without a communications department, the communications officer reports to the operations officer.

Weapons Officer. In ships that have a weapons department, this officer is the department head and is also responsible for the ordnance equipment. In ships without a deck department, the weapons officer is also responsible for equipment associated with deck seamanship. Assistants to the weapons officer may include the first lieutenant (in ships without a deck department), anti-submarine warfare (ASW) officer, missile officer, gunnery officer, ordnance officer, Marine detachment officer, fire-control officer, and department training assistant.

Combat Systems Officer. When a combat systems department exists, it is headed by the combat systems officer, who is responsible for the supervision and direction of the ship's combat systems, including ordnance equipment. Assistants to the combat systems officer may include the ASW officer, missile officer, fire-control officer, ordnance officer, gunnery officer, electronics material officer, Naval Tactical Data System (NTDS) maintenance officer, systems test officer, and department training assistant.

Older ships will have a combat systems officer or a weapons officer, but not both. Newer cruisers and destroyers may have both.

Air Officer. In ships with an air department, the air officer is assigned as head of that department and is responsible for the supervision and direction of launching and landing operations and for the servicing and handling of aircraft. The air officer is also responsible for salvage, firefighting, aviation fuels, aviation lubricants, and safety precautions. Assistants to the air officer include an assistant air officer, catapult officer, arresting-gear officer, aviation fuels officer, and training assistant.

Aviation Officer. In air-capable ships with a Navy helicopter detachment embarked but without a permanent air officer assigned, the officer in charge of the helicopter detachment is the head of the aviation department. This officer is responsible for the specific missions of the embarked aircraft.

Embarked Air Wing Commander. An officer of the rank of captain commands an air wing and reports to the battle group commander. When the air wing embarks aboard a carrier, the air wing commander also reports to the CO as a department head. This officer (commonly referred to as CAG, for carrier air group) has responsibility for the readiness and tactical operation of the air wing. A deputy CAG is generally assigned to supervise the tactical training and indoctrination of the air wing and the coordination and supervision of the various squadrons and detachments of the wing.

Aircraft Intermediate-Maintenance Officer. In ships with an aircraft intermediate-maintenance department, this officer will be responsible for the supervision and direction of the intermediate-maintenance effort of aircraft embarked or assigned to the ship.

Aircraft Maintenance Officer. In aviation units that have an aircraft maintenance department, this officer is responsible for supervising and directing that department's support of unit aircraft.

First Lieutenant. In ships with a deck department, the first lieutenant is the department head responsible for supervising the use of deck seamanship equipment; and in ships without a weapons department or combat systems department, he or she is also responsible for the ordnance equipment. Assistants to the first lieutenant may include the ship's boatswain, weapons officer, first division officer, second division officer, and department training officer.

Engineering Officer. This officer, commonly referred to as the chief engineer, or Cheng, is responsible for the operation, safety, and maintenance of all propulsion, electrical, and auxiliary machinery. As the ship's damage-control officer, the engineering officer is also responsible for overseeing the damage-control organization. The following assistants may be assigned to the engineering officer: main propulsion assistant (MPA), auxiliaries officer, electrical officer, damage-control assistant (DCA), and department training officer.

Maintenance Management Officer. In CVs/CVNs, this officer is responsible for coordinating the planning and execution of ship maintenance and the documentation of ship maintenance requirements at the depot, intermediate, and organization levels.

Submarine Ship's Diving Officer. This officer is assigned in a submarine, and the duty may be a collateral duty of the engineering officer or the damage-control assistant. The diving officer reports directly to the CO in matters concerning safe submerged operations and to the XO in matters concerning the administration and training of personnel. If this individual is not also the engineering officer, the diving officer keeps the engineering officer apprised of technical matters concerning the submerged operation of the ship.

Reactor Officer. In ships that have a reactor department, the reactor officer is responsible for the operation, care, maintenance, and safety of the reactor plants and their auxiliaries. This officer receives all orders concerning these responsibilities directly from the CO, and makes all corresponding reports directly to the CO, but reports to the XO for administrative matters.

There is special responsibility attached to the operation of reactor plants: the reactor officer and the engineering officer must cooperate closely in matters pertaining to the propulsion plant. Assistants to the reactor officer may include the reactor-control assistant, the reactor mechanical assistant, and the reactor watch officers.

Repair Officer. In ships with a repair department, such as tenders, this officer is responsible for repairs and alterations on designated ships and aircraft. The repair officer conducts timely planning, scheduling, accomplishment, and inspection of work to ensure its satisfactory completion in accordance with prescribed methods and standards. Assigned assistants may include the assistant repair officer, hull repair officer, weapons repair officer, machinery repair officer, electrical repair officer, diving and salvage officer, department training officer, and other officers as appropriate for the mission of the ship.

Supply Officer. The supply officer is responsible for procuring, receiving, storing, issuing, transferring, selling, accounting for, and maintaining all stores and equipment in the ship. The supply officer oversees the operation of the ship's galleys and messes, resale operations, laundry, post office, and disbursing office. In all but the smallest ships, the supply officer will be an officer of the supply corps. Assistants to the supply officer may include a disbursing officer, ship's store officer, food service officer, ship's services officer, postal officer, and others as required.

Medical Officer. In ships with one or more officers of the medical corps assigned, the most senior such officer will be head of the medical department. The medical officer is responsible for maintaining the health of the crew and for ship's sanitation and hygiene. This officer may be assisted by one or more assistant medical officers, physician's assistants, or officers of the medical service corps. In smaller ships without an assigned medical corps officer, a physician's assistant or senior corpsman who is qualified for independent duty may fill this position.

Dental Officer. In ships with one or more officers of the dental corps assigned, the senior such officer will be head of the dental department. This officer is responsible for overseeing the dental health of the crew and may have additional responsibilities to care for the crews of other ships. In ships without a dental department, maintenance of dental records and arrangements for dental care at shore facilities are the responsibilities of the medical officer or senior corpsman.

Watchstanding

In addition to duties related to officers' specific billet assignments, the ship's watch organization assigns other authority and responsibilities.

Senior Watch Officer. Under the XO, the senior watch officer is responsible for the assignment and general supervision of all deck watch officers and enlisted watchstanders in port and under way. This officer maintains records concerning the qualifications of all watchstanders, coordinates their training, and prepares appropriate watch bills.

Watchstanding. The Watch Officer's Guide, published by the Naval Institute Press, is a good source of information and guidance on deck watchstanding. It covers deck watches, log writing, shiphandling, rules of the nautical road, and other safety-at-sea issues. It also covers the duties of the OOD in port.

Chapter 10 of this book describes the ship's watch bill.

Training Responsibilities

All officers are responsible for training their assigned personnel.

Executive Officer. The XO is responsible, under the CO, for forming a planning board for training and for ensuring that the board produces a training plan with necessary subsidiary plans. The XO is responsible for monitoring the execution of the training plan and for testing its effectiveness by scheduling drills, exercises, inspections, and critiques.

Department Heads. Department heads are responsible for executing that part of the training plan pertaining to their departments and for supervising their division officers' training efforts.

Division Officers. Division officers prepare the personnel of their divisions for the responsibilities relating to their ratings, administrative assignments, and battle station and watch qualifications. They must monitor their battle bill, watch bill, and emergency bill assignments to ensure that their divisions can fulfill their obligations. In addition, division officers are responsible for the individual training, counseling, and education of their personnel.

Planning Board for Training (PBFT).   A PBFT is normally conducted once each week and is attended by all of the department heads and key executive assistants. This board, headed by the XO, establishes and monitors the command's training program.

The *SORM* sets forth in detail the requirements of a training program. The process begins with the establishment of a long-range program covering the period of a year. A quarterly plan, a monthly plan, and a summary and record of type-commander training are developed from the long-range plan. Many other subsidiary "General Military Training" (GMT) programs are included, such as drug- and alcohol-abuse prevention programs, career-benefits counseling, sexual-harassment prevention, and safe-driving programs.

Training Records.   Each division officer must keep comprehensive records of the training accomplished by divisional personnel, both as individuals and as teams.

8

THE AMERICAN SAILOR

THE AMERICAN BLUEJACKET CAN DO ANYTHING, ANYTIME, ANYWHERE, PROVIDED HE
IS LED BY AN EQUALLY CAPABLE OFFICER.

—*Fleet Admiral Chester Nimitz*

THE TASK OF LEADERSHIP IS NOT TO PUT GREATNESS INTO HUMANITY, BUT TO ELICIT
IT, FOR THE GREATNESS IS ALREADY THERE.

—*John Buchnan*

The most important task that will be entrusted to you as an officer is ensuring the safety of your ship or unit and the personnel in your charge. The next most important task, and the one that will occupy most of your time, is leading the American sailor.

In order to provide effective guidance and counseling to your enlisted personnel to help them achieve their own career milestones, you should understand not only the career opportunities open to these men and women but also something of the historical background and demographics of the Navy's enlisted force.

Chapter 18 offers some additional words on leadership.

British Influence on Our Navy

Our early Navy drew much of its professional expertise and many of its methods of operation from the British Royal Navy. This was to be expected, since most of its officers were of British descent, the only gun-making foundries were British, and other key supplies and equipment were of British manufacture. However, the character of American Navy personnel differed from that of their British counterparts.

The reasons for the divergence are simple. British officers were chosen for their political connections and aristocratic origins rather than for skill, bravery, or leadership ability. (Lord Nelson was a partial exception to this rule. The son of a clergyman who belonged to a class below the aristocracy, he spent many years at sea as a boy and man. He was a captain at twenty but spent many years watching political appointees pass him by before being recognized as a superior naval leader and being rewarded with high command.) The average officer was an overbearing man of high social status, and the lower-class enlisted man was kept in a very subservient position.

The British who emigrated to America brought with them the seagoing traditions and abilities of their homeland, but they rejected some elements of the British class system. A few American naval officers were actually elected by the crew, although this system ultimately proved impractical. Most officers and captains were chosen for their professional skill and experience, and not for political reasons, although there were some exceptions.

American enlisted men, meanwhile, were technically capable men who knew how to fight and sail. They were rough, ignorant, and argumentative, and they were regarded as second-class citizens. But they brought to their task the initiative, aggressiveness, and spirit of independence that had prompted them to leave Great Britain in the first place. They were worthy ancestors of today's fighting men and women.

Demography of the Navy

In the decade prior to 1997, the size of the Navy was reduced by nearly 40 percent. Navy enlisted-force strength figures for 1997 showed the following:

Grade	Numbers
E-9	3,120
E-8	7,282
E-7	26,547
E-6	62,013
E-5	76,235
E-4	68,262
E-1–E-3	101,175
Total	344,634

The Navy's enlisted force is 19.2 percent African American and 8.2 percent of Hispanic heritage; 6.8 percent are members of other minority groups, and 12.5 percent are women. Enlisted members come from all states of the union and from backgrounds across the entire social and economic spectrum. Ninety-five percent of new accessions are high school graduates, many have some college background, and 66 percent score above average in aptitude on the standardized entrance examination.

Enlistment and Basic Training

In order to enlist in the Navy, men and women must be between the ages of eighteen (seventeen with parental consent) and thirty-four. They must be citizens of the United States or immigrant aliens with immigration and naturalization papers. Enlistees must pass both an armed-forces physical examination and the Armed Services Vocational Aptitude Battery (ASVAB) test. Terms of initial enlistment range from three to six years. After enlisting at a military entrance processing station (MEPS), most enlistees are placed on delayed entry until the beginning of boot camp at Recruit Training Command (RTC), Great Lakes, Illinois.

Boot camp is a challenging eight-week introduction to Navy life consisting of classroom instruction, physical-readiness training, military drill, and field instruction in areas such as ship familiarization, deck seamanship, and military customs and courtesies. Following recruit training, many enlisted personnel go directly to "A" schools for training in particular enlisted ratings, or to apprenticeship training programs intended to prepare them for their first assignments.

The Enlisted Rating System

Pay Grades. The term *rank* is not properly used in reference to an enlisted member; the correct term for an enlisted member's level of seniority is *pay grade.* Pay grades range from E-1 for a new recruit to E-9 for a master chief petty officer (E-10 for the one enlisted member holding the position of Master Chief Petty Officer of the Navy, or MCPON). Figure 8.1 illustrates the insignia and titles of the enlisted pay grades.

Ratings and Rates. The term used to identify an enlisted member's specialty is *rating.* All petty officers (i.e., members in pay grade E-4 and above) have a rating. Examples of ratings are quartermaster, yeoman, machinist's mate, and so on. Each rating has its own insignia that, when combined with pay-grade in-

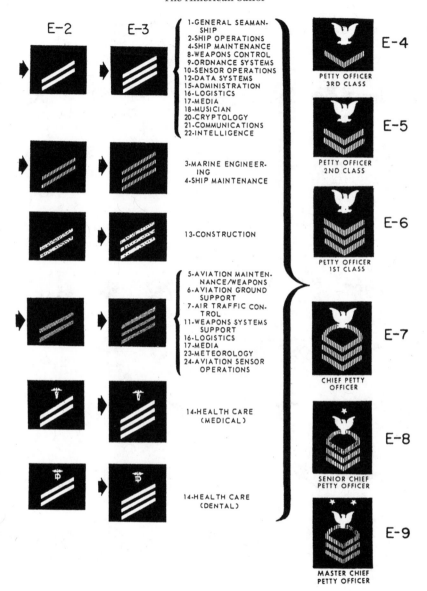

Fig. 8.1. Insignia of enlisted pay grades.
Source: Naval Orientation, NAVEDTRA 12043, April 1992.

Fig. 8.2. Navy enlisted rating insignia.

signia, forms a rating badge worn on the enlisted uniform. Figure 8.2 illustrates some rating insignia. The combination of pay grade and rating (e.g., engineman second class) is called the member's *rate*.

General Ratings and Designated Strikers. Members in pay grades E-1 through E-3 are categorized into six general ratings, also called general apprenticeships: seaman, fireman, constructionman, airman, hospitalman, and dentalman. Each general rating is associated with a broad career field (e.g., firemen are in the engineering field) and with career progression into specific ratings. Members in pay grades E-1 through E-3 who are already assigned a rating are called designated strikers. Enlisted members may become designated strikers through successful completion of "A" school, by passing an advancement exam but not being selected for advancement, or as a result of on-the-job training.

Navy Enlisted Classification (NEC) Codes. NEC codes augment the rating system to identify specific skills of enlisted members. NECs are divided into three groups: principal, component, and related. Principal NECs are stand-alone skills that generally encompass a group of component NECs. Related NECs are similar to principal NECs but are not prerequisites for them.

Enlisted Detailing and Assignment Policy

Detailing. The detailing system used for enlisted personnel is virtually identical to that used for officers. Each rating or group of related ratings has a detailer, and each command has an enlisted placement officer overseeing the assignment of enlisted personnel to that command. In addition, each rating has a community manager, who maintains control over manning and makes decisions affecting assignment policy and career progression in that rating.

Sea-Shore Rotation. Each rating has a sea-shore rotation, designating the normal length of sea and shore tours for sailors in that rating. This notional rotation reflects the rating's relative proportions of billets afloat and ashore. Some shore-intensive ratings substitute overseas tours for sea tours.

Pay and Allowances. There are some subtle differences between the administration of pay and allowances for enlisted personnel and that for officers. Although all officers and enlisted members with dependents are entitled to receive a housing allowance, single enlisted members in the most junior pay grades who are serving aboard ship are not entitled to this allowance and are expected to reside on board. Single sailors on shore duty may also be required to reside in bachelor quarters on base if adequate quarters are available. There are some differences in the administration of basic allowance for subsistence (BAS) for officers and for enlisted members, but these differences are being phased out.

Home-Basing.   The home-basing program allows sailors the opportunity to establish themselves and their families in an area of fleet concentration. Sailors who choose to participate can count on having most, if not all, of their tours in the same geographic area, allowing them the opportunity to buy homes, establish spouses' careers, and provide greater stability to school-aged children.

Members Married to Members.   Enlisted detailers make every effort to co-locate married service couples in the same geographic area, consistent with the needs of the service. In addition, detailers attempt to avoid involuntary assignment to sea duty for both members of dual-career couples at the same time, although they are not prohibited from doing so.

Career Force.   Sailors who have served at least six years are considered to be part of the career force, and they receive some special consideration in their assignments and benefits.

Reenlistment and Retention

Unlike many private enterprises that have the luxury of being able to recruit journeyman skilled workers and middle-level managers from outside the organization, the Navy is wholly dependent on its ability to produce and retain an experienced "home-grown" work force. For this reason it is absolutely essential that significant numbers of the most promising petty officers make the decision to reenlist when eligible, and to stay for a full career. Unfortunately for the Navy, in many cases the most valuable enlisted members are the same individuals whose experience, skills, and knowledge make them attractive to employers outside the Navy. As a division officer, you will be in a position to assist the Navy in retaining these key sailors by providing them information on reenlistment bonuses and special reenlistment programs, described later in this chapter, and helping them progress in their careers.

Selective Reenlistment Bonus (SRB).   In order to remain competitive with the outside job market, the Navy has devised a system of reenlistment bonuses for petty officers in the most critical skills. The amounts of these SRBs, which vary with rating and pay grade, are adjusted twice each year on the basis of available funding and reenlistment patterns. In 1997, twelve thousand enlisted sailors were eligible to receive SRB amounts up to $30,000. Sailors eligible to reenlist with SRB must submit their reenlistment applications to BUPERS between thirty and ninety days prior to their reenlistment dates.

Enlisted Navy Career Options for Reenlistment (ENCORE). Although the Navy needs to provide incentives for its most valuable personnel to stay in, it also needs to place controls on personnel desiring to reenlist, both to prevent overmanning in popular ratings and to screen out members with poor performance records or a history of disciplinary problems. The mechanism used for screening first-term members requesting reenlistment for a second term is the ENCORE program. BUPERS regularly adjusts ENCORE requirements for each rating, depending on the manning situation in that rating. Ratings are classified into three basic career/reenlistment objective (CREO) groups: CREO group 1 is undermanned, CREO group 2 is manned at desired levels, and CREO group 3 is overmanned. Sailors in CREO groups 1 and 2 are automatically approved to reenlist with the recommendation of their CO; those in CREO group 3 must normally have reached at least pay grade E-4 in order to obtain BUPERS authorization. ENCORE also provides an incentive for personnel who are denied the opportunity to reenlist in overmanned CREO group 3 ratings to convert to undermanned ratings that offer better advancement potential.

Petty Officer Quality-Control Program. In the case of career-force individuals with severe performance or behavior deficiencies, unit COs are responsible for making the determination on whether they should be permitted to reenlist.

Extension of Enlistment. Under some circumstances, sailors approaching the end of their current enlistments may extend their enlistments from one month to forty-eight months, in one-month increments. Authorized reasons for extensions include remaining on board to complete a cruise or deployment, to have sufficient obligated service remaining to execute a set of orders or attend formal training, to match the end of active obligated service (EAOS) with the end of a tour (called projected rotation date, or PRD), or to await advancement examination results.

Reenlistment Ceremonies. Reenlistment is a major event in a sailor's career and should be accorded an appropriate and meaningful ceremony to mark the occasion. The officers and senior petty officers in the sailor's chain of command, as well as his or her family, friends, and shipmates, normally attend. An officer of the reenlistee's choosing administers the oath. Most commands provide photographic coverage and forward press releases to base newspapers as well as the sailor's hometown newspapers, and provide other recognition such as refreshments, a period of special liberty, and other selected privileges and benefits.

Training and Qualification

Enlisted Warfare Qualifications. Warfare qualification is a formal system of recognizing the initiative, technical competence, and broadened expertise of enlisted personnel serving in different types of combatant commands. Figure 8.3 illustrates the different types of enlisted warfare qualifications. Attainment of a warfare qualification, which E-3s and junior petty officers are encouraged to pursue, is a recognized milestone in the professional development of any sailor. In recognition of the critical importance of this broad expertise among the senior enlisted ranks, beginning in 1997 sailors assigned to sea duty are required to complete qualification in that command's primary warfare mission prior to advancement to petty officer first class or more senior pay grades. In practice, attainment of a warfare qualification is nearly a prerequisite for selection to any competitive program.

Goal-Card Program. Under the Navy's goal-card program, each first-term sailor is issued a card as a tool to aid in setting and accomplishing goals. Goal cards provide job descriptions as well as information on advancement, educational opportunities, and the educational value of training, and they serve as individualized career plans for first-term enlistees. Recruiters issue goal-card packets to new recruits after they have signed their contracts. The packets include a pocket goal card that is updated at boot camp and periodically thereafter with the assistance of the sailor's chain of command once he or she enters the fleet.

Navy National Apprenticeship Program. This program provides enlisted personnel with qualified apprenticeship training that meets the requirements of the U.S. Department of Labor. Using a combination of existing "A" schools, other classroom train-

SUBMARINE

SURFACE WARFARE

AVIATION WARFARE SPECIALIST

SPECIAL WARFARE

EXPLOSIVE ORDANCE DISPOSAL

Fig. 8.3. Enlisted warfare insignia.
Source: U.S. Navy.

ing, and formalized on-the-job training, sailors can become certified as journeymen in one of seventy-four different trades during their first enlistment.

Rating Entry and Conversions

Rating Entry for General Apprentices (REGA). The primary method of entry into a rating for general apprentices who enter the Navy without guarantee of an "A" school is through on-the-job training followed by a passing score on an advancement examination. In order to provide an appropriate distribution of enlisted skills, the REGA program divides ratings into those that are open (meaning that an undesignated general apprentice in the appropriate pipeline may take the appropriate advancement exam and compete for advancement to third class petty officer in that rating) and those that are closed. A sailor can generally enter a closed rating only following completion of the appropriate "A" school. Commanding officers can request "A" school quotas for promising sailors desiring to enter these ratings.

Conversions. In order to improve their opportunities for upward mobility or to pursue areas of personal interest, enlisted personnel may request to change their ratings. Approval of a lateral conversion from one rating to another is contingent upon the member's release from his or her current detailer and acceptance by the detailer and/or community manager of the new rating. Normally, sailors may only convert from ratings in the CREO 2 or 3 categories to ratings in the CREO 1 (undermanned) category.

Selective Conversion and Reenlistment (SCORE) and Selective Training and Reenlistment (STAR) Programs. Under the SCORE program, a sailor may change his or her rating at reenlistment and be guaranteed attendance at "A" or "C" (advanced-training) school in the new rating. This program is reserved for superior performers who are within one year of their end of active obligated service. In some cases an eligible recipient may be automatically advanced to E-5 following completion of training. The STAR program provides similar benefits for members reenlisting to remain in their present ratings.

Forced Conversion. Personnel who are no longer qualified to serve in their current ratings, because of security considerations, medical concerns, inaptitude, or other reasons, may be involuntarily converted to other ratings. Forced conversion is not a disciplinary tool but may be required in cases where a significant disciplinary infraction has resulted in the loss of a member's security clearance. In addition, a sailor or CO may request a no-fault conversion to a former rating when the sailor fails to succeed in a new rating through no fault of his or her own.

Enlisted Advancement and Development

Unlike officers, who are *promoted* to the next rank, the proper term for an enlisted career progression is *advancement*.

An electronics technician performs routine equipment maintenance on board the aircraft carrier USS *Kitty Hawk.* PHAN Arron Herr

Requirements for Advancement. Requirements for enlisted members to be advanced between pay grades vary, although an absolute requirement is a favorable recommendation by the member's CO. Other requirements generally include a minimum amount of time spent in the previous pay grade, completion of applicable correspondence courses and practical qualifications, and a passing score on a standardized advancement examination. Selectees for advancement to pay grades E-4 through E-6 are determined numerically, through computation of a "final multiple" score that takes into account evaluation grades, advancement exam score, personal awards, time in grade, and other factors. Members who pass the advancement exam but are not selected for advancement are called "passed, not advanced," or PNA. Although eligibility to be considered for selection to E-7 is determined by an advancement exam, selectees for advancement to pay grades E-7 through E-9 are determined by selection boards, which carefully review the members' overall records in much the same manner as officer promotion boards.

Command Advancement Program (CAP).   Commanding officers of ships and selected shore commands are authorized to advance a small number of enlisted personnel to pay grades E-4 through E-6 outside of the normal advancement process. Sailors who advance under this program must meet most of the normal requirements for advancement in rate, although they need not have passed the advancement examination.

Career Milestones.   The two most significant milestones in the career of an enlisted person are advancement to petty officer third class at the E-4 level and advancement to chief petty officer at the E-7 level. The first marks a member's initial entry into leadership, as petty officer third class is the level at which an enlisted member first becomes entrusted with overseeing others. Advancement to chief petty officer is an even more significant milestone and is marked by an elaborate initiation ceremony conducted by the chiefs' mess under the supervision of the command master chief.

Professional Development Board (PDB).   Each command has established a PDB that augments a sailor's chain of command to provide a visibly fair and impartial opportunity for enlisted personnel to attain positions of greater responsibility. The PDB periodically reviews each sailor's record to provide guidance and counseling on career progress. In addition, the PDB reviews applications and requests for striker designations, rating conversion, commissioning programs, and other avenues for professional growth. Normally the command master chief chairs the PDB; other members of the board include the command career counselor, the leading chief petty officer of the member appearing before the board, and the educational services officer.

Educational Opportunities.   Enlisted members as well as officers have numerous opportunities to further their formal education with the Navy's assistance. In addition to the off-duty educational programs described in chapter 17, sailors may apply to the Enlisted Education Advancement Program (EEAP), which provides an opportunity for highly qualified and career-motivated personnel to attend school full-time to obtain associate or bachelor's degrees while on active duty.

Commissioning Programs

Many sailors dream of becoming commissioned officers. There are a number of programs designed specifically to help enlisted personnel achieve this goal.

Limited Duty Officer (LDO) and Chief Warrant Officer (CWO) Programs.   These programs are targeted toward senior enlisted members who already possess unique experience in technical fields. Unlike most other commissioning programs, these two programs do not require a college degree for application, but exceptional evaluation and fitness report marks are a necessity.

Applicants to the LDO program must be in pay grades E-6 through E-8, with between eight and sixteen years of service. Applicants to the CWO program must be in pay grade E-7 or above (or they may be E-6s who have been selected for E-7), with between twelve and twenty-four years of service.

Upon commissioning, LDOs and CWOs are assigned to duties that utilize their specific expertise.

Seaman to Admiral Program.   The name notwithstanding, enlisted members in pay grade E-5 and above with more than four years of service are eligible to apply to this commissioning program. No college degree is required for application to this program, which leads to a commission in the unrestricted line. Following an initial operational tour, selectees are provided the opportunity to obtain their college degrees while serving on active duty.

Enlisted Commissioning Program (ECP) and Medical Enlisted Commissioning Program (MECP).   These programs allow enlisted members who have several years of college credit to return to school while on active duty to complete their degrees and earn a commission. These members attend universities associated with Naval ROTC units at their own expense for up to thirty-six months. Upon graduation they are commissioned as unrestricted line officers (ECP) or nurse corps officers (MECP).

Broadened Opportunity for Officer Selection and Training (BOOST). This program is for active-duty service members (as well as civilians) who seek college degrees and commissions but whose academic background may not qualify them for immediate entry into Navy commissioning programs. Selectees receive ten months of intensive academic instruction at the Naval Education and Training Center in Newport, Rhode Island, to help prepare them for entry into the U.S. Naval Academy or Naval ROTC.

Naval ROTC, U.S. Naval Academy, and Officer Candidate School (OCS). Enlisted members are eligible to apply directly to Naval ROTC and the U.S. Naval Academy in the same manner as their civilian counterparts, although some age waivers are available for current or former active-duty members. Enlisted members who have previously completed their college degrees may apply to OCS.

Separations and Retirement

Unlike officers, who serve at the pleasure of the President and who may request to resign, sailors enlist for specific periods of time and under normal circumstances may elect to be separated only upon completion of an enlistment period.

Administrative Separations. Enlisted members may be administratively separated prior to completing an enlistment for reasons including conscientious objection, certain designated physical or mental conditions, parenthood, pregnancy/childbirth, hardship, personality disorder, a desire to further their education, status as a surviving family member, weight-control failure, and defective enlistments and inductions. Separations may be voluntary or involuntary. Appendix 3 discusses involuntary administrative separations.

High-Year Tenure (HYT). As with officers, who are generally separated from the Navy after twice failing to select for promotion, enlisted members are separated if they fail to reach the next pay grade prior to reaching a certain number of years of service. High-year tenure limits for each pay grade are as follows:

Grade	Years
E-3	6 (8 if the individual passes the advancement exam but is not selected for advancement)
E-4	10
E-5–E-6	20
E-7	24
E-8	26
E-9	30

COs may grant waivers to remain on active duty past HYT limits for members in pay grades E-3 through E-5 who are awaiting advancement results, and under certain other limited circumstances. BUPERS considers other waiver requests on a case-by-case basis.

Fleet Reserve and Retirement. Enlisted members with twenty years of active service may request to be transferred to the fleet reserve. In most respects fleet-reserve status is identical to retired status and entitles an individual to retirement pay and benefits. At the end of thirty years of service, to include time in the fleet reserve, enlisted members may be retired. This transition occurs automatically for members in the fleet reserve.

9

ORAL AND WRITTEN COMMUNICATION

THERE IS NO REST FOR A MESSENGER TILL THE MESSAGE IS DELIVERED.

—*Joseph Conrad*

MAKE EVERYTHING AS SIMPLE AS POSSIBLE, BUT NOT SIMPLER.

—*Albert Einstein*

It is doubtful that as a junior officer you will become known as an especially skilled orator or as a gifted writer, but it is not necessary for you to attain this level of accomplishment at this stage of your career. What is critically important is for you to be reasonably competent in both skills in order to communicate effectively with other members of your command and to prepare messages and correspondence to assist the commanding officer in communicating with outside commands and agencies.

Oral Communication

No doubt you have already had numerous opportunities to observe oral presentations by a variety of senior officers. Although not every senior officer is capable of rousing and inspiring oratory, virtually all are reasonably adept at speaking to a large group without evident discomfort, and of presenting a well-organized and informative lecture that is attuned to the needs of that particular audience. For some of these officers, this ability to speak comfortably in public may have been a gift that required little practice to master, but for most it is a skill that they have honed over many years of practice and experience.

Although the thought of addressing a large group of people in a formal setting may still fill you with dread, be assured that you will almost certainly be afforded frequent opportunities to practice your skills as a speaker in more mundane settings before being thrust into the spotlight. Your earliest such opportunities will be holding morning quarters with your own division, but as you gain in seniority and experience your comfort level will increase, and you will gradually be tasked with giving increasingly complex presentations to larger groups.

Voice Qualities. The human voice has several qualities that distinguish it. The most important are pitch, resonance, projection, and a less definable attribute that we will call tension. These are physical vocal traits that you are born with, but to some extent you can improve upon or control them.

Pitch is the average frequency of tones produced by the vocal cords. A low-pitched voice is more pleasing to the ear than a high-pitched voice, even though the latter carries farther. Nervousness or stress tend to increase the pitch of your voice, but you can counteract this by mastering proper breathing techniques. Watch an opera singer closely. You will see that her chest does not move appreciably, because she uses her lower abdomen for breathing. This technique is not what most of us are used to, particularly if we have engaged in sports, so it will take some time to learn but is well worth the effort. Try to speak using your diaphragm and lower abdomen muscles for breathing. At the same time consciously relax your chest muscles. You will find that you can learn to speak with a minimum use of the muscles of your upper chest and that your throat and voice can be made to relax in the process. This will lower the pitch of your voice and increase resonance and projection. Most important, it will decrease the discernible tension in your voice.

Resonance is the ability of your voice-producing apparatus to resonate to the vibrations of the vocal cords and produce tones and overtones. Greater resonance makes a voice sound richer and more pleasant in the same way that an orchestra produces richer and more pleasant sounds than does a single violin. Good resonance is a function of the internal cavities and shape of the throat, sinuses, and skull. You can improve your resonance by use of the opera-singer exercise described above.

Projection is the property of a voice that helps it carry over long distances. Clearly, the ability to project your voice in a noisy situation can be an important tactical skill, as with the conning officer giving directions to the helm in an emergency situation in a crowded and turbulent pilothouse. In addition, the ability to project your voice well will benefit your ability to make yourself heard to a large group without tiring or straining your vocal cords. The opera-singer exercise will help here too, as will keeping your mouth pointed in the direction you wish your voice to be projected and opening it as wide as possible to maximize the sound waves you produce.

Tension is a combination of pitch and resonance and is directly affected by stress. The voice of a relaxed speaker is more pleasing to the audience and carries far more authority than the wavering voice of a nervous, tense speaker. In addition to this quality of the voice itself, nervous speakers tend to speak faster, as if to rush through the presentation and get it over with as quickly as possible. This kind of rapid-fire delivery tends to antagonize an audience.

To help avoid the "jitters" that can lead to vocal tension, before you make a presentation practice the breathing exercises described earlier and try to focus on something else during the hour or so immediately preceding your talk. Some speakers find that it eases their nervousness to pick out one person in the back of the room and talk directly to him or her. Too much caffeine, as from coffee or caffeinated soft drinks, can accentuate your nervousness and should probably be avoided immediately before your presentation.

Grammar, Diction, and Delivery. The most vibrant, beautiful voice can easily be marred by a delivery that includes faulty grammar, limited vocabulary, poor pronunciation, a regional accent so pronounced as to be unintelligible to the average listener, repeated use of stock phrases ("you know" being one of the worst offenders), or other verbal idiosyncrasies that detract from the speaker's message.

The rules of grammar are considerably relaxed in oral communications; you may augment your spoken words with nonverbal gestures and take other liberties to emphasize your ideas or accommodate the mood of the conversation. Nevertheless, a speaker's disregard for or utter ignorance of appropriate grammar will become apparent in the course of a conversation or presentation and may have a subtle or overt effect on the listeners' trust. Similarly, verbal eccentricities such as the use of obscure words or reliance on profanity or other offensive language to make a point can interfere with your ability to communicate effectively.

The most important rule to remember in oral communications is that your aim is to share your thoughts as clearly and simply as possible with your listeners, to make it easy for them to understand what you want them to know. This doesn't mean you should talk "down" to your listeners, but you also shouldn't try to impress them with your intellect or your worldliness; such a goal is almost certain to backfire.

Communications with Seniors.   A good rule to follow when giving a report to your boss is to remember the guideline taught to all beginning journalists: start with the important facts first, the "who, what, when, where, why, and how" of the situation. Save the lengthy explanations for after you have communicated your main points, and try to ensure that your report does not raise more questions in your boss's mind than it answers.

Many superiors take a dim view of a junior who begins every report with a lengthy preface, particularly when they recognize a pattern in which this preface takes the form of a series of excuses leading up to the ultimate bad news. Putting the bad news first can prevent the buildup of anxiety in your listeners as they wait to find out what you are trying to say, and it will often make them more willing to hear you out without interruption. However, when the news is exceedingly bad, as in a report of an accident involving members of the crew, a superior is likely to appreciate hearing early on a sentence such as, "No one was seriously injured."

Another good rule is never to bring the boss a problem without also suggesting (and demonstrating your ability to implement) an appropriate solution. Inexperienced officers may find it difficult to apply this rule consistently, particularly in an emergency situation, but the report "I have a surface contact on a collision course" is incomplete unless followed with "Recommend altering course 30 degrees to starboard to open the closest point of approach to two thousand yards." Such reports demonstrate your decision-making ability and enhance your superiors' view of your competence.

Communications with Juniors.   When giving orders to juniors, in order to help them develop their own decision-making ability, it is a good idea to tell them *what* you want done without specifying exactly *how* you want it done. At the same time, you should ensure that you are making clear exactly what results you expect from their efforts. Once you become familiar with your subordinates' individual personalities and abilities and they become familiar with your expectations, you may be able to use a kind of verbal shorthand that eliminates much of the explicit detail in such orders.

It is important to get into the habit of giving frequent feedback to your subordinates on their day-to-day performance. You can easily work this kind of communication into your daily routine, and it will pay big dividends for you and your organization over the long run. Telling your chief, "Overall I was happy with the work you did on the performance evaluations, but I noticed some format errors, and I would like you to be careful not to repeat them the next time," is better than saying nothing about the errors and losing your temper the next time the chief makes the same mistake.

A time-honored rule of communicating with subordinates is "Praise in public, reprimand in private." When one of your sailors does a good job, mention it at quarters in front of the whole division. The average sailor may pretend not to care or even to be embarrassed by such attention, but in reality the public praise will serve as a reward for the kind of performance you want to encourage in your subordinates. On the other hand, when you have a criticism of subordinates, you will do better to take them aside and express your concerns privately, to avoid embarrassing them in front of others. Public reprimands are rarely effective in correcting poor performance and can frequently aggravate a troublesome situation.

Although seniors are not obliged to give subordinates justification for their orders, the best leaders typically explain their reasons to subordinates when time permits. Subordinates who understand the reasons for an order not only appreciate that the senior took the time to explain it but are much more likely to carry it out enthusiastically and thoroughly.

Making a Speech. As you increase in seniority you will find yourself invited to give talks to groups of people who want to hear about your experiences or who have a particular interest in one of your areas of expertise. For the novice speechmaker, the best method to ensure that you give a relaxed, professional delivery is to rehearse extensively. After you write your speech, practice into a tape recorder, in front of a mirror, or with a friend. This exercise will serve several functions. If you use the tape recorder or a particularly honest friend, your rehearsal will give you insight into how your delivery is coming across and will allow you to improve the mechanics of your technique. In addition, the added familiarity you gain with the subject matter of the speech will allow you to be more comfortable, and the partial memorization that results will ensure your ability to make more eye contact with your audience than you do when using notes.

If your speech will be followed by a question-and-answer period, try to anticipate the questions you are likely to be asked, and rough out some notes to use in an answer to each. Even if you are not asked the particular questions you anticipate, you will likely find that the notes you made will come in handy in your answers to other questions.

Once you have given a few speeches from prepared texts, try to take the next step by leaving the copy of the verbatim text at home and instead relying on a series of file cards with short notes on them. If you can develop the ability to glance briefly at your notes to refresh your memory as to your next point and then look up from your notes while you are speaking, it will prevent those panicked moments when you lose your place in the text, and it will also allow you to look directly at your audience, greatly enhancing your credibility as a speaker. In addition to the intangible benefits of being able to make more eye contact with your audience, your voice will project better because you will be speaking out into the room, rather than down toward the podium.

If you will be using an unfamiliar sound system, you should try to familiarize yourself with its use beforehand. With a stationary microphone, you must adjust it so that you don't have to hunch over to maintain an appropriate distance from it (normally no more than several inches), and you must take care to maintain a constant distance between your mouth and the microphone to avoid creating distracting fluctuations in the sound level. Lapel microphones are considerably more flexible and easier to use.

Giving a Training Lecture or Briefing. A training lecture is generally given to a group of subordinates or peers, while a briefing is generally given to a senior or group of seniors. These two types of presentation have much in common; in both cases you are the recognized subject-matter expert and are being tasked with sharing your expertise with a group, and in both cases you are likely to make use of such presentation tools as overhead or 35 mm slides, computer presentation software, and videotapes or other audiovisual aids.

Ideally, substantial effort should go into your preparations for a training lecture or briefing. First, you need to prepare an outline of the important points you plan to cover, with amplifying data for each point. Translate these points into a series of "slides," which can take the form of full-sized transparencies or 35 mm slides, a computer-generated projection, or a paper handout. The preparation of good slides is an art form. You should strive to include sufficient information to reinforce your verbal message with visual cues, and to jog the memory of your audience if they review the slides at a later time following your presentation; but you don't want so much detail that your audience has to choose between reading the slides and listening to you. If you use paper handouts, you should plan to include sufficient "white space" for your listeners to take notes directly on the pages.

In your preparations, make sure you are gearing your presentation to the knowledge level of your audience. You don't want to bore them by reviewing information with which they are already very familiar, but you also don't want to lose them by assuming knowledge they do not have. As with your preparations for a speech, it is a good idea to try to anticipate the questions the audience will ask and to prepare answers in advance. Experienced briefers often prepare "backup slides," with amplifying information to be used if the audience requests additional information in a particular area. Such foresight generally reflects very favorably on the briefer.

It has been said that a good training lecture or brief has the following format: tell them what you are going to tell them, tell them, then tell them what you told them. The introductory portion ("tell them what you are going to tell them") should preview for the audience the major points you plan to cover so that they don't start wondering during your presentation where you are going with a particular thought. During the body of your presentation ("tell them") it can be useful to hold your audience's attention by saying something like "I plan to show five advantages to this new technique" or "We will discuss the four basic types of fires," and then tick off each point in some manner as you cover it. It is a good habit to close your training lecture or brief ("tell them what you told them") with a short recap of the important points you covered.

Listening Skills. Just as important as the skill of speaking is the skill of listening. Learn to give your full attention to a subor-

A commanding officer communicates with his crew over closed circuit television.
PHAN Robert Baker

dinate's report, without allowing your attention to be diverted by the paperwork in your "in" box or a ringing telephone (unless, of course, it represents an emergency). Although you may find it necessary to ask questions to help coax the information out of the speaker, you should try to avoid excessive interruptions, which may cause the speaker to lose his or her train of thought or become flustered. When a superior is providing oral direction, it is good practice to take notes so that you will later be able to remember exactly what you have been told to do. Many officers carry small "wheelbooks" in their back pockets for just this purpose.

Televised Presentations. With the advent of closed-circuit television systems on board most Navy ships, it is no longer only the most senior officers who must concern themselves with television appearances. The same general guidelines apply for television appearances as for "in-person" presentations, with a few additional rules.

As is true with still photographs, television tends to accentuate the negative aspects of your appearance. If your shirt isn't tucked in properly or your hair is unkempt, it will be painfully noticeable on television, so take extra pains with your appearance as you prepare for the presentation. A camera with a red light showing is "on." Many experienced officers state that the best method of addressing the camera is to make eye contact with it just as if you were speaking to one individual.

If you are asked to give an interview for a non-Navy broadcast, make sure that your appearance is cleared with the appropriate public affairs office. Be aware that your talk will not likely be used on the air in its entirety. An otherwise good interview can be ruined by one sentence that gives false information or the wrong impression when taken out of context.

Written Communication

All officers will spend a considerable amount of time writing documents, messages, and correspondence and, as they become more senior, proofreading the written efforts of others. With the wide availability of spell-checking tools and other electronic means of proofreading, there is less excuse than ever for sloppily edited work.

It is becoming increasingly common for all officers, except for the most senior, to do their own word processing, requiring a familiarity with word-processing software as well as a good understanding of the fundamentals of Navy correspondence, records, and documents. This section will not make you an expert on these rules but will provide you with a general overview of the different types of commonly used written communications.

The primary reference for most forms of written correspondence is SECNAVINST 5216.5. SECNAVINST 5215.1 governs instructions and notices. The *Naval Institute Guide to Naval Writing* is another excellent reference.

Naval Writing Standards

It is a common misconception that naval writing is supposed to be bureaucratic, bloated, difficult to comprehend, and couched in impenetrable technical jargon. Nothing could be farther from the truth. In fact, for a number of years the Navy has been actively working to encourage a style of writing that is simple, direct, and easily understood. A few general rules will help you to develop this style in your own work.

Be Organized.   As in oral communications, remember the "who, what, when, where, why, and how" of journalism. Get to the key issues quickly to avoid wasting your readers' time; if you believe that amplifying details may be required, include them after your main points. A chronological record of events is rarely the most effective method of communicating your information.

Be Brief.   Don't write a long paragraph if you can get the same ideas across in a short one. Avoid swelling your prose with legalese (e.g., *pursuant, notwithstanding,* or *aforesaid*), unnecessary stock phrases (e.g., *in order to, be advised,* or *in the event of*), and don't use long words (e.g., *utilize* or *procure*) when short ones (e.g., *use* or *buy*) will do just as well. Don't be afraid to use contractions.

Take the Active Voice.   Nothing makes writing appear bureaucratic and overblown faster than using the passive voice. Don't say, "It is believed by the investigating officer that the casualty was caused by lack of oversight on the part of the watch supervisor." Instead say, "I believe that the watch supervisor's lack of oversight caused the casualty." It is highly appropriate to use the personal pronoun in most such situations.

Naval Correspondence and Documents

Letters.   A Navy letter is an official piece of correspondence, in most cases from the commanding officer or commander of one unit to the commanding officer or commander of another unit. Letters may be signed by the commanding officer or by another member of the command to whom the CO has delegated "by direction" authority. Typically a number of officers in a command have "by direction" signature authority for routine correspondence in their areas of responsibility. With this authority goes the understanding that the officer signing "by direction" speaks directly for the commanding officer.

Navy letters are generally printed on command letterhead stationery and follow a strict format as illustrated in figure 9.1, from SECNAVINST 5216.5. The SSIC, or standard subject identification code, listed in the upper right-hand corner, is a code that permits correspondence to be routed and filed as appropriate for the subject matter. SECNAVINST 5210.11 contains a complete listing of these four- and five-digit codes. Underneath the SSIC is a line containing a locally assigned numerical code corresponding

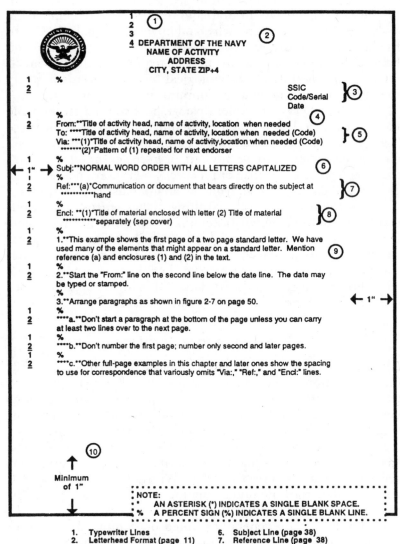

Fig. 9.1. A Navy letter.
Source: SECNAVINST 5216.5.

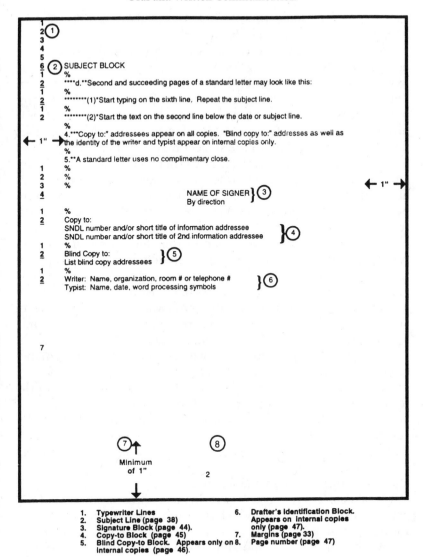

1. Typewriter Lines
2. Subject Line (page 38)
3. Signature Block (page 44).
4. Copy-to Block (page 45)
5. Blind Copy-to Block. Appears only on internal copies (page 46).
6. Drafter's Identification Block. Appears on internal copies only (page 47).
7. Margins (page 33)
8. Page number (page 47)

to the drafter of the correspondence and a serial number corresponding to the letter itself. Serial numbers are not required on unclassified correspondence but are normally used to assist in correspondence management. If used, serial numbers are assigned sequentially, beginning with the number 001 on the first day of each new year. Beneath this line is the date, which may be stamped after the letter has been signed.

To ensure routing to the appropriate individual within the command on the receiving end of a letter, the specific office code may be designated in parenthesis in the "To" (address) line. A "via" command is an intermediate level in the chain of command; the format for such a command's endorsement of a letter is discussed below. "References" (listed in the "Ref" line) are other documents that pertain to the subject matter but are not included with the correspondence; these are designated by letters. "Enclosures" (listed in the "Encl" line) are supporting documents that are included in the correspondence; these are designated by numbers. All listed references and enclosures are discussed, in order, in the body of the letter.

The only exception to the rule that letters are from commanding officers is for letters from individuals on personal or career matters. Examples of such official personal letters include correspondence with selection boards or detailers or requests for augmentation. For identification purposes, the "From" line in such a personal letter always lists the officer's rank, full name, and social security number/designator, and unless otherwise directed such letters are normally sent via the drafter's commanding officer and other intermediates in the chain of command.

Intermediate activities (designated as "via" addressees in the letter) endorse correspondence and forward it to the next "via" addressee or to the ultimate addressee as appropriate. Normally the first word of the first paragraph of an endorsement is *Forwarded*. (This may be expanded into a phrase such as *Forwarded, recommending approval,* or other appropriate remark.) Figure 9.2 shows the format for an endorsement.

When corresponding with a civilian business or other non-DoD activity, use standard business-letter format in place of Navy-letter format. Figure 9.3 provides an example of such correspondence.

Memoranda. A memorandum is a less formal means of communication used between individuals in the same command or different commands. With a few exceptions, the signer of a memorandum speaks only for himself or herself rather than as an official representative of the commanding officer. The general format of a memorandum is similar to that of a Navy letter, except that a memorandum is normally written on plain paper or preprinted forms rather than on letterhead, and the word *MEMORANDUM*

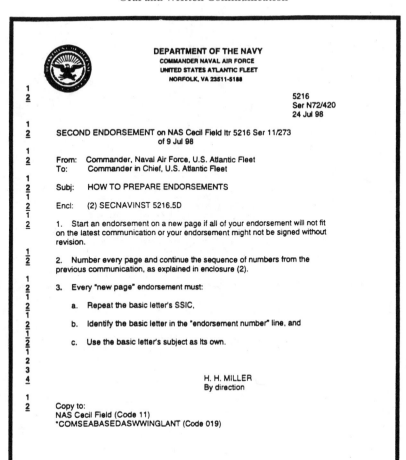

DEPARTMENT OF THE NAVY
COMMANDER NAVAL AIR FORCE
UNITED STATES ATLANTIC FLEET
NORFOLK, VA 23511-5188

1
2

5216
Ser N72/420
24 Jul 98

1
2

SECOND ENDORSEMENT on NAS Cecil Field ltr 5216 Ser 11/273
of 9 Jul 98

1
2

From: Commander, Naval Air Force, U.S. Atlantic Fleet
To: Commander in Chief, U.S. Atlantic Fleet

1
2
1

Subj: HOW TO PREPARE ENDORSEMENTS

2
1

Encl: (2) SECNAVINST 5216.5D

2

1. Start an endorsement on a new page if all of your endorsement will not fit on the latest communication or your endorsement might not be signed without revision.

1
2

2. Number every page and continue the sequence of numbers from the previous communication, as explained in enclosure (2).

1
2
1

3. Every "new page" endorsement must:

2
1

   a. Repeat the basic letter's SSIC,

2
1

   b. Identify the basic letter in the "endorsement number" line, and

2
1
2
1

   c. Use the basic letter's subject as its own.

2
3
4

H. H. MILLER
By direction

1
2

Copy to:
NAS Cecil Field (Code 11)
*COMSEABASEDASWWINGLANT (Code 019)

*Prior endorser included because second endorsement is significant.

2

Fig. 9.2. A Navy endorsement.
Source: SECNAVINST 5216.5.

is typed or printed at the top of the page. Memoranda are generally typed, although very informal ones may be handwritten.

The "From" and "To" lines in a memorandum identify the sender and recipient by name and/or position. The signature

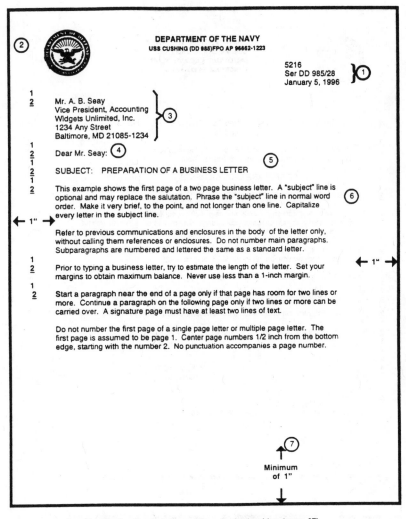

Fig. 9.3. A business letter.
Source: SECNAVINST 5216.5.

block of a memorandum does not list the signer's organizational title, although his or her name may be typed underneath for clarity. Although it is technically incorrect to use a complimentary close in a memorandum, it is still common (and in many commands, expected) for a junior to close a memorandum to a senior with "Very respectfully" and for a senior to close a memorandum to a junior with "Respectfully." In very informal correspondence these complimentary closes may be abbreviated as "V/r" and "R."

Figure 9.4 illustrates a simple informal memorandum. SECNAVINST 5216.5 discusses in detail more formal and specialized memorandum formats used for particular purposes, such as a memorandum for the record or a memorandum of agreement.

Point Papers. The point paper (and its close relative, the discussion paper or talking paper) is a document produced by staff members to provide condensed briefing information on key issues to busy flag officers and other senior officials. A point paper should be short (no more than one page long) and should list in bullet format the background, discussion, and drafter's recommendation(s) pertaining to the issue identified in the subject line. Figure 9.5 illustrates the format for a point paper.

Instructions and Notices. An instruction is a directive containing information of continuous reference value or requiring continuous action; it remains in effect until canceled or superseded. A notice is a directive that contains information that is of value for one time or a brief duration (not more than one year); a notice is always self-canceling after a specified date. Both instructions and notices are filed in numerical order according to the same SSICs used to file Navy letters.

Any commander or commanding officer may issue instructions and notices as necessary in the administration of his or her responsibilities. Instructions issued by the Secretary of the Navy (SECNAVINSTs), Chief of Naval Operations (OPNAVINSTs), and other high-ranking officials are termed "general instructions" and carry the force of law. Every command maintains a file of all the instructions and notices that govern its operation. It is becoming increasingly common for such files to be distributed and maintained on floppy disk or CD-ROM rather than on paper.

Naval Messages. The naval message is the primary means of rapid, official communications between Navy commands. A message is transmitted electronically, permitting almost immediate and highly secure communications between ships at sea,

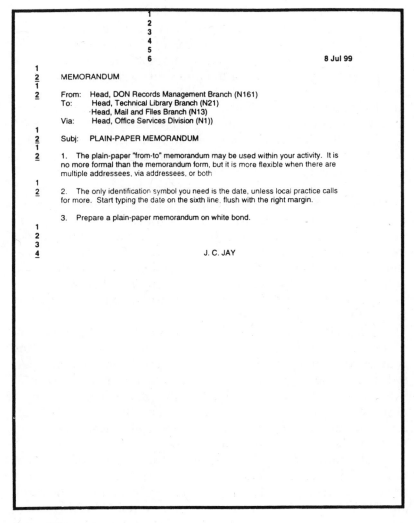

1
2
3
4
5
6   8 Jul 99

1
2
1
2   MEMORANDUM

        From: Head, DON Records Management Branch (N161)
        To: Head, Technical Library Branch (N21)
                ·Head, Mail and Files Branch (N13)
        Via: Head, Office Services Division (N1))
1
2
1
2   Subj: PLAIN-PAPER MEMORANDUM

        1.   The plain-paper "from-to" memorandum may be used within your activity. It is
        no more formal than the memorandum form, but it is more flexible when there are
        multiple addressees, via addressees, or both
1
2   2.   The only identification symbol you need is the date, unless local practice calls
        for more. Start typing the date on the sixth line, flush with the right margin.

        3.   Prepare a plain-paper memorandum on white bond.
1
2
3
4   J. C. JAY

Fig. 9.4. A Navy memo.
Source: SECNAVINST 5216.5.

shore commands, DoD activities and other government agencies, and even foreign military units.

To ensure proper handling and routing to their destinations, Navy messages must be very carefully formatted. Fortunately, a software program in use throughout the fleet called MTF (for

---

POINT (TALKING) PAPER (#)

CLASSIFICATION (Typed here   Rank and Name
and stamped top and bottom   Office Code/Telephone #
of page)   Date of Preparation

Subj: SAMPLE POINT (TALKING) PAPER FORMAT (*) (Unclassified if possible)

BACKGROUND (*)

(*) Why you are writing this paper. Brevity, clarity, and graphic representation are key
ingredients of point papers. Use cascading indentation to organize subordinate points.

DISCUSSION (*)

-       (*)   To prepare a "Talking Paper" substitute those words for "Point Paper."

-       (*)   Might contain problems pros and cons, present status, and outlook for future.

-       (*)   Other points which will aid in your preparation of point papers:

        --   Point papers should be concisely written in bulletized format. Indent subordinate
                  points in cascading style. Continuation lines start directly under the first word of
                  the paragraph.

        --   Point papers should not exceed one page.

        --   Who has been involved and concurs or non-concurs.

-       (*)   Type on 8 1/2 x 11 paper with a 1-inch margin all around. Increase left margin if
                  binding is anticipated.

RECOMMENDATION (*)

(*) State what recommended approach should be. State whether recommendation concerns
discussion of plans and policies that have not been approved by higher authority.

Classified by _____
Declassify on _____

"#"-Denotes highest classification of Point (Talking) Paper
"*"- Denotes the highest classification within section/paragraph

Fig. 9.5. A Navy point paper.
Source: SECNAVINST 5216.5.

Message Text File) Editor makes proper formatting a relatively simple matter. More specific rules apply to certain types of messages, such as those used to report emergencies, and before you are tasked with drafting such messages you will receive more detailed instructions.

Electronic Mail.   Many commands now have the ability to send and receive electronic mail messages (e-mail) via the Internet. The format of an e-mail message depends on whether or not it is considered to be official correspondence. In formal e-mail correspondence, follow the standard format for a naval letter, with the full name of the "signer" indicated at the close. Less formal correspondence may follow the memorandum format, and no specific format is required in very informal electronic correspondence.

Correspondence by Facsimile (Fax).   When time is critical, it may be necessary to transmit a piece of correspondence by fax rather than through the mail system. When you send or receive correspondence by fax, it is of no less importance and must be treated in the same manner as mailed correspondence. You may use a cover sheet to direct an outgoing fax to the appropriate person at the receiving command, although a small fax transmission stick-on form is also available, and its use may save time and telephone charges.

When filing faxed correspondence, remember that thermal fax paper tends to fade dramatically over time. If you need to retain a copy of the fax for more than a few months, make a photocopy.

Classification Markings.   Information that requires protection against unauthorized disclosure is classified as Top Secret, Secret, or Confidential depending on its potential for damage to national security. Additional designations, including "For Official Use Only," NOFORN (for information "Not Releasable to Foreign Nationals"), COMSEC ("Communications Security" materials), and so on, may be used in conjunction with classification markings but are not themselves considered classifications. OP-NAVINST 5510.1, *Department of the Navy Information and Personnel Security Program Regulations,* contains detailed guidance for the assignment of classifications and marking of documents.

Classified information may only be disclosed to individuals with the appropriate clearance and "need to know" (also called "access"), meaning that the individual must have the information to do his or her job. No one has a right to classified material solely on the basis of rank, position, or security clearance.

Only those commands with facilities adequate to safeguard classified material are authorized to hold it. In general, all classified material must be held in such a manner as to prevent unauthorized access by personnel without the appropriate clearance or need to know, usually by means of safes or other secure storage areas. Any person in possession of classified material is responsible for preventing its unauthorized disclosure and for returning the material to the appropriate secure storage.

Classified instructions, correspondence, messages, and other material must be appropriately marked in a manner that ensures proper safeguarding of the information. These markings must leave no doubt as to the level of classification, which parts contain classified information, how long the material must remain classified, and any additional protective measures required.

The overall classification of a document is marked at the top and bottom center of the front and back covers, the title page, and the front and back pages. Each internal page of the document may be marked with the overall classification of the entire document, or the highest classification of the information on that particular page. Classification markings must be highly visible—generally larger than the capital letters used in the text and, whenever possible, marked in red. Rubber stamps used with red ink are a common means of conspicuously annotating classification markings. In addition to page markings, each section, part, paragraph, or other portion of a classified document is marked with the appropriate symbol to indicate the highest classification of the information in that portion: (TS) for Top Secret, (S) for Secret, (C) for Confidential, or (U) for Unclassified.

10

SHIP'S ORGANIZATION AND REGULATIONS

GENERALLY, MANAGEMENT OF THE MANY IS THE SAME AS THE MANAGEMENT OF THE FEW. IT IS A MATTER OF ORGANIZATION.

—Sun Tzu

ORGANIZATIONS AND REGULATIONS ARE NECESSARY TO COVER NINETY PERCENT OF WHAT HAPPENS ON A SHIP. IF THIS MUCH IS TAKEN CARE OF AUTOMATICALLY, THE OTHER TEN PERCENT CAN BE GIVEN THE FULL ATTENTION IT SHOULD HAVE.

—Admiral Robert L. Dennison

An organized ship—one whose crew members know their duties, know how these duties relate to the routines of others, and know what can and cannot be done in the daily routine of living—is an efficient ship, and its crew is a happy one. A ship lacking organization is lax and unsure, and its crew is indifferent.

General Principles of Organization

Planning an Organization. Chapters 2, 3, and 4 of OPNAVINST 3120.32, the *Standard Organization and Regulations Manual (SORM),* describe some of the basic principles of Navy organization. Although you should take time to read those chapters, this section covers most of the basic principles discussed there.

Funk and Wagnalls *Standard College Dictionary* defines *organize* as follows: "to bring into systematic relations the parts of a whole." The *SORM* defines *organization* as "the orderly arrangement of materials and personnel by functions." It states that sound organization is a requisite for good administration, that it is designed to carry out the objectives of command, and that it is based on a division of activities and an assignment of responsibilities and authority to individuals within the organization. Further, to ensure optimum efficiency, a command must assign essential functions as specific responsibilities of appropriate individuals or groups, and there must be a clear understanding of duties, responsibility, and authority.

Definitions. The *SORM* gives definitions of several basic terms you should be familiar with:

• *Accountability* is the obligation of an individual to render an account of the discharge of his or her responsibilities to a superior. An individual assigned both authority and responsibility also accepts a commensurate accountability, which means answering for his or her success or failure.

• *Authority* is the right to make a decision in order to fulfill a responsibility, the right to discharge particular obligations, and the right to require action of others.

• *Delegating* is the act whereby a person in authority tasks another to act on his or her behalf. Authority may be delegated; responsibility may never be delegated.

• *Duties* are the tasks that an individual is required to perform.

• *Responsibility* is accountability for the performance of duty.

There is nothing new about these terms, nor are they unique to the Navy. The same terms and the same elements of organization apply in any organizational setting.

Setting up an Organization. Chapter 2 of the *SORM* lists the steps necessary to establish an organization. Your ship, unless newly commissioned, will already have one, but you may wish to modify the organization of your own division. If so, you will need to do the following:

• Prepare a statement of objectives or missions and tasks
• Familiarize yourself with the principles of organization
• Group functions logically so that they can be assigned to appropriate segments of the organization
• Prepare manuals, charts, and functional guides
• Establish policies and procedures
• Inform key personnel of their individual and group responsibilities
• Set up controls to ensure achievement of objectives

Principles of Organization

Chapter 1 of the *SORM* discusses three principles of organization: unity of command, span of control, and delegation of authority.

Unity of Command.　One person should report to only one superior. One person should have control over one segment of the organization. Lines of authority should be clear-cut, simple, and understood by all.

Span of Control.　Ideally, a supervisor should be responsible for a group of three to seven individuals. Organizations should be structured so that at higher levels of the organization, a supervisor who is responsible for overseeing a large group directly oversees three to seven supervisors, each supervising three to seven lower-level supervisors, and so on.

Delegation of Authority.　Authority delegated to a subordinate should be commensurate with his or her ability and should be delegated to the lowest level of competence. Regardless of delegation, officers remain ultimately responsible for the performance of their subordinates.

Organizational Authority and Directives

Organizational Authority.　*Navy Regulations* arts. 1020–39 are the source of authority for naval personnel. Exact limits and kinds of authority stem from guidance promulgated by ship, department, division, and other manuals and regulations accompanying the corresponding organization.

Organizational Directives.　The basic directive for the organization of Navy ships is in *Navy Regulations*. Art. 0804 states that all commands are to be organized and administered in accordance with law (as set forth in *Navy Regulations*) and with the orders of competent authority, and that all orders and instructions of the CO are to conform to these directives.

Art. 0826 requires commanding officers to take action as appropriate to prevent unauthorized access to their equipment and installations and to safeguard their personnel and facilities against espionage, sabotage, damage, theft, acts of terrorism, and natural disasters.

The *SORM* is the next echelon of directive. This volume is inclusive, covering shipboard organization in detail.

The authority on the organization for the particular type of command is the type commander (TYCOM). There is a type commander assigned for each warfare area (surface, air, and subsurface) in both the Atlantic and Pacific Fleets. For example, Commander, Surface Force, Atlantic, is in charge of surface ships in the Atlantic Fleet, and Commander, Submarine Force, Pacific, is in charge of submarines in the Pacific Fleet. Type commanders may promulgate standard organization and regulations manuals for each class of ship under their command.

Finally, there is the ship's own organization. It must conform with the *SORM* as well as with applicable type-commander directives.

Each ship has its own organizational directive, regulations, and standing orders; a battle bill including a condition watch system; watch, quarter, and station bills; a safety program; a training program; and necessary boards and committees. The *SORM* includes regulations for organizing miscellaneous bills and committees, not all of which are required on every ship.

Organization for Battle

A combatant ship was built to fight, and a ship's allowance of officers and enlisted personnel is based on the manning level required to fulfill that duty. A crew member's position in the battle organization, and the qualifications required to fulfill that position, should be a source of pride. Many a ship's cook or barber has become a gun-mount captain or key person in a missile-loading system.

Conditions of Readiness. Each ship must have a watch organization for each of the conditions of readiness appropriate to that ship. The conditions of readiness are as follows:

- Condition I: General quarters. All hands at battle stations, all armaments and sensors fully operational and loaded.
- Condition II: Modified condition I for specific missions.
    —Condition II AS: Antisubmarine-warfare stations manned at condition I level, remaining stations manned at level of condition III or IV.
    —Condition II AW: Antiair-warfare stations manned at condition I level, remaining stations manned at level of condition III or IV.

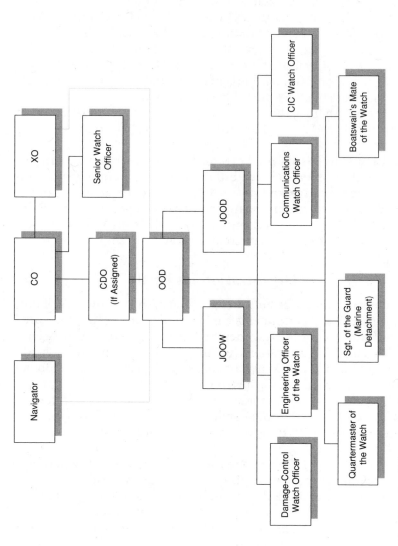

Fig. 10.1. Condition IV watch organization.

- Condition III: Normal wartime cruising. Approximately one-third of the crew on watch, armament manned to match threat.
- Condition IV: Normal peacetime cruising, or in port when watch organization must be able to get the ship under way. Figure 10.1 illustrates a typical condition IV watch organization.
- Condition V: Normal peacetime in port. Figure 10.2 illustrates a typical condition V watch organization.

Administrative Organization

Although a ship's primary mission is to fight, it remains a fact that a far larger proportion of a crew's time, even during war, is spent on routine and administrative matters. Administration requires an organization of its own, known as the ship's organization plan. Chapters 2 and 3 of the *SORM* describe in great detail the form of the standard organization of any ship. Each ship refines this organization to provide for the functions, duties, responsibilities, and authority of each officer and petty officer on board.

The normal chain of command is from the CO through the XO through the department heads, division officers, and work center supervisors to the individual sailors. Larger ships may have additional levels in the chain of command.

Department Heads. In addition to the specific duties and responsibilities assigned to a department head by virtue of his or her billet, each also has certain general duties. A department head represents the CO in all matters pertaining to the department and must conform to the CO's orders and policies. All personnel in a department are subordinate to the department head. A department head normally reports to the XO but may confer directly with the CO whenever he or she believes that such action is necessary. In such cases the department head must back-brief the XO promptly. The department head is responsible for maintaining the general condition of the equipment in that department, and for promptly reporting any problems to the XO and CO, particularly conditions relating to the safety or operation of equipment. A department head may not disable equipment without the permission of the CO. Chapter 7 describes the specific duties of each department head.

Division Officers. The next level below department head is division officer. Division officer billets are normally filled by junior officers, although in some cases senior enlisted members

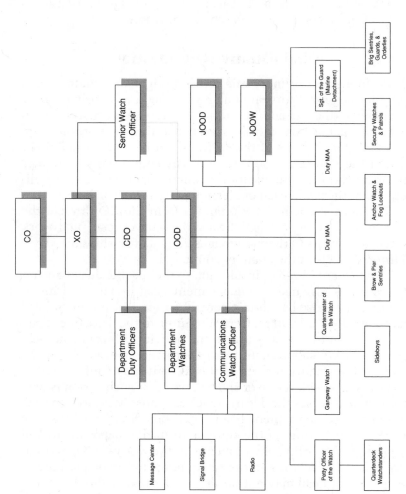

Fig. 10.2. Condition V watch organization.

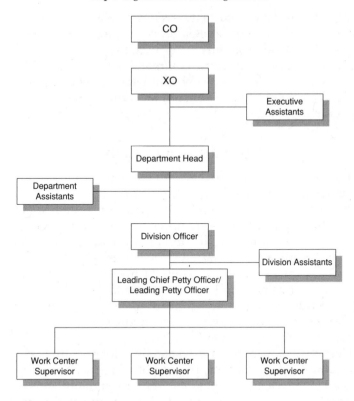

Fig. 10.3. Division chain of command.

may serve as division officers. Chapter 7 describes the specific responsibilities of each division officer. A division officer is assisted in his or her duties by a leading petty officer (LPO) or leading chief petty officer (LCPO), one or more work center supervisors (WCSs), and various special assistants as illustrated in figure 10.3. The *Division Officer's Guide,* published by the Naval Institute Press, is an excellent handbook for division officers and describes their duties in detail.

Boards and Committees. Many organizational functions lend themselves to administration by boards and committees. *SORM* art. 304 describes the composition and purpose of many such boards and committees. A board or committee is a group of persons organized under a chairman, president, or senior member to evaluate problems and make recommendations to the proper authority for their solution. Boards and committees are generally policy-recommending groups, as opposed to policy-making groups; recommendations concerning command policy or function must generally be forwarded through the chain of command for approval by the XO or CO. Enlisted personnel as well as officers may serve on boards.

Watch Organization

Chapter 4 of the *SORM* covers watch organization, both in port and under way, in great detail.

Development of a Watch Organization. The *SORM* describes the standard watches required for the safety and operation of the ship. Two watches, the officer of the deck (OOD) and the engineering officer of the watch (EOOW), are required to be continuous except as specified. The CO may eliminate any other functions that do not apply to that particular ship. Each ship generates written guidelines to delineate the responsibilities of each watchstander, as well as the corresponding system for qualifying personnel for those positions.

Certain departments are responsible for manning specified watch stations; for example, the engineering department usually mans all engineering watches. The senior watch officer is responsible for all watches that are not the responsibility of a particular department, such as quarterdeck watches in port. The senior watch officer maintains duty-section assignments and records of individual watch-station qualifications, and periodically publishes watch assignments in watch bills and in the plan of the day.

The standard daily watch schedule is as follows:

0000–0400	Mid watch
0400–0800	Morning watch
0800–1200	Forenoon watch
1200–1600	Afternoon watch
1600–1800	First dog watch
1800–2000	Second dog watch
2000–0000	Evening watch

Commanding officers may prescribe longer or shorter watch rotations as required by the conditions under which the watches are stood and the number of qualified personnel available.

A junior officer stands watch in the combat information center (CIC) on board the destroyer USS *Benfold*. PH1 Stephen Batiz

When a ship is in port, duty personnel are normally assigned a day's duty from 0800 to 0800 on the following day. Duty personnel must remain on board for the duration of the duty day, except as required in the performance of their duties, and may be assigned specific watches or other duty-section responsibilities for that day.

Relieving the Watch. Watches are customarily relieved at fifteen minutes prior to the hour; for example, oncoming watchstanders assigned to the 1200–1600 watch relieve the offgoing watchstanders at 1145. Prior to relieving a watch, the oncoming watchstander inspects all appropriate spaces and equipment and is on station in sufficient time to be familiarized with the overall situation and equipment status and to obtain a thorough turnover from the offgoing watchstander prior to the designated time for relieving the watch. In the case of an underway OOD, this can require the oncoming watchstander to begin the turnover process as much as a half-hour prior to the beginning of the watch. The senior watchstander at each station is not relieved until all subordinate watches have been relieved.

The standard procedure for relieving a watch is as follows:

• The oncoming watchstander performs any required tours or inspections and, when applicable, receives permission from the appropriate individual (watch supervisor, OOD, etc.) to relieve the watch.

• Relief reports to the offgoing watchstander, "I am ready to relieve you."

• Offgoing watchstander replies, "I am ready to be relieved."

• The oncoming and offgoing watchstanders tour the watch station and review the tactical and equipment situation, including any orders to the watch and unexecuted signals.

• When the oncoming watchstander is satisfied that he or she is completely informed regarding the status of the watch, he or she relieves the watch by saying, "I relieve you."

• The offgoing watchstander states, "I stand relieved."

• The oncoming and/or offgoing watchstanders, as appropriate, report the watch relief to the individual from whom permission was received to relieve the watch.

• On stations that maintain a log, the log is annotated to indicate relief of the watch, and the offgoing watchstander signs the log prior to leaving the watch station.

Personnel Qualification Standard (PQS) and Job Qualification Requirements (JQRs). Under the PQS program, individuals must be certified at a minimum level of competency before they qualify to perform specific duties or to stand particular watches. A PQS book for a watch station or duty specifies the minimum knowledge and skills an individual must demonstrate in order to ensure the safety, security, or proper operation of a ship, aircraft, or support system. The objective of PQS is to standardize and facilitate these qualifications. The JQR system is similar to PQS, but JQRs are locally produced to meet the specific training requirements of a particular command. Commands are required to maintain a list of all personnel who are qualified in each applicable PQS and JQR watch station or duty as well as a list of those individuals authorized to "sign off" each type of PQS and JQR.

Unit Bills

A unit bill sets forth policy and directions for assigning personnel to duties or stations for specific purposes or functions. The *SORM* requires that each bill have a preface stating its purpose, assigning responsibility for its maintenance, and giving background information. A bill should set forth a procedure for interpreting the responsibilities of each person with regard to the functions discussed in the bill. Chapter 6 of the *SORM* contains bills for every possible contingency or evolution. The bills in the *SORM* are intended as a guide for type commanders and commanding officers.

There are three types of bills: administrative, operational, and emergency. Examples of administrative bills are those for cleaning, formation and parade, and berthing and locker assignments. Examples of operational bills include special sea and anchor detail (set when entering or leaving port, or maneuvering in restricted waters), underway replenishment, and helicopter operations. Emergency bills include bills for aircraft crash and rescue, man-overboard recovery, and emergency steering. In addition, there are a number of bills for special circumstances, such as antiswimmer attack, evacuation of civilians, and handling of prisoners of war.

Watch, Quarter, and Station Bill

The watch, quarter, and station bill is the division officer's summary of the allocation of personnel to duties and assignments for each of the bills in use. As its title indicates, it lists the watches, berthing assignments, and bill assignments for each person in a division. Keep it up-to-date as changes occur, accounting for personnel who have transferred in or out of your division. It should also be neat and be posted for ready reference by all personnel. A standard tabular form is used, which can be obtained from the Navy supply system.

Organization Communications

No organization can function unless the will of the CO is known to those who are to carry it out. No less important is the flow of information up the chain of command, to provide the CO with the information he or she needs to make sound decisions.

Methods of Communication. Every ship has several methods of communication, in addition to the familiar oral and written means discussed in detail in chapter 9.

Voice transmission systems provide an effective means of internal communications aboard ship. The 1MC, or general announcing system, is a one-way transmitter whereby orders or information can be announced to particular areas or to the entire ship. A variety of two-way voice transmission systems, including the 21MC and others, provide communications links between multiple watch stations. MC systems have disadvantages in that they require electrical power to operate, their transmissions are degraded by battle noise, and a one-way system cannot ensure that messages are received.

Ships also have a ship's service telephone system linking stations throughout the ship. Theoretically this is an administrative system that was not designed to issue operational orders, but it can be so used in an emergency.

The most reliable internal communications system on board is the sound-powered phone system. As the name implies, this system requires no electrical power to operate and so is ideally suited for use in emergency situations. Its components are rugged and less susceptible to casualty than other communications systems, and headphones worn by sound-powered telephone operators provide some protection against distracting external noise. Numerous individual circuits exist within the system, connecting watch stations that need to communicate with each other; when required, circuits can be cross-connected to allow stations on different circuits to communicate directly with each other. Some circuits in this system are manned during normal underway watches; others are manned for special evolutions such as general quarters, refueling, flight operations, or special sea and anchor detail. The primary disadvantage of this system is that it requires training and discipline on the part of the phone talkers. Strict "repeat-back" procedures are required to ensure that transmissions are not garbled as they are passed from one station to another.

Many ships augment the sound-powered phone system with portable walkie-talkie-type radios for emergency internal communications. Although such radios are less cumbersome to use than the sound-powered phone system, their range below decks can be compromised by the metal hull partitions, and for this reason it can be risky to rely on them in an emergency. Radios are also commonly used for short-range external communications, such as with the crew of a small boat or with a line-handling detail.

When no other means of communication between stations exists, runners may be used to pass messages between them. In damage-control situations, preprinted message pads facilitate the passing of information between the scene of the casualty and damage-control central.

The general, chemical and collision alarms sound over the 1MC system; each has a distinctive sound that everyone in the crew should recognize. Additional specialized alarm systems, such as high-temperature alarms and flooding alarms, are monitored by particular watch stations.

11

STAFF ORGANIZATION AND FUNCTIONS

NO MILITARY OR NAVAL FORCE, IN WAR, CAN ACCOMPLISH ANYTHING WORTHWHILE
UNLESS THERE IS BACK OF IT THE WORK OF AN EFFICIENT, LOYAL AND DEVOTED STAFF.

—*Lieutenant General Hunter Liggett*

AND SO, WHILE THE GREAT ONES DEPART TO THEIR DINNER,
THE SECRETARIAT WORKS—AND GETS THINNER AND THINNER.

—*British military jingle*

Staffs are assigned to flag officers or other senior officers who are in command of a group of subordinate commands. A commander who is not a flag officer normally has the title Commodore.

Staffs are absolutely essential for the smooth functioning of a military organization. No commander, however versatile and intelligent, can unassisted hope to gather and collate all of the information available, make a reasoned and correct decision, organize assigned personnel and forces, and then issue detailed orders for the execution of the decision. A staff is the organization that exists to assist the commander in all of these functions.

Staffs vary widely in size, from the handful of officers and dozen enlisted personnel on the staff of a destroyer squadron commander to the hundreds of personnel assisting the Chairman of the Joint Chiefs of Staff. A staff may have a largely administrative function if assigned to a commander in the administrative chain of command, or an operational function if assigned to an operational commander, or both if assigned to a commander who has a role in both chains of command.

General Staff Functions

A staff exists for one purpose: to assist the commander in carrying out the functions of command for which he or she is responsible. These include operational functions and supporting functions. Operational functions are the missions assigned to the command: making decisions, evaluating intelligence, and formulating plans for executing missions. Supporting functions provide for the welfare of assigned personnel, for training, for personnel management, and for supply and allocation of resources.

The magnitude of these functions will vary with the commander's mission. For example, an administrative commander is concerned mainly with support to the fleet: personnel administration, basic-phase training, and maintenance and repair of ships and aircraft. These support tasks form the basis for operational functions. An operational commander is more concerned with advanced training for combat and with planning, supervising, and evaluating the execution of combat operations.

Regardless of the mission and size of a staff organization, some basic functions are common to all staffs.

Effective staff organization ensures the staff's ability to furnish maximum assistance to the commander. In addition, efficient staff work, which relies on a good organizational structure, is essential to the accomplishment of the commander's mission. For this reason staff organizations follow a standardized plan for dividing the work of the staff, for assigning personnel to positions on the staff, and for delegating authority and assigning duties within the staff organization.

Liaison with Other Commands. The following discussion of duties applies to all types of staffs.

Coordinated teamwork is the essence not only of successful military operations but of efficient staff functioning as well. The operations of a naval task force or battle group, often involving all the elements of the armed forces of the United States and of allied powers, require extensive liaison both within and between commands. Staff officers must conduct liaison in a courteous and cooperative manner, keeping the commander fully informed, as tentative agreements reached at staff levels are not binding on the commander. The vast scope of naval and joint operations, particularly in amphibious operations, and the complex interrelation of forces and types make good staff work essential.

Providing Information and Advice to the Commander. It is not sufficient for a staff officer to bring a problem to the commander's attention and then wait for guidance on how to resolve it. When a staff officer presents an issue to the commander for decision, it should normally be in the format of a smooth (never rough-draft) decision paper as described in chapter 9. Staff officers are responsible for researching all aspects of the issues in their areas and for providing detailed but succinct information to the commander, along with thoughtful recommendations for action. A good staff officer never asks the commander, "What do you want to do?" or "How should we handle this?" although the officer should be flexible enough to accommodate changes in plans if the commander overrules his or her recommendation.

A staff officer must be willing to tell the commander that a planned action would be a mistake. As Major General Orland Ward, USA, said in 1934, "A yes man on a staff is a menace to the commander. One with the courage to express his convictions is an asset."

Navy Staff Organization

A staff's organization will depend on its mission and size. In recent years the Navy has been moving toward a more standardized staff organization, similar to the one in use at the Office of the Chief of Naval Operations, which in turn is patterned after the Joint Staff. Although the division heads, sometimes called assistant chiefs of staff or deputy chiefs of staff, are all on the same level organizationally, they may be of widely disparate ranks. The chain of staff authority extends from the commander to the chief of staff (or chief staff officer) and on down through each division, but it does not cross from one division to another. A typical staff organization is shown in figure 11.1.

In the Navy, every function of the commander, except decision making, is assigned to a staff division. The commander makes all decisions. The Navy does not have a special staff group (with a signal officer, engineer officer, etc.) as the command organizations of other services do. In the Navy, all officers, whether line or staff corps, are fully integrated into the staff chain of command.

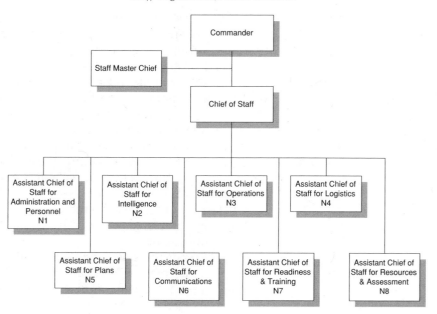

Fig. 11.1. Organization of the Navy staff.

Navy Staff Functions

Chief of Staff or Chief Staff Officer. The chief of staff (COS) is the senior officer on an admiral's staff. The comparable officer on a commodore's staff is called the chief staff officer (CSO). The COS or CSO functions much as an executive officer does. He or she keeps the commander informed of the condition and situation of the command, of subordinate commands, and of other commands in the theater of operations; advises the commander on administrative matters; supervises administrative work; and coordinates staff activities. The COS or CSO signs routine correspondence for the commander, except those concerning policy, action on legal papers, or approvals of action, and acts for the commander on issues for which the commander's policy is known, such as requests for repairs and maintenance, endorsements of routine correspondence, and orders to subordinate officers other than flag officers. If the admiral delegates this authority, his or her chief of staff may exercise nonjudicial-punishment authority for the admiral.

Flag Secretary. The flag secretary is a personal aide who on many staffs acts as assistant chief of staff for administration. He or she is responsible for routing, filing, and managing incoming and outgoing correspondence and message traffic, for managing the commander's directives and instructions, for administering the flag office, and for supervising the preparation of evaluations and fitness reports.

Flag Lieutenant. As the personal aide to a flag officer, the flag lieutenant looks out for such matters as salutes, honors, presentations of awards, official calls, uniforms, entertainment, invitations, and liaisons with other organizations. He or she schedules the commander's calls, maintains the commander's schedule, arranges transportation, and keeps the chief of staff, staff duty officer, OOD of the flagship, and other interested persons advised as to the commander's prospective movements.

In addition, the flag lieutenant tends the side upon the arrival and departure of the commander, visiting flag and general officers, and other dignitaries and serves as flag signal officer. In this latter capacity the flag lieutenant is responsible to the staff communications officer, and on many flagships he or she is responsible for all visual signaling to and from the flagship and for the performance of all signal personnel, whether assigned to the ship or to the staff.

Principal Assistants and Deputies. Assignments and titles of staff division heads depend in large measure on the mission of the staff. Administrative staffs have different primary functions from operational staffs, and their organization reflects that difference. Although no staff will have an assistant or deputy chief of staff in every one of the positions described below, the following numbering system is fairly standard throughout the Navy.

N1, Administration and Personnel. The officer heading the administration division is often also the flag secretary. In addition to the duties already discussed for the flag secretary, he or she advises the commander on the formulation of command administrative policies and handles all administrative matters for assigned staff personnel. N1 also supervises training for enlisted staff members.

N2, Intelligence. The head of the intelligence division formulates and implements policies pertaining to combat intelligence, counterintelligence, propaganda, psychological warfare, and public information. The intelligence officer also keeps the commander and staff informed as to the capabilities of present and potential enemies by the collection, evaluation, interpretation, and dissemination of information regarding the enemy, hydrography, terrain, and weather. Through liaison with subordinate, parallel, and higher commands, and by use of all existing sources of intelligence, including aviation, satellite, and submarine visual and photographic reconnaissance, he or she strives to maintain accurate and current intelligence on all actual and potential enemies.

N3, Operations.   The operations division is the primary executive element of the staff. The operations officer is responsible for the functions that relate to organization and command: training; preparing and issuing directives for combat operations and training exercises; and managing related reports. He or she also prepares operation orders; prepares the command employment schedule; issues the necessary movement orders; keeps track of the location and movement of ships and units assigned to the command; and advises the commander on the assignment of ships and other units to task groups to perform specific tasks.

N4, Logistics.   The logistics division is responsible for advising the commander on all matters relating to logistics and material. Logistics is essential to strategy and the execution of operations and is emphasized throughout the planning process. The assistant chief of staff for logistics prepares studies for proposed operations and the logistics annex for all operational orders and plans. He or she maintains full liaison with subordinate, parallel, and senior commands.

N43, Maintenance.   This officer oversees the maintenance and repair of assigned ships and equipment. On some staffs, particularly those with an administrative mission, N43 is not subordinate to N4 but has equal status on the staff.

N46, Shore Installation Management.   This officer oversees management of shore installations assigned to the commander. As with N43, in some circumstances this officer may report directly to the chief of staff instead of being subordinate to N4.

N5, Plans.   This officer prepares and develops operation plans, monitors force levels and structure, and makes plans to carry out all assigned missions of the commander under peacetime, limited-war, or general-war conditions.

N6, Communications.   This officer is responsible for providing adequate rapid communication within the command and with other commands, and for operation of the message center.

N7, Readiness and Training.   This officer conducts readiness inspections, reviews inspection reports, and oversees training of individuals, ships, units, and special task organizations.

N8, Resources and Assessment.   This officer is the commander's representative in the development of primary mission assessment and procurement.

Other Staff Officers.   In addition to the positions described above, staffs may include a chaplain, medical officer, staff judge advocate, public affairs officer, meteorologist, and other specialists. These officers are typically assigned three-digit numerical codes beginning with the number 01.

Staff Duty Officers.   The chief of staff designates certain staff officers to take turns being staff duty officer on watch at sea and to perform a day's duty in port. In port, the staff duty officer receives routine reports and acts on routine matters as necessary in the absence of other staff officers. He or she regulates the use of staff boats and tends the side on all occasions of ceremony or when officers of command or flag rank are visiting; sees all message traffic; and takes prompt action on any messages requiring immediate attention. In the absence of the flag secretary, the staff duty officer examines incoming mail and takes appropriate action as required.

The duties of the staff duty officer assume special importance when, in the absence of the commander and chief of staff, he or she is called upon to make decisions in an emergency or other urgent situation. For this reason it is imperative that officers on duty keep informed as to the status quo, the policies of the commander, and the appropriate actions to be taken in various situations. In port, in an emergency, and in the absence of the admiral and chief of staff, the staff duty officer may refer the situation to the senior unit CO present.

When the flagship is under way, the staff duty officer represents the admiral in much the same way as the OOD represents the CO. He or she must remain abreast of the formation and location of ships and units, of the navigational situation, and of any significant scheduled events. The staff duty officer makes reports to the admiral and chief of staff as required.

Relationships between Staff and Flagship Personnel

Officers serving in a flagship or on the staff of an embarked commander are involved daily in relationships between members of the staff and flagship crew.

Relationship between Flag and Flagship Officers. A flagship crew plays a dual role. The CO is at all times responsible for the safety of the ship and its performance, but the CO and the ship are answerable to the embarked commander. While under way, the flagship maneuvers as directed by the signals from the officer in tactical command (OTC). When the embarked commander is OTC, he may verbally direct the flagship to maneuver, in which case the flagship must notify other ships in company.

The embarked commander takes over responsibility for the operation of all communications of the flagship, absorbing into his or her organization the members of the flagship communication unit. This unit is then responsible to the flagship for all communications.

Staff Officers' Responsibilities. Staff officers embarked in a ship must always be careful to respect the flagship's unity of command. When making requests to the ship in the name of the admiral, staff officers should always make requests directly to the CO or XO and preface them with "The admiral desires that you. . . ."

All officers and enlisted personnel who serve in a ship, except for the commander, are subject to the authority of the CO and to his or her discipline and punishment. Staff officers have no authority of their own; all of their authority comes from the admiral.

Shore leave and liberty for staff members should conform as closely as possible to that of the flagship. Flag watch, quarter, and station bills should be kept up-to-date, and flag personnel, unless excused by proper authority, should observe calls to general drills promptly. Staff compartments, lockers, and berthing and messing areas should be kept in a condition on a par with or better than that of similar ship facilities.

12

THE ARMED FORCES OF
THE UNITED STATES

WE LIVE IN A WORLD IN WHICH STRENGTH ON THE PART OF PEACE-LOVING NATIONS
IS STILL THE GREATEST DETERRENT TO AGGRESSION. WORLD STABILITY CAN BE DE-
STROYED WHEN NATIONS WITH GREAT RESPONSIBILITIES NEGLECT TO MAINTAIN THE
MEANS OF DISCHARGING THOSE RESPONSIBILITIES.

—*President Harry S. Truman*

OUR GENERATION, LIKE THE ONE BEFORE US, MUST CHOOSE. WITHOUT THE THREAT
OF THE COLD WAR, WITHOUT THE PAIN OF ECONOMIC RUIN, WITHOUT THE FRESH
MEMORY OF WORLD WAR II'S SLAUGHTER, IT IS TEMPTING TO PURSUE OUR PRIVATE
AGENDAS—TO SIMPLY SIT BACK AND LET HISTORY UNFOLD. WE MUST RESIST THE
TEMPTATION.

—*President William J. Clinton*

Organization for National Security

The Commander in Chief.   The President of the United States
is, by provision of the Constitution, Commander in Chief of the
Armed Forces. Several agencies that are part of the Executive Of-
fice of the President advise the President in security matters.
These agencies include the National Security Council and the
Central Intelligence Agency.

The National Command Authority (NCA).   The NCA consists of the President and the Secretary of Defense, who have the
sole authority for making certain types of defense-related decisions. The commanders in chief (CINCs) of the operational forces
report to the NCA.

The National Security Council (NSC).   Established by the
National Security Act of 1947 and modified by the Goldwater-

Nichols Department of Defense Reorganization Act of 1986, the NSC has as statutory members the President, Vice President, Secretary of State, and Secretary of Defense. The Director of the Central Intelligence Agency and Chairman of the Joint Chiefs of Staff are statutory advisers to the NSC. The Counselor to the President, the White House Chief of Staff and Deputy Chief of Staff, and the National Security Adviser also normally attend NSC meetings. The 1947 act provides that the secretaries and under secretaries of the other executive departments and of the military departments may serve as members of the NSC, when appointed by the President with the advice and consent of the Senate. A civilian executive secretary, appointed by the President, heads the NSC staff. The staff includes officers and civilian officials from the Departments of State and Defense and the four military services. The secretariat conducts the routine business of the NSC.

The NSC advises the President on domestic, foreign, and military policies and problems relating to national security, so as to enable the military services and other departments and agencies of the government to cooperate more effectively in matters involving national security. The duties of the NSC are to assess and appraise the objectives, commitments, and risks of the United States in relation to the actual and potential military power of the nation, to consider policies of common interest to departments and agencies of the government concerned with national security, and to make recommendations to the President on subjects that may affect the national policy of the government.

The Central Intelligence Agency (CIA). A Director, appointed by the President with the advice and consent of the Senate, administers the Central Intelligence Agency. The Director may be either a military officer or a civilian. If an officer, he or she is completely separated from the military service while serving as Director.

The CIA coordinates the intelligence activities of the government. It advises the NSC concerning the intelligence activities of the government that relate to national security; makes recommendations to the NSC for coordination of these intelligence activities; correlates and evaluates intelligence; disseminates such intelligence within the government, using existing agencies where appropriate; and performs additional intelligence services that the NSC determines.

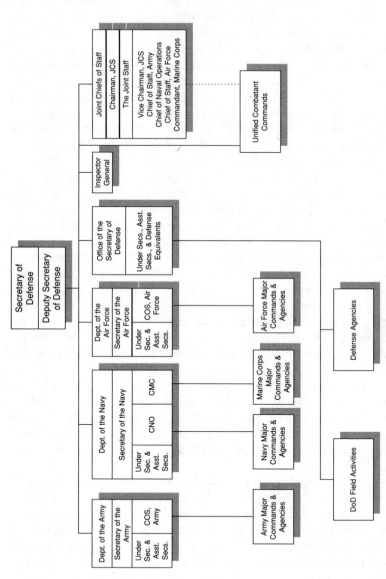

Fig. 12.1. Organization of the Department of Defense.

The Department of Defense

Mission.   The Department of Defense (DoD) was established following World War II in order to unify the military departments under a single cabinet-level secretary. The National Security Act of 1947 marked the beginning of the modern military organization. The act created the National Military Establishment (renamed DoD by a 1949 amendment) and established civilian secretaries for the Departments of the Navy, Army, and newly created Air Force. The DoD is responsible for providing the military forces needed to deter war and protect the security of the United States. The organization of the Department of Defense is shown in figure 12.1.

The Secretary of Defense.   The Secretary of Defense is the principal assistant to the President in all matters relating to the DoD. The Secretary is a civilian appointed by the President with the advice and consent of the Senate. Under the President, and subject to the provisions of the National Security Act, the Secretary exercises control over the department.

The Goldwater-Nichols DoD Reorganization Act of 1986 clarified the Secretary's position in the operational chain of command, which runs from the President (as Commander in Chief) through the Secretary directly to the combatant commanders.

The Deputy Secretary of Defense.   The Deputy Secretary of Defense is responsible for the supervision and coordination of the activities of the DoD as directed by the Secretary. He or she acts for and exercises the powers of the Secretary in his or her absence or disability.

Office of the Secretary of Defense.   Various agencies, offices, and positions created under the National Security Act, together with certain other agencies that assist the Secretary of Defense, are referred to as the Office of the Secretary of Defense, or OSD. They constitute the primary staff of the Secretary. The principal members of this staff are as follows:

• The Deputy Secretary of Defense acts on all matters in the Secretary's absence.

• The Under Secretary of Defense for Acquisition and Technology is responsible for all matters involving acquisition, research and development, environmental security, logistics, space, and nuclear, chemical, and biological defense programs.

- The Under Secretary of Defense (Comptroller) is responsible for budgeting matters and for liaison with the appropriation committees of Congress.
- The Under Secretary of Defense for Personnel and Readiness oversees force management policy, health matters, and reserve affairs.
- The Under Secretary of Defense for Policy handles policy matters including international security affairs, strategy and requirements, and special operations and low-intensity conflict.
- The Assistant Secretary of Defense for Command, Control, Communications, and Intelligence is responsible for all matters involving those areas.
- The Assistant Secretary of Defense for Legislative Affairs acts as liaison to the appropriate committees of Congress on all legislative matters except for those pertaining to appropriations.
- The Assistant Secretary of Defense for Public Affairs handles public affairs and media relations.
- The General Counsel to the Department of Defense handles all legal matters.
- The Director of Operational Test and Evaluation oversees the testing and evaluation of new technologies and equipment.
- The Assistant to the Secretary of Defense for Intelligence Oversight oversees intelligence matters as assigned by the Secretary.
- The Director of Administration and Management acts as executive and office manager to the Secretary.

Defense Agencies.   The following DoD agencies operate under the control of the Secretary of Defense:

- Ballistic Missile Defense Organization
- Defense Advanced Research Projects Agency
- Defense Commissary Agency
- Defense Contract Audit Agency
- Defense Finance and Accounting Service
- Defense Information Systems Agency
- Defense Intelligence Agency
- Defense Investigative Service
- Defense Legal Services Agency
- Defense Logistics Agency
- Defense Security Assistance Agency

- Defense Special Weapons Agency
- National Imagery and Mapping Agency
- National Security Agency/Central Security Service
- On-Site Inspection Agency

The National Security Act. The National Security Act of 1947, incorporated into Title 50 of the United States Code and amended several times in subsequent years, is the basic military legislation of the United States.

The policy section of the act reads, "It is the intent of Congress to provide a comprehensive program for the future security of the United States; to provide for the establishment of integrated policies and procedures for the departments, agencies and functions of the Government relating to national security." In so doing, the act:

- Provides for three military departments, separately administered, for the operation and administration of the Army, the Navy (including the Marine Corps), and the Air Force, with their assigned combatant and service components
- Provides for coordination and direction of the three military departments and four services under the Secretary of Defense
- Provides for strategic direction of the armed forces, for their operation under unified control, and for the integration of the services into an efficient team of land, naval, and air forces

Unification was accomplished by giving the Secretary of Defense authority, direction, and virtual military control over the four services. The Secretary also has authority to eliminate duplication in procurement, supply, transportation, storage, health services, and research.

At the same time, the law established that there would not be a single uniformed chief of staff over all the armed forces and the general staff, reinforcing the concept of civilian control of the military.

Administrative vs. Operational Chain of Command

Within the organization of the U.S. military, an important distinction is drawn between the administrative and operational chains of command.

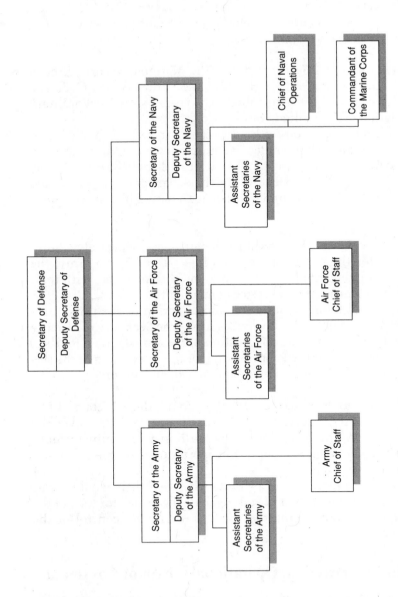

Fig. 12.2. U.S. Armed Forces administrative chain of command.

Administrative Chain of Command. The administrative chain of command is assigned to recruit, organize, supply, equip, train, service, mobilize, demobilize, administer, and maintain the forces of the four military services. This organization is responsible for providing fully trained and equipped combatant units to the operational commanders. The administrative chain of command, which includes the Secretaries of the Army, Navy, and Air Force as well as the Chiefs of Staff of the Army and Air Force, the Chief of Naval Operations, and the Commandant of the Marine Corps, is not directly involved in the employment of combatant forces. The administrative chain of command is illustrated in figure 12.2.

Operational Chain of Command. The operational chain of command is responsible for the employment of the forces provided by the administrative chain of command, in order to carry out missions in support of the national defense. The operational chain was further clarified by the Goldwater-Nichols DoD Reorganization Act of 1986, which specified that the operational chain of command runs from the President through the Secretary of Defense directly to the commanders of the combatant commands. Figure 12.3 illustrates the operational chain of command.

The Joint Chiefs of Staff

History. The authority of the President as Commander in Chief of the Army and Navy was formerly exercised through the Secretaries of War and Navy. During World War II the President felt a need for more personal control and wanted direct access to his military advisers as well as improved coordination between the Army and Navy. He ordered the organization of the Joint Chiefs of Staff (JCS), with Admiral William D. Leahy as Chief of Staff to the Commander in Chief and presiding member of the JCS. The first members of the JCS were General George C. Marshall, Chief of Staff of the Army, and Admiral Ernest J. King, Chief of Naval Operations (CNO). Lieutenant General H. H. Arnold, Chief of the Army Air Corps, was added as a third member. These four officers, later promoted to five-star rank, conducted the global warfare of World War II.

The original National Security Act of 1947 established the Joint Chiefs of Staff as planners and advisers but excluded them from the operational chain of command. Nevertheless, members

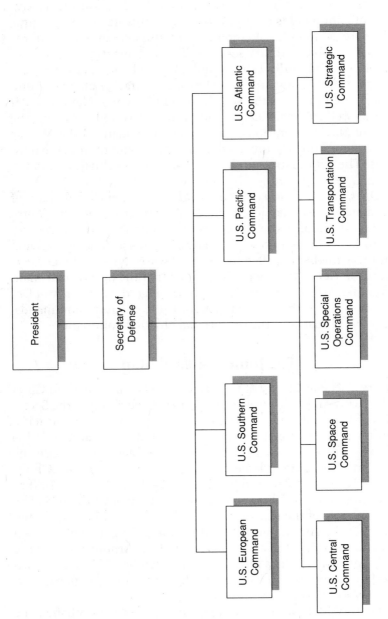

Fig. 12.3. U.S. Armed Forces operational chain of command.

of the JCS were allowed to serve also as executive agents for unified commands, in which capacity they were in the operational chain of command. A 1953 amendment to the act withdrew this authority from members of the JCS, and today, as clarified by the Goldwater-Nichols DoD Reorganization Act of 1986, the members are clearly outside the operational chain of command, although they do act as advisers to the President and the Secretary of Defense.

Composition and Functions. The composition and functions of the Joint Chiefs of Staff are outlined in Title 10 of the United States Code. The Joint Chiefs of Staff are headed by the Chairman, who serves as the principal military adviser to the President, the National Security Council, and the Secretary of Defense. In presenting advice, the Chairman consults with the other members of the JCS and presents the full range of military advice and opinions, unless doing so would cause undue delay. The Chairman may transmit communications to the commanders of the combatant commands from the President and the Secretary of Defense but does not exercise military command over any combatant forces.

The Goldwater-Nichols DoD Reorganization Act of 1986 created the position of Vice Chairman of the Joint Chiefs of Staff, who performs such duties as the Chairman may prescribe. By law, the Vice Chairman is the second ranking member of the armed forces and replaces the Chairman in his or her absence or disability. Although the Vice Chairman was not originally included as a member of the JCS, the National Defense Authorization Act of 1992 made the Vice Chairman a full voting member.

In addition to the Chairman and Vice Chairman, the other members of the JCS are the Chief of Staff of the Army, the Chief of Naval Operations, the Chief of Staff of the Air Force, and the Commandant of the Marine Corps. These other members of the Joint Chiefs of Staff also serve as military advisers to the President, the National Security Council, and the Secretary of Defense and may present their advice individually or collectively. After first informing the Secretary of Defense, any member of the JCS may make such recommendations to Congress relating to the Department of Defense as are considered appropriate.

The military service chiefs are often said to "wear two hats." As members of the Joint Chiefs of Staff, they offer operational advice to the President, the Secretary of Defense, and the NSC. Un-

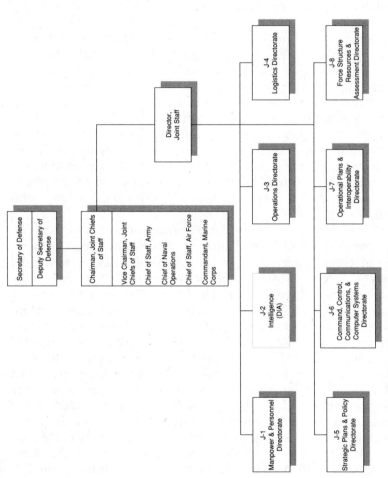

Fig. 12.4. Organization of the Joint Staff.

der the administrative chain of command, as chiefs of military services they are responsible to the secretaries of their respective departments. Their responsibilities as members of the Joint Chiefs of Staff take precedence over their duties as chiefs of the military services.

The JCS is supported by the Joint Staff, composed of approximately equal numbers of officers from the Army, the Navy–Marine Corps team, and the Air Force. In practice, the Marines make up about 20 percent of the number allocated to the Department of the Navy. The Joint Staff has no direct operational authority over combatant forces. The Chairman of the Joint Chiefs of Staff, after consultation with other JCS members and with the approval of the Secretary of Defense, selects the Director, Joint Staff, to assist in managing the Joint Staff. By law, the direction of the Joint Staff rests exclusively with the Chairman of the Joint Chiefs of Staff. As the Chairman directs, the Joint Staff also may assist the other JCS members in carrying out their responsibilities. The organization of the Joint Staff is illustrated in figure 12.4.

In the joint arena, a body of senior flag or general officers assists in resolving matters that do not require JCS attention. Each service chief appoints an operations deputy who works with the Director, Joint Staff, to form the subsidiary body known as the Operations Deputies. They meet in sessions chaired by the Director, Joint Staff, to consider issues of lesser importance or to review major issues before they reach the Joint Chiefs of Staff. With the exception of the Director, this body is not part of the Joint Staff. There is also a subsidiary body known as the Deputy Operations Deputies, composed of the Vice Director, Joint Staff, and a two-star flag or general officer appointed by each service chief. Issues come before the Deputy Operations Deputies to be settled at their level or forwarded to the Operations Deputies. The Director, Joint Staff, is authorized to review and approve issues when there is no dispute between the services, when the issue does not warrant JCS attention, when the proposed action is in conformance with JCS policy, or when the issue has not been raised by a member of the Joint Chiefs of Staff.

Operation. A problem for the JCS may be presented by the President or the Secretary of Defense; it may be brought up by one of the chiefs; it may be forced on them by the exigencies of war or national emergency; it may come to them through JCS representation on the Military Committee of NATO; or it may come up internally in the course of making or reviewing plans. However it originates, it is presented to the JCS on paper through the Joint Secretariat (the administrative staff of the JCS). From the Joint Secretariat the problem is referred to the appropriate Joint Staff directorate. The appropriate directorate studies the problem, coordinates it with other Joint Staff directorates, the services, and other affected agencies and government departments. Usually agreement is reached between all concerned; however, a dissenting view is occasionally passed forward with the completed action. If necessary, a decision brief, attended by the Joint Chiefs, is used to resolve differences.

Two or three times a week in peacetime and several times a day during war or a national emergency the Joint Chiefs meet in the JCS conference room in the Pentagon. Usually present are each chief and principal assistants, the Director of the Joint Staff, and the Chairman. Other officers and civilian officials may be invited to attend; occasionally a JCS action officer is invited. The chiefs may discuss the subjects informally among themselves or may allow presentations to be made.

The majority of JCS decisions are unanimous, although an occasional major decision is split.

Combatant Commands

Structure. Unified commands, also known as combatant commands, are composed of forces from two or more services, have a broad or continuing mission, and are normally organized on a geographical basis or by mission. The number of combatant commands is not fixed by law or regulation and so may vary. All forces not assigned to a combatant command remain in their departments, as does the administration of the forces assigned to combatant commands.

The current combatant commands are as follows.

U.S. European Command (EUCOM). EUCOM, located in Stuttgart, Germany, was established in 1952. EUCOM exercises joint operational command of the U.S. forces in the European theater and serves as NATO's Supreme Allied Commander, Europe. Component commands are:

- U.S. Army Forces, Europe
- U.S. Naval Forces, Europe
- U.S. Air Forces in Europe

U.S. Southern Command (SOUTHCOM). SOUTHCOM, headquartered in Miami, Florida, is responsible for all U.S. military activities in South America and Central America, with emphasis on drug suppression, counterinsurgency, nation assistance, military professionalism, and treaty implementation programs. Component commands are:

- U.S. Army, South
- U.S. Atlantic Fleet
- Twelfth U.S. Air Force
- Special Operations Command, South
- Joint Task Force Bravo (a temporary organization)

U.S. Atlantic Command (LANTCOM). LANTCOM, located in Norfolk, Virginia, was established in 1993. The Commander in Chief of the U.S. Atlantic Command also serves as NATO's Supreme Allied Commander, Atlantic. The four component commands assigned to LANTCOM are:

- U.S. Atlantic Fleet
- U.S. Air Force Air Combat Command
- U.S. Army Forces Command
- U.S. Marine Corps Forces, Atlantic

U.S. Pacific Command (PACCOM). PACCOM is the oldest of the nine unified commands, established in 1947 as an outgrowth of the command structure used during World War II. Located at Camp H. M. Smith, Hawaii, PACCOM is responsible for U.S. military activities in an area stretching from the west coast of the U.S. mainland to the east coast of Africa, and from the Arctic to the Antarctic, including the states of Alaska and Hawaii. Subordinate commands include:

- U.S. Army, Pacific
- U.S. Pacific Fleet
- U.S. Marine Corps Forces, Pacific
- U.S. Pacific Air Forces
- U.S. Forces, Japan
- U.S. Forces, Korea
- U.S. Special Operations Command, Pacific
- U.S. Alaskan Command

U.S. Central Command (CENTCOM). CENTCOM is located at MacDill Air Force Base, Tampa, Florida. Established in 1983, CENTCOM is responsible for U.S. military affairs in the Middle East, Southwest Asia, Northeast Africa, and the Arabian Gulf. Component commands include:

- U.S. Army Forces, Central Command
- U.S. Central Command Air Forces
- U.S. Naval Forces, Central Command
- U.S. Marine Corps Forces, Central Command
- U.S. Special Operations Command Central

U.S. Special Operations Command (SOCOM). SOCOM was activated in 1987 to provide command, control, and training for all special operations forces in the United States. SOCOM is located at MacDill Air Force Base, Florida. Its components include:

- U.S. Army Special Operations Command
- U.S. Air Force Special Operations Command
- U.S. Naval Special Warfare Command
- Joint Special Operations Command
- John F. Kennedy Special Warfare Center and School
- U.S. Air Force Special Operations School
- U.S. Naval Special Warfare Center

U.S. Transportation Command (TRANSCOM). TRANSCOM, located at Scott Air Force Base, Illinois, is responsible for rapidly moving U.S. troops, equipment, and supplies by land, sea, or air to or from any place in the world whenever necessary. Component commands are:

- U.S. Air Force Air Mobility Command (AMC)
- U.S. Army Military Traffic Management Command (MTMC)
- U.S. Navy Military Sealift Command (MSC)

U.S. Space Command (SPACECOM). SPACECOM, headquartered at Peterson Air Force Base, Colorado Springs, Colorado, was established in 1985 to consolidate all military space efforts under the direction of one commander in chief. SPACECOM has four primary missions: space support (satellite command and control operations), force enhancement (satellites that provide ballistic-missile warning, communications, weather, and navigation and positioning support), space control (ability to use space and to deny an adversary the use of space-based support), and force application (planned acquisition of a ballistic-missile defense system). Component commands are:

- U.S. Army Space Command
- U.S. Naval Space Command
- U.S. Air Force Space Command

U.S. Strategic Command (STRATCOM). STRATCOM (located in Omaha, Nebraska) was established in 1992 to unify U.S. strategic forces under a single commander. STRATCOM is responsible for overseeing the U.S. strategic nuclear force structure, modernization and arms control, integration of strategic nuclear policies, and preparation of forces for use if deterrence should fail. Execution of these forces can be authorized only by the National Command Authority. STRATCOM's forces include:

- Minuteman III and Peacekeeper intercontinental ballistic missiles
- Sea-launched ballistic missiles based on submarines
- B-52H and B-1B bombers and support aircraft

The Department of the Army

Mission. The Department of the Army is charged with providing support for national and international policy and the security of the United States by planning, directing, and reviewing the military and civil operations of the Army establishment.

The U.S. Army includes land-combat and service forces; of the four services, the Army has a primary interest in all operations on land.

Functions of the Department of the Army. The functions of the Army, as set forth in DoD Directive 5100.1 of 25 September 1987, are as follows:

(1) The Army, within the Department of the Army, includes land combat and service forces and any organic aviation and water transport assigned. The Army is responsible for the preparation of land forces necessary for the effective prosecution of war and military operations short of war, except as otherwise assigned and, in accor-

M-1 Abrams tanks of the U.S. Army First Armored Division operating in Bosnia-Herzegovina. DoD photo by PFC R. Alan Mitchell

dance with integrated joint mobilization plans, for the expansion of the peacetime components of the Army to meet the needs of war.

(2) The primary functions of the Army are:

(a) To organize, train, and equip forces for the conduct of prompt and sustained combat operations on land—specifically, forces to defeat enemy land forces and to seize, occupy, and defend land areas.

(b) To organize, train, equip, and provide forces for appropriate air and missile defense and space control operations, including the provision of forces as required for the strategic defense of the United States, in accordance with joint doctrines.

(c) To organize, equip, and provide Army forces, in coordination with the other Military Services, for joint amphibious, airborne, and space operations and to provide for the training of such forces, in accordance with joint doctrines. Specifically, the Army shall:

1. Develop, in coordination with the other Military Services, doctrines, tactics, techniques, and equipment of in-

terest to the Army for amphibious operations and not provided for elsewhere.

2. Develop, in coordination with the other Military Services, the doctrines, procedures, and equipment employed by Army and Marine Corps forces in airborne operations. The Army shall have primary responsibility for developing those airborne doctrines, procedures, and equipment that are of common interest to the Army and the Marine Corps.

3. Develop, in coordination with the other Military Services, doctrines, procedures, and equipment employed by Army forces in the conduct of space operations.

(d) To organize, train, equip, and provide forces for the support and conduct of special operations.

(e) To provide equipment, forces, procedures, and doctrine necessary for the effective prosecution of electronic warfare operations and, as directed, support of other forces.

(f) To organize, train, equip, and provide forces for the support and conduct of psychological operations.

(g) To provide forces for the occupation of territories abroad, including initial establishment of military government pending transfer of this responsibility to other authority.

(h) To develop doctrines and procedures, in coordination with the other Military Services, for organizing, equipping, training, and employing forces operating on land, except that the development of doctrines and procedures for organizing, equipping, training, and employing Marine Corps units for amphibious operations shall be a function of the Marine Corps coordinating, as required, with the other Military Services.

(i) To organize, train, equip, and provide forces, as directed, to operate land lines of communication.

(j) To conduct the following activities:

1. Functions relating to the management and operation of the Panama Canal, as assigned by the Secretary or Deputy Secretary of Defense.

2. The authorized civil works program, including projects for improvement of navigation, flood control, beach erosion control, and other water resource developments in the United States, its territories, and its possessions.

3. Certain other civil activities prescribed by law.

(3) A collateral function of the Army is to train forces to interdict enemy sea and air power and communications through operations on or from land.

(4) Army responsibilities in support of space operations include the following:

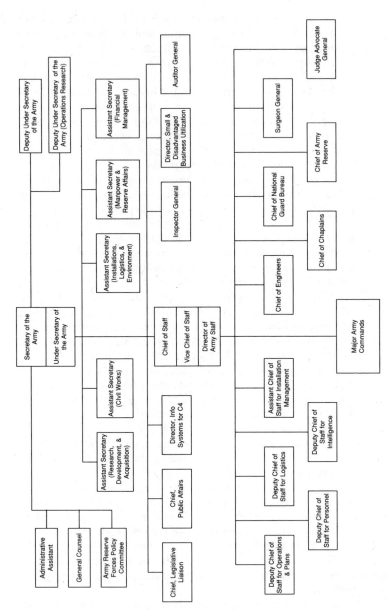

Fig. 12.5. Organization of the Department of the Army.

(a) Organizing, training, equipping, and providing Army forces to support space operations.

(b) Developing, in coordination with the other Military Services, tactics, techniques, and equipment employed by Army forces for use in space operations.

(c) Conducting individual and unit training of Army space operations forces.

(d) Participating with other Services in joint space operations, training, and exercises as mutually agreed to by the Services concerned, or as directed by competent authority.

(e) Providing forces for space support operations for the Department of Defense when directed.

(5) Other responsibilities of the Army. With respect to close air support of ground forces, the Army has specific responsibility for the following:

(a) Providing, in accordance with inter-Service agreements, communications, personnel, and equipment employed by Army forces.

(b) Conducting individual and unit training of Army forces.

(c) Developing equipment, tactics, and techniques employed by Army forces.

Structure of the Department of the Army. The Secretary of the Army is responsible to the Secretary of Defense for overseeing the administrative chain of command of the department (i.e., organizing, training, and equipping a strategic land combat force). Figure 12.5 shows the structure of the Department of the Army.

The Secretary of the Army is assisted by five assistant secretaries:

• The Assistant Secretary of the Army for Civil Works supervises Army functions for conservation, development, and management of national water resources for flood control, navigation, and the environment, and directs the foreign activities of the Corps of Engineers.

• The Assistant Secretary of the Army for Financial Management directs and manages the department's financial management activities.

• The Assistant Secretary of the Army for Installations, Logistics, and Environment determines long-range strategic direction and policy for Army installations and oversees installations, logistics, environment, and safety programs.

- The Assistant Secretary of the Army for Manpower and Reserve Affairs exercises overall supervision of manpower within the Army and oversees all personnel policies.
- The Assistant Secretary of the Army for Research, Development, and Acquisition manages the Army's acquisitions, directs research and development efforts, and oversees procurement and contracting.

The Chief of Staff of the Army, in addition to serving as a member of the JCS, is the primary military adviser to the Secretary of the Army and is responsible for planning, developing, executing, reviewing, and analyzing Army programs. The Chief of Staff is assisted by the following officers:

- The Deputy Chief of Staff for Operations and Plans oversees force structure, establishes requirements and priorities for personnel distribution, and coordinates joint and external matters.
- The Deputy Chief of Staff for Personnel provides and maintains properly trained personnel to accomplish the Army's missions.
- The Deputy Chief of Staff for Logistics develops and supervises logistics concepts, policies, procedures, plans, and systems.
- The Deputy Chief of Staff for Intelligence oversees intelligence activities, including signals and human intelligence, imagery and measurements, counterintelligence, and security countermeasure activities.
- The Assistant Chief of Staff for Installation Management is responsible for promulgating policies pertaining to the operation of Army installations.

Organization of the Army. The Army is organized into three general communities: combat arms, combat support arms, and combat service support arms.

Combat arms are the branches of the Army that directly engage in combat. They include:

- Air defense artillery
- Armor
- Aviation (combat)
- Corps of engineers (combat)
- Field artillery

- Infantry
- Special Forces

Combat support arms provide operational assistance. These branches include:

- Chemical corps
- Intelligence
- Military police
- Signal corps

Combat service support arms are not directly involved in combat. These branches provide logistics, personnel, and administrative functions and include:

- Adjutant general corps
- Chaplain corps
- Civil affairs personnel
- Finance corps
- Judge advocate general corps
- Medical corps
- Ordnance corps
- Quartermaster corps
- Transportation corps

General Structuring of Army Forces. In the field, the Army is divided into armies made up of corps and divisions, all of which contain a balance of combat arms, combat support arms, and combat service support arms to make them effective and independent. The units of the Army, from the lowest echelon up, are as follows:

- A squad/section consists of nine to ten soldiers and is led by a noncommissioned officer, normally a sergeant (E-5) or staff sergeant (E-6).
- A platoon consists of two to four squads (16–44 soldiers) and is led by a lieutenant (O-1/O-2).
- A company consists of three to five platoons (62–190 soldiers) and is led by a captain (O-3). Artillery units of similar size are designated as batteries, and armored or air cavalry units of similar size are designated as troops.
- A battalion consists of four to six companies (300–1,000 soldiers) and is led by a lieutenant colonel (O-5). A battalion is

self-sufficient and capable of independent operations, and it may consist of personnel in combat arms, combat support arms, and/or combat service support arms. Armored or air cavalry units of similar size are designated as squadrons.

• A brigade consists of two to five organic or attached battalions/squadrons (3,000–5,000 soldiers) and is led by a colonel (O-6). Armored cavalry, Ranger, and Special Forces units this size are categorized as regiments or groups.

• A division consists of three brigades (10,000–15,000 soldiers) and is led by a major general (O-8). Divisions are numbered and are assigned missions including infantry, airborne, air assault, light or mechanized infantry, or armored, based on their structure.

• A corps consists of two or more divisions (20,000–45,000 soldiers) and is led by a lieutenant general (O-9). This is the deployable level of command required to synchronize and sustain combat operations.

• An army consists of two or more corps (50,000+ soldiers) and is led by a general (O-10). An army may be a theater army, the army component of a unified command; a field army, constituted from existing assets and structured to meet specific operational requirements; or an army group, formed to control the operations of two or more armies.

Warfighting Units of the Army. The Army is represented in eight of the nine combatant commands, as follows:

• U.S. Army Forces, Europe (U.S. European Command)
• U.S. Army, South (U.S. Southern Command)
• U.S. Army Forces Command (U.S. Atlantic Command)
• U.S. Army, Pacific (U.S. Pacific Command)
• U.S. Army Forces, Central Command (U.S. Central Command)
• U.S. Army Special Operations Command (U.S. Special Operations Command)
• U.S. Army Military Traffic Management Command (U.S. Transportation Command)
• U.S. Army Space Command (U.S. Space Command)

Army Reserve and National Guard. The Army is a total force, comprising both active and reserve forces. The reserve component consists of nearly 370,000 National Guard personnel (mostly in combat units) and 215,000 Army Reserve personnel (mostly in combat support and combat service support units). Current guard and reserve units make up almost 61 percent of combat arms, 56 percent of combat support, and 68 percent of combat service support personnel. In recent years the Army's reserve components have played a more prominent role in peacekeeping, humanitarian work, and civil assistance operations, as well as in operations such as Joint Endeavor in Bosnia, which mobilized almost eight thousand guard and reserve soldiers for public affairs, firefighting, fire support, aviation, logistics, maintenance, civil affairs, and psychological operations.

Army Commissioning Programs. The Army relies on three separate programs to produce its officer accessions: Reserve Officers Training Corps (ROTC), the U.S. Military Academy, and Officer Candidate School (OCS). ROTC provides about 75 percent of the Army's officers and consists of over twenty thousand participating students at approximately three hundred colleges and universities nationwide. The U.S. Military Academy, in West Point, New York, was established in 1802 for the purpose of training commissioned officers. The academy's four-year curriculum combines military science and other subjects and commissions its graduates as second lieutenants. OCS, at the U.S. Army Infantry Center, Fort Benning, Georgia, is a fourteen-week program of intense instruction for previous college graduates that commissions 150–300 officers per year.

The Department of the Air Force

Mission. The Department of the Air Force and the U.S. Air Force were established in 1947 by the National Security Act, which severed the Air Force from the Army. The Air Force includes air combat, missile, and service forces. It is organized, trained, and equipped for prompt and sustained offensive and defensive combat operations in the air. The mission of the Air Force is to defend the United States through the control and exploitation of air and space.

Functions of the Department of the Air Force. The functions of the Air Force, as set forth in DoD Directive 5100.1 of 25 September 1987, are as follows:

(1) The Air Force, within the Department of the Air Force, includes aviation forces, both combat and service, not otherwise as-

Close-up of a F-16CJ of the U.S. Air Force 78th Fighter Squadron/20th Fighter Wing, operating near the Saudi Arabian–Iraqi border. A1C Greg L. Davis

signed. The Air Force is responsible for the preparation of the air forces necessary for the effective prosecution of war and military operations short of war, except as otherwise assigned and, in accordance with integrated joint mobilization plans, for the expansion of the peacetime components of the Air Force to meet the needs of war.

(2) The primary functions of the Air Force include:

(a) To organize, train, equip, and provide forces for the conduct of prompt and sustained combat operations in the air—specifically, forces to defend the United States against air attack in accordance with doctrines established by the JCS, gain and maintain general air supremacy, defeat enemy air forces, conduct space operations, control vital air areas, and establish local air superiority except as otherwise assigned herein.

(b) To organize, train, equip, and provide forces for appropriate air and missile defense and space control operations, including the provision of forces as required for the strategic defense of the United States, in accordance with joint doctrines.

(c) To organize, train, equip, and provide forces for strategic air and missile warfare.

(d) To organize, equip, and provide forces for joint amphibious, space, and airborne operations, in coordination with the other Military Services, and to provide for their training in accordance with joint doctrines.

(e) To organize, train, equip, and provide forces for close air support and air logistic support to the Army and other forces, as directed, including airlift, air support, resupply of airborne operations, aerial photography, tactical air reconnaissance, and air interdiction of enemy land forces and communications.

(f) To organize, train, equip, and provide forces for air transport for the Armed Forces, except as otherwise assigned.

(g) To develop, in coordination with the other Services, doctrines, procedures, and equipment for air defense from land areas, including the United States.

(h) To organize, train, equip, and provide forces to furnish aerial imagery for use by the Army and other agencies as directed, including aerial imagery for cartographic purposes.

(i) To develop, in coordination with the other Services, tactics, techniques, and equipment of interest to the Air Force for amphibious operations and not provided for elsewhere.

(j) To develop, in coordination with the other Services, doctrines, procedures, and equipment employed by Air Force forces in airborne operations.

(k) To provide launch and space support for the Department of Defense, except as otherwise assigned.

(l) To develop, in coordination with the other Services, doctrines, procedures, and equipment employed by Air Force forces in the conduct of space operations.

(m) To organize, train, equip, and provide land-based tanker forces for the in-flight refueling support of strategic operations and deployments of aircraft of the Armed Forces and Air Force tactical operations, except as otherwise assigned.

(n) To organize, train, equip, and provide forces, as directed, to operate air lines of communications.

(o) To organize, train, equip, and provide forces for the support and conduct of special operations.

(p) To organize, train, equip, and provide forces for the support and conduct of psychological operations.

(q) To provide equipment, forces, procedures, and doctrine necessary for the effective prosecution of electronic warfare operations and, as directed, support of other forces.

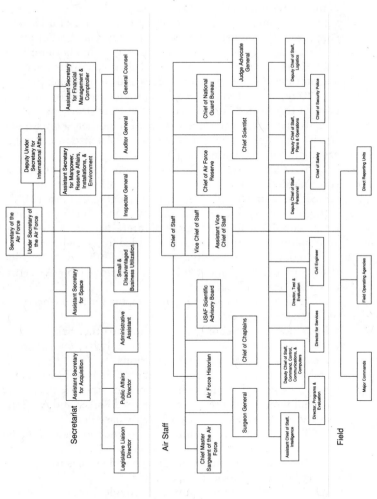

Fig. 12.6. Organization of the Department of the Air Force.

(3) Collateral functions of the Air Force include the following:

(a) Surface sea surveillance and anti–surface ship warfare through air operations.

(b) Antisubmarine warfare and antiair warfare operations to protect sea lines of communications.

(c) Aerial minelaying operations.

(d) Air-to-air refueling in support of naval campaigns.

(4) Air Force responsibilities in support of space operations include:

(a) Organizing, training, equipping, and providing forces to support space operations.

(b) Developing, in coordination with the other Military Services, tactics, techniques, and equipment employed by Air Force forces for use in space operations.

(c) Conducting individual and unit training of Air Force space operations forces.

(d) Participating with the other Services in joint space operations, training, and exercises as mutually agreed to by the Services concerned, or as directed by competent authority.

(5) Other responsibilities of the Air Force include:

(a) With respect to amphibious operations, the Air Force shall develop, in coordination with the other Services, tactics, techniques, and equipment of interest to the Air Force and not provided for by the Navy and Marine Corps.

(b) With respect to airborne operations, the Air Force has specific responsibility to:

1. Provide Air Force forces for the air movement of troops, supplies, and equipment in joint airborne operations, including parachuted and aircraft landings.

2. Develop tactics and techniques employed by Air Force forces in the air movement of troops, supplies, and equipment.

(c) With respect to close air support of ground forces, the Air Force has specific responsibility for developing, in coordination with the other Services, doctrines and procedures, except as provided for in Navy responsibilities for amphibious operations and in responsibilities for the Marine Corps.

Structure of the Department of the Air Force.   The Secretary of the Air Force is responsible to the Secretary of Defense for overseeing the administrative chain of command of the department. Figure 12.6 shows the structure of the Department of the Air Force.

The principal assistants to the Secretary of the Air Force are as follows:

- The Under Secretary of the Air Force is responsible for all actions of the Air Force on behalf of the Secretary of the Air Force and is acting Secretary in the Secretary's absence.
- The Deputy Under Secretary for International Affairs is responsible for the direction, guidance, and supervision of the international activities of the Department of the Air Force.
- The Assistant Secretary for Acquisition supervises, directs, and oversees the management of Air Force acquisition programs and provides advice on acquisition matters to the Secretary of the Air Force.
- The Assistant Secretary for Space serves as principal Air Force adviser to the Secretary on all manner of Air Force space activities.
- The Assistant Secretary for Manpower, Reserve Affairs, Installations, and Environment is responsible for the management of all matters pertaining to the formulation, review, and execution of plans and programs for Air Force military and civilian personnel, Air Force Reserve and Air National Guard forces, installations, and the environment.
- The Assistant Secretary for Financial Management and Comptroller provides financial advice to the Secretary of the Air Force, the Chief of Staff of the Air Force, and other senior Air Force officials.

The Office of the Secretary of the Air Force also includes a general counsel, auditor general, inspector general, administrative assistant, public affairs director, legislative liaison director, small and disadvantaged business utilization director, and various statutory boards and committees.

The Chief of Staff, U.S. Air Force, is appointed by the President, with the consent of the Senate, from among Air Force general officers, normally for a four-year term. The Chief of Staff serves as a member of the Joint Chiefs of Staff and is the principal uniformed adviser to the Secretary of the Air Force.

The Chief of Staff presides over the Air Staff, transmits Air Staff plans and recommendations to the Secretary of the Air Force, and acts as the Secretary's agent in carrying them out. The Chief of Staff is responsible for the efficiency of the Air Force and the preparation of its forces for military operations; supervises the administration of Air Force personnel assigned to unified combatant commands; and supervises support of these forces assigned by the Air Force as directed by the Secretary of Defense.

The Chief of Staff has the following principal assistants:

- Vice Chief of Staff
- Assistant Vice Chief of Staff
- Deputy Chief of Staff for Personnel
- Deputy Chief of Staff for Plans and Operations
- Deputy Chief of Staff for Logistics
- Deputy Chief of Staff for Command, Control, Communications, and Computers
- Assistant Chief of Staff for Intelligence

Additional members of the Air Staff include the following: a civil engineer, chief master sergeant of the Air Force, chief of safety, chief of security police, Air Force historian, chief scientist, chief of the Air Force Reserve, chief of the National Guard Bureau, the U.S. Air Force Scientific Advisory Board, judge advocate general, director of test and evaluation, director of programs and evaluation, surgeon general, chief of chaplains, and director for services.

Organization of the Air Force. The Air Force's basic warfighting unit is the wing. Composite wings operate more than one kind of aircraft and may be configured as self-contained units designated for quick deployment anywhere in the world. In addition, wings can have specialized missions such as training or intelligence. Wing organizations generally include operations, logistics, and support groups.

In descending order of command, the elements of the Air Force include major commands, numbered air forces, wings, groups, squadrons, and flights.

Air Force Major Commands. There are eight major commands in the Air Force:

- The Air Combat Command organizes, trains, and equips nuclear-capable forces for the U.S. Strategic Command and theater air combat forces for the five geographic U.S. combatant commands (U.S. Atlantic Command, U.S. European Command, U.S. Pacific Command, U.S. Central Command, and U.S. Southern Command).

- The Air Education and Training Command conducts recruiting and training programs, including basic military training, officer training, advanced training, and technical training.
- The Air Mobility Command provides forces for airlift and sustainment of U.S. armed forces (and for humanitarian missions).
- The Air Force Material Command conducts research and development for weapons systems (this command was created by the merger of the Air Force Logistics Command and the Air Force Systems Command).
- Air Forces in Europe is the air component of the U.S. European Command.
- Pacific Air Forces is the air component of the U.S. Pacific Command.
- The Air Force Space Command utilizes space to provide support for combat forces and is responsible for the Air Force's ICBM forces.
- The Air Force Special Operations Command provides Air Force special operations forces for worldwide deployment and assignment to regional combatant commands.

In addition to the eight major commands, thirty-seven field operating agencies and three direct reporting units report to Headquarters, U.S. Air Force. Field agencies are assigned specialized missions such as intelligence, security, communications, reserve administration, civil engineering, and personnel. Direct reporting units are the Eleventh Wing in Washington D.C., the Air Force Operational Test and Evaluation Center, and the U.S. Air Force Academy.

Air Force Reserve and Air National Guard. The active Air Force is augmented by the Air Force Reserve and the Air National Guard. Air Force Reserve aircrews perform up to 30 percent of the Air Mobility Command's peacetime flying missions, and its fighters, bombers, tankers, transports, and rescue aircraft are fully integrated into the Air Force under the total-force concept. In addition, civil engineering, security police, medical, and communications personnel serve in the reserve.

Air National Guard personnel perform mostly supporting roles in airlift, aerial refueling, communications, intelligence, civil engineering, and medical support.

Air Force Commissioning Programs. The Air Force trains future officers in Air Force ROTC programs at nearly 150 colleges and universities, at the U.S. Air Force Academy in Colorado Springs, Colorado, and in a thirteen-and-a-half-week course of instruction at Officer Training School (OTS) located at Maxwell Air Force Base in Montgomery, Alabama.

13

THE DEPARTMENT OF THE NAVY

IT FOLLOWS THEN, AS CERTAIN AS NIGHT SUCCEEDS DAY, THAT WITHOUT A DECISIVE NAVAL FORCE WE CAN DO NOTHING DEFINITIVE, AND WITH IT EVERYTHING HONORABLE AND GLORIOUS.

—*President George Washington*

EVERY DANGER OF A MILITARY CHARACTER TO WHICH THE UNITED STATES IS EXPOSED CAN BE MET BEST OUTSIDE HER OWN TERRITORY—AT SEA.

—*Rear Admiral Alfred Thayer Mahan*

Mission and Functions

The Department of the Navy is to "be organized, trained and equipped primarily for prompt and sustainable combat incident to operations at sea" (*Navy Regulations* art. 0202). The National Security Act of 1947, as amended in 1949, governs the role of the Navy in national defense. The Goldwater-Nichols Department of Defense Reorganization Act of 1986 streamlined the operational chain of command and provided detailed descriptions of the roles of the Secretary of the Navy, the Chief of Naval Operations, and the Commandant of the Marine Corps.

Functions of the Department of the Navy.   The functions of the Navy, as set forth in DoD Directive 5100.1 of 25 September 1987, are as follows:

(1) The Navy, within the Department of the Navy, includes, in general, naval combat and service forces and such aviation as may be organic therein. The Marine Corps, within the Department of Navy, includes not less than three combat divisions and three air wings and such other land combat, aviation, and other services as may be organic therein. The Coast Guard, when operating as a Service

within the Department of the Navy, includes naval combat and service forces and such aviation as may be organic therein.

(a) The Navy and Marine Corps, under the Secretary of the Navy, are responsible for the preparation of Navy and Marine Corps forces necessary for the effective prosecution of war and military operations short of war, except as otherwise assigned and, in accordance with the integrated joint mobilization plans, for the expansion of the peacetime components of the Navy and Marine Corps to meet the needs of war.

(b) During peacetime, the Department of Transportation is responsible for maintaining the United States Coast Guard in a state of readiness so that it may function as a specialized Service in the Navy in time of war or when the President directs. The Coast Guard may also perform its military functions in times of limited war or defense contingency, in support of Naval Component Commanders, without transfer to the Department of the Navy.

(2) The primary functions of the Navy and/or Marine Corps are:

(a) To organize, train, equip, and provide Navy and Marine Corps forces for the conduct of prompt and sustained combat incident to operations at sea, including operations of sea-based aircraft and land-based naval air components—specifically, forces to seek out and destroy enemy naval forces and to suppress enemy sea commerce, to gain and maintain general naval supremacy, to control vital sea areas and to protect vital sea lines of communication, to establish and maintain local superiority (including air) in an area of naval operations, to seize and defend advanced naval bases, and to conduct such land, air, and space operations as may be essential to the prosecution of a naval campaign.

(b) To maintain the Marine Corps, which shall be organized, trained, and equipped to provide Fleet Marine Forces of combined arms, together with supporting air components, for service with the fleet in the seizure or defense of advanced naval bases and for the conduct of such land operations as may be essential to the prosecution of a naval campaign. In addition, the Marine Corps shall provide detachments and organizations for service on armed vessels of the Navy, provide security detachments for the protection of naval property at naval stations and bases, and perform such other duties as the President or the Secretary of Defense may direct. However, these additional duties must not detract from, or interfere with, the operations for which the Marine Corps is primarily organized. These functions do not contemplate the creation of a second land army.

(c) Further, the Marine Corps shall:

1. Develop, in coordination with the other Military Services, the doctrines, tactics, techniques, and equipment employed by landing forces in amphibious operations. The Marine Corps shall have primary responsibility for the development of those landing force doctrines, tactics, techniques, and equipment which are of common interest to the Army and the Marine Corps.

2. Train and equip, as required, forces for airborne operations, in coordination with the other Military Services, and in accordance with joint doctrines.

3. Develop, in coordination with the other Military Services, doctrines, procedures, and equipment of interest to the Marine Corps for airborne operations and not provided for by the Army, which has primary responsibility for the development of airborne doctrines, procedures, and techniques, which are of common interest to the Army and Marine Corps.

(d) To organize and equip, in coordination with the other Military Services, and to provide naval forces, including naval close air support and space forces, for the conduct of joint amphibious operations, and to be responsible for the amphibious training of all forces assigned to joint amphibious operations in accordance with joint doctrines.

(e) To develop, in coordination with the other Services, the doctrines, procedures, and equipment of naval forces for amphibious operations and the doctrines and procedures for joint amphibious operations.

(f) To organize, train, equip, and provide forces for strategic nuclear warfare to support strategic deterrence.

(g) To furnish adequate, timely, reliable intelligence for the Coast Guard.

(h) To organize, train, equip, and provide forces for reconnaissance, antisubmarine warfare, protection of shipping, aerial refueling and minelaying, including the air and space aspects thereof, and controlled minefield operations.

(i) To provide the afloat forces for strategic sealift.

(j) To provide air support essential for naval operations.

(k) To organize, train, equip, and provide forces for appropriate air and missile defense and space control operations, including the provision of forces as required for the strategic defense of the United States, in accordance with joint doctrines.

(l) To provide equipment, forces, procedures, and doctrine

necessary for the effective prosecution of electronic warfare operations and, as directed, support of other forces.

(m) To furnish aerial photography, as necessary, for Navy and Marine Corps operations.

(n) To develop, in coordination with the other Services, doctrines, procedures, and equipment employed by Navy and Marine Corps forces in the conduct of space operations.

(o) To provide sea-based launch and space support for the Department of Defense when directed.

(p) To organize, train, equip, and provide forces, as directed, to operate sea lines of communication.

(q) To organize, train, equip, and provide forces for the support and conduct of special operations.

(r) To organize, train, equip, and provide Navy and Marine Corps forces for the support and conduct of psychological operations.

(s) To coordinate with the Department of Transportation for the peacetime maintenance of the Coast Guard. During war, the Coast Guard will function as a Military Service. The specific wartime functions of the Coast Guard are as follows:

1. To provide an integrated port security and coastal defense force, in coordination with the other Military Services, for the United States.

2. To provide specialized Coast Guard units, including designated ships and aircraft, for overseas deployment required by naval component commanders.

3. To organize and equip, in coordination with the other Military Services, and provide forces for maritime search and rescue, icebreaking, and servicing of maritime aids to navigation.

(3) The collateral functions of the Navy and Marine Corps include the following:

(a) To interdict enemy land power, air power, and communications through operations at sea.

(b) To conduct close air and naval support for land operations.

(c) To furnish aerial imagery for cartographic purposes.

(d) To be prepared to participate in the overall air and space effort, as directed.

(e) To establish military government, as directed, pending transfer of this responsibility to other authority.

(4) Navy and Marine Corps responsibilities in support of space operations include:

(a) Organizing, training, equipping, and providing Navy and Marine Corps forces to support space operations.

(b) Developing, in coordination with the other Military Services, tactics, techniques, and equipment employed by Navy and Marine Corps forces for use in space operations.

(c) Conducting individual and unit training of Navy and Marine Corps space operations forces.

(d) Participating with the other Services in joint space operations, training, and exercises, as mutually agreed to by the Services concerned or as directed by competent authority.

(5) Other responsibilities of the Navy and Marine Corps include:

(a) Providing, when directed, logistic support of Coast Guard forces, including procurement, distribution, supply, equipment, and maintenance.

(b) Providing air and land transport essential for naval operations and not otherwise provided for.

(c) Providing and operating sea transport for the Armed Forces other than that which is organic to the individual Services.

(d) Developing, in coordination with the other Services, doctrine and procedures for close air support for naval forces and for joint forces in amphibious operations.

History

The government of the United States is founded upon a single document, the Constitution. The Constitution contains provisions for governing the armed forces that have not changed since the document was written.

The Congress, under the powers granted to it by the Constitution, has passed many laws forming and regulating the Navy. In turn, the Secretary of the Navy has approved regulations and orders giving detail to these regulations.

In 1798, *Navy Regulations* provided for the establishment "at the seat of the government an executive known as the Department of the Navy, and a Secretary of the Navy, who shall be the head thereof."

A board of naval commissioners, with three members, was created by an act of 7 February 1815.

On 31 August 1842 the "bureau system" was established by Congress.

The congressional acts of 11 July 1890, 3 March 1891, and 20 June 1940 provided an under secretary and an assistant secretary.

On 3 March 1915 the Office of the Chief of Naval Operations was provided for by an act of Congress.

On 12 July 1921 Congress created the Bureau of Aeronautics, and on 24 June 1926 Congress authorized the Assistant Secretary for Air.

By 1942, *Navy Regulations* read as follows:

> The business of the Department of the Navy not specifically assigned by law shall be distributed in such manner as the Secretary of the Navy shall judge to be expedient and proper among the following bureaus:
>
> First, a Bureau of Yards and Docks.
> Second, a Bureau of Naval Personnel.
> Third, a Bureau of Ordnance.
> Fourth, a Bureau of Ships.
> Fifth, a Bureau of Supplies and Accounts.
> Sixth, a Bureau of Medicine and Surgery.
> Seventh, a Bureau of Aeronautics.

The National Security Act established the DoD in 1949 as an executive department of the government to include the military departments of the Army, Navy, and Air Force. The Secretary of the Navy was demoted to subcabinet rank. The titles of these positions have changed over the years. In 1966 the Naval Material Command was organized, and in subsequent years various bureaus have been retitled as commands.

Congress and the Department of the Navy

Of the three branches of government, the legislative branch has the sole power to appropriate funds. From this and from the constitutional responsibility to "raise armies and navies" Congress derives the power to determine the nature of the Navy and Marine Corps and the amount of money used to purchase and operate ships and weapons and to pay personnel. Both the Senate and the House have committees on armed forces. These committees hold annual hearings for the purpose of authorizing ships and weapons. The appropriations committees of both houses then appropriate money for their construction and additional funds for supplies, pay, and other support.

The Navy Department has a Chief of Legislative Affairs, several legislative officers, and an office in the House and the Senate to provide rapid liaison with the committees and members.

The Comptroller of the Navy, under the supervision of the Assistant Secretary of the Navy for Financial Management, directs the preparation of the Navy budget and supplementary appropriation requests, which are forwarded to the Comptroller of DoD. The budget is based on requirements carefully screened by the Joint Chiefs of Staff.

Proposals for legislation affecting the Navy may be originated by members of Congress, by the Navy Department, or by other offices of DoD. Wherever they originate, they are referred to appropriation committees of the Congress for hearing and further processing.

Titles 10 and 37 of the United States Code, which are widely available in print and on the Internet (see Sources), contain most of the laws affecting the Navy.

Organization of the Department of the Navy

Figure 13.1 shows the basic organization of the Department of the Navy. The department is unique within DoD in that it includes two separate services, the Navy and the Marine Corps, having their own distinct, although interrelated, missions and chains of command.

Organization of the Secretariat. Figure 13.2 shows the organization of the Office of the Secretary of the Navy. The Secretary is overall in charge of construction, manning, armament, equipment, and maintenance of all vessels and aircraft and performs other duties as assigned by the Secretary of Defense. The Secretary of the Navy has direct cognizance over all officers and enlisted personnel and over all public and legislative relations.

Four assistant secretaries assist the Secretary of the Navy:

• The Assistant Secretary of the Navy for Research, Acquisition, and Development manages the department's acquisitions, directs research and development efforts, and oversees procurement and contracting.

• The Assistant Secretary of the Navy for Installations and Environment determines long-range strategic direction and policy for Navy installations and oversees installations, logistics, environment, and safety programs.

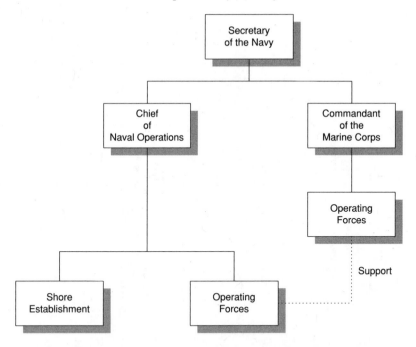

Fig. 13.1. Organization of the Department of the Navy. The dashed line marked "Support" indicates the cooperative support of the Navy–Marine Corps team. Each of the operating forces supports the other.

• The Assistant Secretary of the Navy for Financial Management and Comptroller directs and manages the department's financial activities.

• The Assistant Secretary of the Navy for Manpower and Reserve Affairs exercises overall supervision of personnel policies for the department.

The Secretary is further assisted by various other groups and individuals:

• The Executive Office of the Secretary is the collective name for the various boards, directors, and chiefs reporting to and performing staff functions for the Secretary and the Secretary's civilian executive assistants.

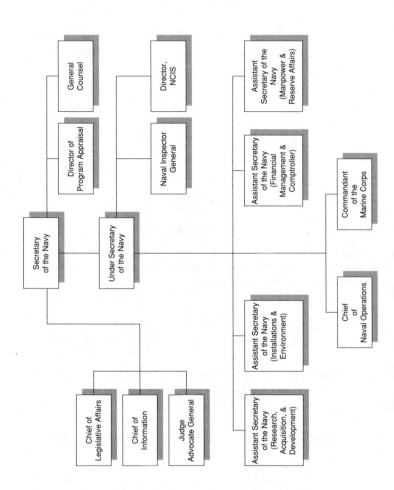

Fig. 13.2. Office of the Secretary of the Navy.

- The Judge Advocate General has cognizance over all major phases of military, administrative, and legislative law pertaining to the operation of the department. The JAG's office reviews the records of court-martial proceedings and other courts and boards, as well as matters of international law.
- The General Counsel is responsible for providing legal services and advice throughout the department in the fields of business and commercial law.
- The Chief of Information (CHINFO) handles all aspects of public information and the public affairs program for the department.
- The Chief of Legislative Affairs assists the senior officials of the Navy in their relations with Congress and handles liaison with individual members of Congress and congressional staff members.
- The Director of Program Appraisal provides appraisals of Navy and defense plans, studies, and proposals.
- The Naval Inspector General is responsible for inquiring and reporting on matters affecting military efficiency or discipline; proposing a program of inspections; and making inspections, investigations, and reports as directed by the Secretary of the Navy or the Chief of Naval Operations.
- The Director, Naval Criminal Investigative Service (NCIS), is responsible for criminal investigations, counterintelligence, and naval security.

The Office of the Chief of Naval Operations

The various offices under the Chief of Naval Operations are collectively referred to as the Office of the Chief of Naval Operations, or OPNAV. Figure 13.3 shows the organization of OPNAV.

Chief of Naval Operations (CNO, OP-00). The CNO is the senior military officer in the Navy and serves as primary naval adviser to the President and the Secretary of Defense and as a member of the Joint Chiefs of Staff (JCS). The CNO, with the Commandant of the Marine Corps (CMC), is responsible for keeping the Secretary of the Navy fully informed on matters considered or acted upon by the JCS.

Vice Chief of Naval Operations (VCNO, OP-09). The VCNO has authority and duties as delegated by the CNO. Orders

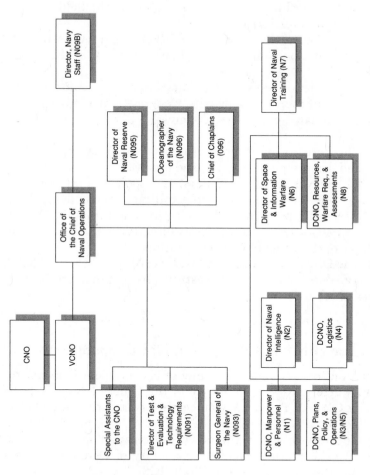

Fig. 13.3. Office of the Chief of Naval Operations.

issued by the VCNO in performing such duties have the same effect as if issued by the CNO.

The VCNO's principal job is to act as executive for the CNO. In addition, the VCNO coordinates the performance of the various boards, staff assistants, deputy chiefs of staff, and directors of major staff offices. The following individuals assist the CNO:

- Director, Navy Staff (N09B)
- Deputy CNO (DCNO), Manpower and Personnel (N1)
- Director of Naval Intelligence (N2)
- DCNO, Plans, Policy, and Operations (N3/N5)
- DCNO, Logistics (N4)
- Director of Space and Information Warfare (N6)
- Director of Naval Training (N7)
- DCNO, Resources, Warfare Requirements, and Assessments (N8)

The position of DCNO, Resources, Warfare Requirements, and Assessments, was established in 1992. Prior to that time a different assistant CNO represented each naval warfare area on the OPNAV staff. The reorganization consolidated all of the warfare areas under a single DCNO, N8, to eliminate the barriers between the warfare communities and ensure that Navy procurement programs were evaluated in terms of their specific contributions to the joint warfighting effort. Reflecting the new emphasis on joint operations in the littoral, the redesigned OPNAV organization parallels the structure and functions of the Joint Staff. Divisions reporting to N8 are as follows:

- Programming Division (N80)
- Assessment Division (N81)
- Fiscal Management Division (N82)
- CINC Liaison Division (N83)
- Expeditionary Warfare Division (N85)
- Surface Warfare Division (N86)
- Submarine Warfare Division (N87)
- Air Warfare Division (N88)
- Special Programs Division (N89)

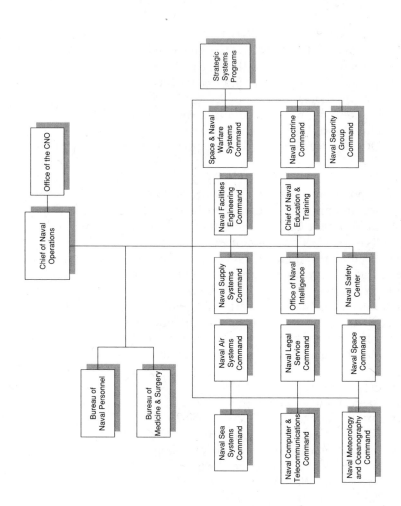

Fig. 13.4. Organization of the Navy shore establishment.

The Shore Establishment

Figure 13.4 illustrates the Navy shore establishment.

Bureau of Naval Personnel (BUPERS). BUPERS, established in 1942, is the successor to the Bureau of Navigation. In 1982 the name BUPERS was changed to Naval Military Personnel Command, which was in turn changed back to BUPERS in 1991. The Chief of Naval Personnel (who is also N1 on the CNO's staff) heads BUPERS. BUPERS is responsible for the procurement, education, training, discipline, promotion, welfare, morale, and distribution of officers and enlisted personnel. The command also has responsibility for all records of medals and awards and for correctional custody units, and it supervises Navy morale, welfare, and recreation (MWR) activities.

Bureau of Medicine and Surgery (BUMED). BUMED, led by the Surgeon General of the Navy (who also serves as N093 on the CNO's staff) provides Navy and Marine Corps members with health-care and quality-of-life services, maintains health records, and conducts research and development for health-related issues.

Naval Sea Systems Command (NAVSEA). NAVSEA develops, acquires, modernizes, and maintains ships, ordnance, and systems for the Navy and Marine Corps. It performs acquisition, in-service support, and technical organization functions to meet naval and joint-forces warfighting requirements.

Naval Air Systems Command (NAVAIR). NAVAIR develops, acquires, and supports naval aeronautical and related technology systems for the operating forces of the Navy and Marine Corps.

Naval Supply Systems Command (NAVSUP). NAVSUP provides supply support to Navy forces worldwide. It supplies parts and equipment to the fleet, performs contracting functions, and operates the Navy Exchange system and other services.

Naval Facilities Engineering Command (NAVFAC). NAVFAC provides products, services, engineering, and construction to support mission requirements, housing, and community facilities. This includes management of installations, environmental programs, base realignment and closure requirements, and engineering planning for contingency operations. NAVFAC also oversees the civil engineering corps and naval construction battalions (Seabees).

Space and Naval Warfare Systems Command (SPAWAR). SPAWAR provides the Navy with command, control, communications, computers, and intelligence as well as undersea, surface, and airborne surveillance resources.

Strategic Systems Programs. This command conducts research and development for strategic weapons systems.

Naval Computer and Telecommunications Command (NCTC). NCTC organizes, trains, and equips computer and telecommunications activities to provide information systems and services to the fleet, support commands, and higher authority. It also manages, processes, and transfers information for command, control, and administration of the Navy.

Naval Legal Service Command. This command provides legal services to ship and shore commands, active-duty military personnel, dependents, and retirees. Legal services include military justice, including trial and defense counsel; command support; legal assistance; civil law, including the handling of personal-property, tort, and military claims; administrative law; and environmental law.

Office of Naval Intelligence. This office supports the operating forces by collecting, processing, analyzing, and reporting intelligence information. It conducts analysis of the design and construction of foreign surface ships, sensors, and weapons systems and provides appraisals of opposition combat tactics. The Director of Naval Intelligence, who also serves as the staff adviser on intelligence matters to the Chief of Naval Operations (N2), oversees the Office of Naval Intelligence.

Chief of Naval Education and Training (CNET). CNET conducts education and training of Navy and Marine Corps officers and enlisted members. CNET's responsibility includes recruit training, specialized-skills training, precommissioning training for officers, warfare-specialty training, and fleet individual and team training. The Chief of Naval Education and Training is also the Director of Naval Training (N7) on the OPNAV staff.

Naval Doctrine Command. This command develops naval concepts and integrated naval doctrine; provides a coordinated Navy–Marine Corps voice in joint- and multinational-doctrine development; and addresses naval and joint doctrine with respect to training, education, operations, exercises, simulations, and war games.

Naval Meteorology and Oceanography Command. This command collects, interprets, and applies global data and information for safety at sea, strategic and tactical warfare, and weapons system design, development, and deployment. The command provides meteorological, oceanographic, and mapping, charting, and geodesy services to the Navy. The Oceanographer of the Navy, N096 on the OPNAV staff, commands this organization.

Naval Space Command. This command provides information and capabilities to shore and afloat naval forces by operating space surveillance, navigation, communication, environmental, and information systems, advocating naval warfighting requirements in the joint arena; by advising, supporting, and assisting the naval services through training; and by developing space plans, programs, policies, concepts, and doctrine.

Naval Security Group Command (NAVSECGRU). NAVSECGRU performs and coordinates the Navy's cryptologic programs. The Commander, Naval Security Group Command, also reports to the Chief, Central Security Service (CSS), as the Navy Element Commander of the CSS and performs cryptologic functions at the national level as the Commander of the Navy's Service Cryptologic Element (SCE).

Commissioning Programs

The Navy trains future officers through a variety of programs. In addition to the programs described below, there are programs specifically designed to commission Navy enlisted members, which are discussed in chapter 8.

Officer Candidate School (OCS). Naval Officer Candidate School, located in Pensacola, Florida, is an intensive thirteen-week course that provides initial training for college graduates to become Navy officers. Officer candidates who are accepted into the Nuclear Propulsion Officer Candidate (NUPOC) program may receive financial assistance during their last two years of college as well as cash bonuses upon acceptance into the program and completion of nuclear-power training. Aviation officer candidates and naval flight officer candidates attend basic and advanced pilot or naval flight officer training upon completion of OCS.

Naval Reserve Officers Training Corps (NROTC) Program. The NROTC program commissions officers into the Navy's unrestricted line and nurse corps as well as the Marine Corps. Two- and four-year NROTC scholarships, offering tuition, fees, a monthly stipend, books, and uniforms, are available at more than sixty colleges and universities. Scholarship midshipmen participate in summer cruises each year. A two- or four-year NROTC nonscholarship college program is also offered. Participants in the college program are eligible to compete for scholarships, receive monthly stipends during their junior and senior years, and participate in summer cruises the summer before they are commissioned.

United States Naval Academy (USNA). The USNA, located in Annapolis, Maryland, is a fully subsidized four-year undergraduate educational program. Naval Academy midshipmen, who must be single, not pregnant, and without legal obligation to support dependents, receive active-duty pay while pursuing bachelor's degrees in a wide variety of majors and commissions as Navy or Marine Corps officers. USNA midshipmen also participate in cruises each summer.

Staff Corps Commissioning Programs. Specialized programs exist to commission officers into the civil engineering corps, nurse corps, medical corps, dental corps, JAG corps, and chaplain corps. Some of these programs provide financial benefits while the candidates complete degree requirements. In addition, established specialists in certain professional and scientific fields may qualify for direct commissions.

The U.S. Marine Corps

History. On 10 November 1775 a resolution of the Continental Congress established the Continental Marines, a group based on an organization in the British Royal Navy. The Marine Corps was established by an act of Congress on 11 July 1798. Congress intended the Marine Corps to be a strong, versatile, fast-moving, and hard-hitting force that would be prepared to prevent potential conflicts by prompt and vigorous action, be able to hold a full-scale aggressor at bay while the United States mobilized, and be ready when the nation was least ready.

In keeping with this intent, the Marine Corps still provides the nation with an expeditionary military organization capable of responding rapidly to threats to American interests by projecting power through its forward-deployed units and by reacting to crises with combat-ready units tailored to meet any contingency.

Tradition. As they enlist, Marines learn that Marine Corps traditions are as much a part of their equipment as their pack and rifle. These traditions are many: devotion to duty and to discipline, loyalty to the country and the corps, self-sacrifice, flexibility, and dependability. Marines reinforce this tradition through meticulous maintenance of their distinctive insignia and uniforms and through a continuously fostered readiness to be the first force called upon to respond to a national emergency.

Missions of the Marine Corps.   Complex global situations require Marine forces that are capable of rapid and discriminate employment across the spectrum of conflict on land, sea, and air. This spectrum ranges from general war to mid- or low-intensity conflicts. The Marine Corps provides forces that may be either visible or discreet, on-scene or poised beyond the horizon, and that possess a conspicuous strike and power-projection capability.

Title 10 of the United States Code assigns the Marine Corps several specific roles and functions. In fulfilling these roles, the Marine Corps performs a wide variety of wartime tasks, including seizure and defense of advanced naval bases, crisis response, forward presence, alliance support, various noncombat operations involved with disaster relief, humanitarian assistance, and counternarcotics efforts, and special operations; Marine Corps special operations can include close-quarter battle, reconnaissance and surveillance, seizure and destruction of offshore facilities such as oil or gas platforms, or hostage rescue.

The Commandant and Headquarters Staff.   The Commandant of the Marine Corps is a member of the Joint Chiefs of Staff and is also directly responsible to the Secretary of the Navy under the administrative chain of command for the procurement, discharge, education, training, discipline, and distribution of Marine Corps officers and enlisted personnel.

The Commandant is assisted by the Assistant Commandant and the Chief of Staff as well as the following deputies:

- Deputy Chief of Staff for Plans, Policies, and Operations
- Deputy Chief of Staff for Manpower and Reserve Affairs
- Deputy Chief of Staff for Programs and Resources
- Deputy Chief of Staff for Aviation
- Deputy Chief of Staff for Installations and Logistics

Organization of the Marine Corps.   Figure 13.5 shows the organization of the Marine Corps. The Marine Corps is organized into two broad categories: operating forces and the support establishment.

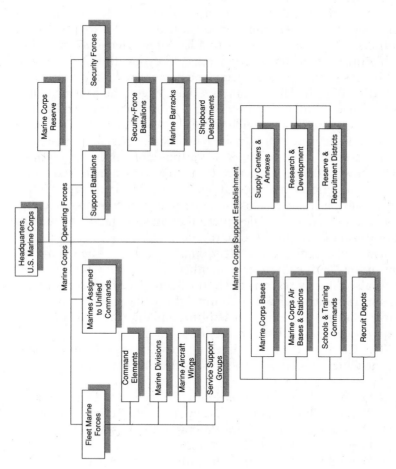

Fig. 13.5. Organization of the Marine Corps.

The major elements of the operating forces are the fleet Marine forces (FMF), and security forces. The FMF are made up of command elements, divisions, aircraft wings, and service support groups. Marine Corps security forces consist of two Marine Corps security-force battalions, Marine barracks in the continental United States and abroad, and Marine detachments aboard ships. The Marine security-force battalions provide Marines to the State Department for embassy security at 138 diplomatic posts in 129 different countries. Support forces account for less than one-quarter of the Marine Corps' total force. They include training and education commands, bases and stations, recruiters, and research and development activities.

Organization for Combat. The Marine Corps organizes for combat by forming integrated, combined-arms Marine air-ground task forces (MAGTFs). These task forces are specifically tailored to the mission and can be rapidly deployed by air or sea. A task force comprises four elements: command, ground combat, aviation combat, and service support. Combining air and ground combat elements with combat service support under a single commander allows close integration of air and ground units into a single force. The size of the task force and its elements are mission-dependent.

Marine Expeditionary Forces and Marine Expeditionary Brigades. The largest MAGTFs are categorized as either Marine expeditionary forces (MEFs) or Marine expeditionary brigades (MEBs). A MEF is made up of a command element, a division, an aircraft wing, and a force service support group. A MEB is smaller than a MEF and consists of a command element, an infantry regiment, an aircraft group, and a brigade service support group. A MEF is normally commanded by a lieutenant general and can include multiple divisions and aircraft wings, together with one or more force service support groups. The Marine Corps currently has three standing MEFs: I and III MEF (Marine Forces, Pacific) and II MEF (Marine Forces, Atlantic). A MEF is self-sustaining for up to sixty days after deployment but can extend operations with external support.

Marine Expeditionary Units. A Marine expeditionary unit (MEU) is the smallest standard task force. With a strength of about twenty-two hundred personnel, a MEU normally consists of a reinforced infantry battalion, a composite aviation squadron (which normally includes attack helicopters, transport helicopters, air refuelers/transport aircraft, light attack fixed-wing aircraft, and command-and-control assets), a MEU service support group, and a command element. A MEU is commanded by a colonel and deploys with fifteen days of supplies. Forward-deployed MEUs provide an immediate sea-based response to meet forward presence and limited power-projection requirements. All forward-deployed MEUs have completed specialized training and are designated special-operations-capable.

Special-Purpose MAGTFs. A special-purpose MAGTF (SP-MAGTF) is task-organized to accomplish specific missions for which a MEF or MEU would be inappropriate. SPMAGTFs can be organized, trained, and equipped to conduct a wide variety of expeditionary operations in response to a crisis or for a peacetime mission. They are designated by location, and their duties cover the spectrum from noncombatant evacuation to disaster relief and humanitarian missions.

Amphibious Warfare. Amphibious warfare integrates all types of ships, aircraft, weapons, and landing forces in an attack against a hostile shore. Initiated in the absence of friendly forces ashore and exploiting the element of surprise, amphibious warfare requires the rapid landing and build-up of forces and equipment to prosecute further combat operations.

An amphibious evolution may range in scale from a small incursion to a full-scale assault. When confronting an enemy of significant combat capability, the role of the amphibious force may be to seize initial entry points for introduction of more extensive follow-on forces.

When a decision is made to "send in the Marines," a MEU is normally the first on the scene. A MEU is also used to fulfill more routine forward deployments around the globe. An amphibious ready group (ARG) is used to get the Marines where they need to go to fulfill their mission. An ARG consists of three to four amphibious-warfare ships designed to bring the MEU to the theater of operations and to land it on a hostile shore. Normally an ARG is commanded by a Navy officer whose title is commander, amphibious task force (CATF). This officer and the Marine Corps MEU commander known as the commander, landing force (CLF), share equal authority in the planning stage of an amphibious evolution. Thereafter the CATF is in charge until the Marines have secured a beachhead and control is shifted to the CLF ashore.

Commissioning Programs. USMC officers may be commissioned following graduation from the U.S. Naval Academy or an NROTC program, or following completion of Officer Candidate School in Quantico, Virginia.

The U.S. Coast Guard

History. Created by an act of Congress on 4 August 1790 at the request of the first Secretary of the Treasury, Alexander Hamilton, the Coast Guard has been variously known as the Revenue Marine, the Revenue Service, and the Revenue Cutter Service. As early as 1799, Congress provided for cooperation between the cutters and the Navy whenever the President directed. An act of Congress in 1915 consolidated the Revenue Cutter Service and the Life-Saving Service into the Coast Guard, which was to operate under the Secretary of the Treasury in peacetime and the Secretary of the Navy in wartime or when directed by the President.

In addition to peacetime service to the country, the Coast Guard has given effective service in wartime. It participated with the Navy in the Quasi War with France in 1798, in the War of 1812, in the Seminole War, and in the Mexican War, and it is said to have fired the first maritime shot of the Civil War (the revenue cutter *Harriet Lane* fired across the bow of the steamer *Nashville* while Fort Sumter was being bombarded).

During World War I the Coast Guard not only hunted submarines but also performed convoy duty, principally between Gibraltar and the British Isles. Peace after World War I brought the Coast Guard its greatest expansion and most difficult duty, the enforcement of Prohibition. With the repeal of Prohibition, the Coast Guard was drastically cut. In 1939 the Lighthouse Service of the Department of Commerce was transferred to the Department of the Treasury and the Coast Guard. In 1940 the Coast Guard established the Atlantic Weather Observation Service for protection of transatlantic air commerce. The Coast Guard Auxiliary (then called the Reserve) was established in 1939 and the Reserve in 1941. By November 1941 the Coast Guard was operating as part of the Navy. During World War II, in addition to guarding the continental coastline, the Coast Guard manned 351 vessels of the Navy. Today the Coast Guard operates under the Department of Transportation in peacetime, and as part of the Department of the Navy in wartime or when directed by the President.

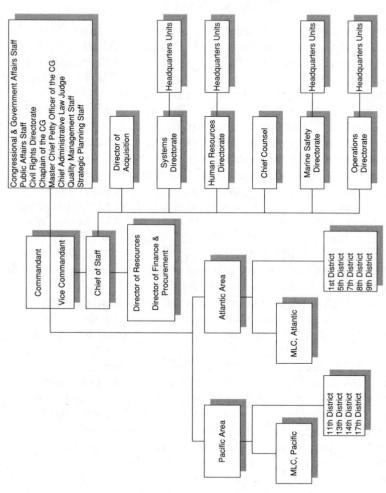

Fig. 13.6. Organization of the Coast Guard.

Organization of the Coast Guard. Figure 13.6 illustrates the organization of the Coast Guard. The operating forces are divided between two area commanders: Commander, Coast Guard Area Atlantic (headquartered in Portsmouth, Virginia), and Commander, Coast Guard Area Pacific (headquartered in Alameda, California). A Maintenance and Logistics Command (MLC) supports each area command, and area commands are further divided into geographic districts, each under a district commander.

Missions of the Coast Guard. The Coast Guard exercises primary maritime authority within U.S. waters. It is a relatively small, decentralized organization capable of rapid response in a wide variety of situations as well as shifts in emphasis on short notice when the need arises. Although operating within the Department of Transportation in peacetime, Title 14 of the United States Code specifies that the Coast Guard is "at all times an armed force of the United States."

The Coast Guard's primary missions are:

• Maritime law enforcement, including enforcement of federal laws on, under, and over the high seas and waters under U.S. jurisdiction, including interdiction of drug smugglers and illegal immigrants and enforcement of fishing regulations within the U.S. Exclusive Economic Zone and any other U.S. territory or possession.

• Maritime safety, including oversight of recreational boating safety, regulation and inspection of commercial vessels, and maintenance of aids to navigation.

• Marine environmental protection, including abatement of damage from oil spills and other pollutants released in the coastal zone and development of national and international pollution response plans.

• National security, including maintaining readiness to provide operating units with the combat capability necessary to function effectively as an armed, naval force. In peacetime, the Coast Guard is responsible for coastal defense planning and exercises. In wartime, it is responsible for conducting port security duties and U.S. coastal defensive operations up to two hundred miles offshore.

Law Enforcement Operations. Title 18, United States Code, sec. 1385, known as the Posse Comitatus Act, proscribes the use of Army and Air Force units for law enforcement except when expressly authorized by the Constitution or Congress. By regulation, this proscription also applies to naval units. Additional laws specify that DoD activities may provide law enforcement agencies, such as the Coast Guard, with support and technical assistance, such as facilities, aircraft, vessels, intelligence, technical expertise, and surveillance.

Posse Comitatus prohibits Navy personnel from directly participating in the search, seizure, or arrest of suspected criminals. When engaged in law enforcement operations (LEOs), which are primarily targeted at interdiction of suspected drug smugglers, Navy ships are augmented with Coast Guard law enforcement detachments. Embarked Coast Guard personnel perform the actual boardings of interdicted suspect drug-smuggling vessels and, if needed, place the smugglers under arrest.

Commissioning Programs. Officers receive commissions in the U.S. Coast Guard following graduation from the U.S. Coast Guard Academy in New London, Connecticut, or completion of Officer Candidate School in Yorktown, Virginia. In addition, direct commissioning programs exist for professionals in specialized fields such as law, aviation, environmental management, and engineering.

14

THE OPERATING
FORCES OF THE NAVY

NOT ONLY ON THE DEEP SEA, THE BROAD BAY, AND THE RAPID RIVER, BUT ALSO UP
THE NARROW MUDDY BAYOU, AND WHEREVER THE GROUND WAS A LITTLE DAMP, THEY
HAVE MADE THEIR TRACKS.

—President Abraham Lincoln

IT WAS THEIR TASK TO KEEP THE SEA LANES OPEN, TO MAINTAIN THE NAVY'S TRADI-
TIONS OF "NOT GIVING UP THE SHIP," AND THIS THEY DID EVEN THOUGH THEY PAID
WITH THEIR LIVES.

—Navy Department press release, 19 July 1942

Chapter 12 described the distinction between the administrative
and operational chains of command. The operating forces, which
report to the National Command Authority through the operational chain of command, carry out assigned missions in direct
support of national defense. Operating forces consist of ships, aircraft squadrons, and other warfighting units.

The operating forces of the Navy consist of several fleets,
shore-based long-range air forces, strategic submarine forces, the
Military Sealift Command (MSC), and shore activities assigned
by the President or the Secretary of the Navy.

The operating forces have a dual chain of command. They report to the Chief of Naval Operations through an administrative
chain of command that is responsible for their training and preparation for employment. Additionally, they report through an operational chain of command to the appropriate combatant command CINCs discussed in chapter 12, to fulfill the Navy's
warfighting missions. Figure 14.1 shows the overall chain of command for Navy operating forces.

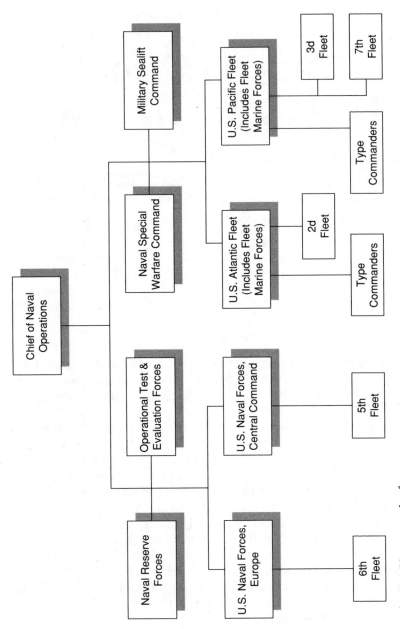

Fig. 14.1. Navy operating forces.

Under the administrative chain of command, operating forces are assigned to type commanders (TYCOMs). TYCOMs are responsible for administrative control of operating units at all times, and for operational control during most phases of training. After the completion of basic and intermediate training, the appropriate numbered-fleet commanders take charge of these forces for advanced training and operations. Some elements of these forces are further assigned to task force or battle force organizations for specific operations and missions including assignment to combatant commands.

Classifications of Ships and Aircraft

Surface Ships.   Commissioned Navy ships with military crews (both surface ships and submarines) are designated by the prefix USS (for United States Ship) preceding the ship's name. In addition to the name, each ship is assigned a hull number, consisting of its designation and its sequential number (e.g., DD-976).

The designations of the major categories of combatant warships are as follows:

CG	Guided-missile cruiser
CV	Aircraft carrier
CVN	Aircraft carrier (nuclear-powered)
DD	Destroyer
DDG	Guided-missile destroyer
FFG	Guided-missile frigate
MCM	Mine-countermeasures ship
MCS	Mine-countermeasures support ship
MHC	Coastal minehunter
PC	Coastal patrol craft

The designations of amphibious-force ships, used to transport Marines and land them ashore, begin with the letter *L*. The current classes of amphibious ships are:

LCC	Command ship
LHA	Amphibious assault ship (general purpose)
LHD	Amphibious assault ship (multipurpose)
LKA	Amphibious cargo ship
LPD	Amphibious transport dock

Sailors carefully ready the lines as the nuclear powered attack submarine USS *Seawolf* prepares to moor. PHC John E. Gay

LPH	Amphibious assault helicopter carrier
LSD	Dock landing ship
LST	Tank landing ship

The designations of auxiliary-force ships, used to replenish, repair, and provide other logistic services to the fleet, begin with the letter *A*. Some of the major classes of auxiliary ships are:

AD	Destroyer tender
AO	Oiler
AOE	Fast combat-support ship
ARS	Salvage ship
AS	Submarine tender

Ships that instead have the USNS prefix before the name (for United States Naval Ship) are Military Sealift Command ships manned with mostly civilian crews. USNS ships have a *T-* preceding the designation, as follows:

T-AE	Ammunition carrier
T-AFS	Combat stores ship
T-AH	Hospital ship

T-AO   Oiler
T-ATF   Fleet tug

Submarines. The U.S. Navy has two categories of submarines:

SSBN   Nuclear-powered ballistic-missile submarine
SSN   Nuclear-powered submarine (fast attack)

Aircraft Squadrons. Aircraft squadrons are designated by a group of two or more letters identifying the type and mission of the squadron, followed by a number identifying the specific squadron. For example, VP-1 indicates a squadron of fixed-wing aircraft with a patrol mission.

The first letter of an aircraft squadron title is the squadron prefix symbol. An *H* denotes a helicopter squadron; a *V* denotes fixed-wing aircraft. In a Marine Corps squadron, this first letter is followed by an *M*.

The next letter in the squadron title is the squadron class symbol, and it indicates the basic mission of the squadron, as follows:

C   Combat support (in helicopter squadrons) or composite (in fixed-wing squadrons)
F   Fighter
M   Mining
O   Observation
P   Patrol
Q   Electronic reconnaissance
R   Airlift/transportation
S   Antisubmarine warfare
T   Training
X   Test/development

A final letter, called a squadron subclass symbol, may be used to denote a modified mission.

Administrative Chain of Command

The administrative chain of command for all Navy operating units is through a type commander to the appropriate fleet commander. Figure 14.2 illustrates the Navy's type-commander organization. All Navy warfighting units are organized into broad categories under one of six type commands: Surface Force, Atlantic

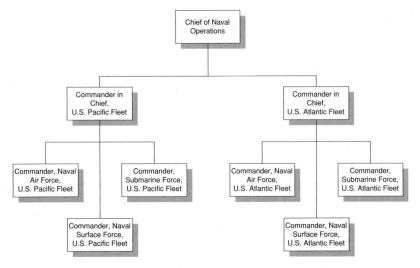

Fig. 14.2. Navy type commanders.

(SURFLANT), Submarine Force, Atlantic (SUBLANT), and Air Force, Atlantic (AIRLANT), which report to Commander in Chief, U.S. Atlantic Fleet (CINCLANTFLT), and Surface Force, Pacific (SURFPAC), Submarine Force, Pacific (SUBPAC), and Air Force, Pacific (AIRPAC), which report administratively to Commander in Chief, U.S. Pacific Fleet (CINCPACFLT). Each type command is further subdivided into groups and squadrons. This organization carries out normal administration, and a ship or unit is always under the administrative control of its type commander, even when under the operational control of a numbered-fleet, task force, or battle group commander. Figure 14.3 shows the administrative chain of command for operating units.

In addition to the type commands discussed above, equivalent administrative commands also reporting to CINCLANTFLT and CINCPACFLT include fleet Marine forces and fleet training commands.

Operational Chain of Command

Operationally, the Navy assigns ships and other units on the basis of geographic location to one of five numbered fleets. The composition of these fleets changes on virtually a daily basis as

The Operating Forces of the Navy

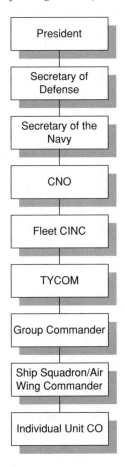

Fig. 14.3. Administrative chain of command for operating units.

assets move in and out of their respective areas of responsibility. As units of the Navy enter the area of responsibility for a particular Navy CINC, they are operationally assigned to the appropriate numbered fleet. When a ship home-ported in Norfolk transits across the Atlantic Ocean and enters the Mediterranean, its operational commander shifts—in this case, from Commander, Second Fleet, to Commander, Sixth Fleet.

The Second and Sixth Fleets serve in the Atlantic and Mediterranean, respectively, and report to the Commander in

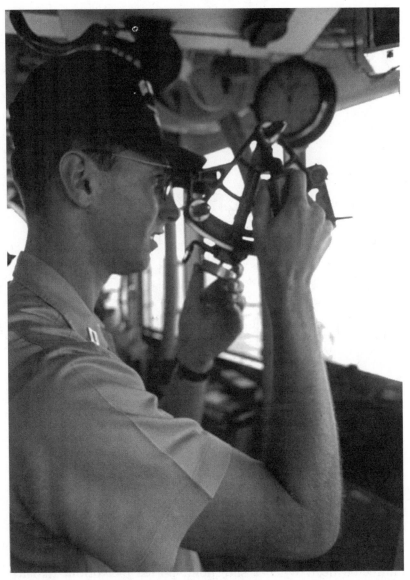

A lieutenant takes a position reading with a sextant on the bridge of the USS *Wisconsin* during Desert Shield. CWO Ed Bailey

Chief, U.S. Atlantic Command (CINCLANT), through the Commander in Chief, U.S. Atlantic Fleet. Similarly, units of the Third and Seventh Fleets report to the Commander in Chief, U.S. Pacific Command (CINCPAC), through the Commander in Chief, U.S. Pacific Fleet; the Third Fleet's area of responsibility is the eastern and northern Pacific Ocean, while Seventh Fleet units serve throughout the western Pacific and Indian Ocean region. Fifth Fleet units serve throughout the Persian Gulf and Middle East; the Commander, Fifth Fleet, reports to the U.S. Central Command (CENTCOM) through U.S. Naval Forces Central Command (NAVCENT).

Below the numbered fleets in the operational chain of command are task forces. A task force may consist of a diverse variety of ships, including aircraft carriers, amphibious ships, combatants, and auxiliary ships brought together to fulfill a particular mission. In order to provide flexibility and ease of communication in meeting the varied military requirements of vast areas, task forces are further divided operationally into task groups, which in turn may be subdivided into task units and task elements; figure 14.4 shows this operational chain of command. Depending on the type and scope of the operation, the force will be assigned a task force or battle force designation under the operational control of the numbered-fleet commander. These subdivisions are designated numerically; for example, Task Unit 77.3.1 is Task Unit 1 of Task Group 3 of Task Force 7 of the Seventh Fleet.

Deploying Units

On any given day, some ships and squadrons from the U.S. Atlantic and Pacific Fleets are on deployment away from home port. Although battle group configurations vary depending on the mission, deploying forces generally follow a few standard configurations.

Carrier Groups. A carrier group is led by an aircraft carrier and also includes an air wing and a contingent of carrier escorts. When the escort ships include destroyers as well as cruisers, the group is referred to as a cruiser-destroyer group.

Destroyer Squadrons (DESRONs). Destroyer squadrons, composed of destroyers, frigates, or a combination of the two, may operate independently or as part of a battle group or task

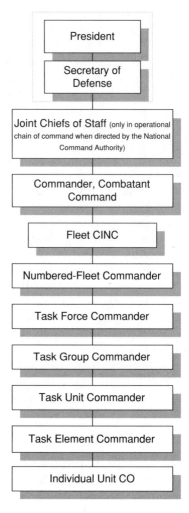

Fig. 14.4. Operational chain of command.

force. When a DESRON deploys with a carrier and its escort ships, the combination is called a carrier task group.

Amphibious Groups. An amphibious group is a group of ships designed to transport Marines. Typically three to four ships will deploy together to form an amphibious ready group (ARG). The ARG configuration may vary but will generally provide the commander with the ability to launch and recover Marines and deploy landing craft.

Marine Expeditionary Forces. Destroyers and other combatants are routinely assigned to work with the Marine expeditionary forces (MEF), providing naval support for amphibious operations.

Combat Support Ships. These ships, including oilers, supply ships, and ordnance ships, deploy alongside the combatant ships of the fleet to perform underway logistics and replenishment support.

Employment Schedules

Fleet commanders draw up annual employment schedules listing the major categories of assignments to the ships and squadrons of their fleets. They also issue quarterly schedules that incorporate the latest known changes and operational details. Type commanders are then able to make up their own annual and quarterly employment schedules using the schedules of fleet commanders as guides. The TYCOMs' employment schedules are normally quite detailed, assigning authority to unit commanders to make required movements.

The current employment cycle of a DDG, for example, consists of eighteen months of training, maintenance, and predeployment exercises followed by a six-month overseas deployment.

Tactical Training Strategy

The Navy's tactical training strategy was designed to achieve maximum combat readiness and interoperability of ships, submarines, and aircraft squadrons between the Atlantic and Pacific Fleets. The requirements of the combatant commander who will ultimately be employing the ship, squadron, or other operating unit are used to develop training objectives. The goal of the training strategy is to prepare unit training teams to be self-sufficient, through an emphasis on stressful, realistic, increasingly difficult but safe training scenarios that stress basic warfighting competencies and skills. Whenever possible, joint training is stressed. "Train the trainers" is the central theme of the strategy.

The unit interdeployment training cycle begins with postdeployment leave and upkeep and ends with the unit fully trained and ready for the next deployment. The major phases of the training cycle are basic, intermediate, and advanced.

Fleet CINCs, through the appropriate TYCOMs and numbered-fleet commanders, are responsible for providing trained and combat-ready forces to meet the requirements of the unified combatant commander (CINCLANT/CINCPAC). The TYCOMs set basic training requirements for their units. TYCOMs are responsible for ensuring that deploying units successfully complete required certifications and assessments. Operational control of units other than SSNs remains with the TYCOM during basic-phase training and shifts to the numbered-fleet commander for the intermediate and advanced phases; fleet CINCs retain operational control of SSNs throughout the training cycle.

Basic-Phase Training. The first step in basic training is the Command Assessment of Readiness and Training (CART), conducted in two phases. Phase I is a self-evaluation conducted by the CO as a unit returns from deployment. Phase II is generally conducted by the CO and his or her immediate superior in command (ISIC) after the leave and upkeep period that follows a deployment.

Tailored Ship Training Availabilities (TSTAs) are the next steps in a unit's basic training. TSTA I concentrates on training the internal training teams that will be responsible for the majority of actual watchstander training on board. TSTA II refines the performance of unit training teams and watch teams in more complicated scenarios. TSTA III allows the CO to build integrated training proficiency with the assistance of Commander, Afloat Training Group Atlantic/Pacific, and TSTA IV is specialized training for certain types of surface ships.

The Final Evaluation Period (FEP) tests the crew under realistically stressful conditions in different readiness conditions. FEP generally includes a major damage-control scenario and weapons-firing exercises.

Intermediate-Phase Training. The intermediate phase of training (beginning no later than 180 days prior to a ship's scheduled deployment date) is normally conducted by the appropriate deploying battle group commander, amphibious ready group commander, or mine countermeasure force commander. This phase focuses on team training for each warfare area and basic multiunit operations including command-and-control procedures.

Advanced-Phase Training. The advanced phase of training continues to develop and refine the integrated battle group warfare skills and command-and-control procedures needed to meet the supported warfare commander's specific mission requirements. Training objectives are tailored to required force structure, capabilities, and mission tasking. The numbered-fleet commander conducts advanced-phase training, which includes a final at-sea exercise designed to train and evaluate the entire battle group in all warfare skills. If necessary, a ship or unit may conduct additional training en route to the overseas deployment.

Battle Efficiency Award

Every eighteen months there is a fleetwide competition for the battle efficiency ribbon, or "Battle E." Each group or squadron commander selects one ship or squadron for the award, on the basis of the unit's performance in logistics and engineering certifications, qualifications, and inspections, competitive exercises, and day-to-day sustained superior performance. All crew members of a winning ship or squadron are authorized to wear the battle efficiency ribbon, and the winning ship displays a painted *E*.

15

THE NAVAL RESERVE

A STRONG NAVAL RESERVE IS ESSENTIAL, BECAUSE IT MEANS A STRONG NAVY. THE NAVAL RESERVE IS OUR TRAINED CIVILIAN NAVY, READY, ABLE, AND WILLING TO DEFEND OUR COUNTRY AND SUPPRESS HER ENEMIES SHOULD THE NEED ARISE AGAIN.

—*Rear Admiral Felix Johnson*

WE ARE WONDERFULLY SERVED TODAY BY THE RESERVES IN WAYS THAT . . . WE COULD ONLY IMAGINE SOME YEARS AGO.

—*Admiral Jay L. Johnson*

In the wake of the recent downsizing following the end of the Cold War, the Naval Reserve plays a larger and more critical role than ever in the Navy's routine operations. Today the Naval Reserve is an important component of the Navy's balanced and affordable force. Every naval officer should have a basic understanding of the organization and role the Naval Reserve plays in meeting peacetime commitments and wartime requirements.

History of the Naval Reserve

The U.S. Naval Reserve was officially established on 3 March 1915, although historians trace its roots to colonial days and the Revolutionary War. Predecessors of the citizen-sailors of today include the members of naval militias in Massachusetts (1888) and then New York, Pennsylvania, and Rhode Island (1889). In 1891 the Office of Naval Militia was established in the Navy Department. Six years later, sixteen states had naval militias whose personnel served with the Regular Navy during the Spanish-American War.

The Division of Naval Affairs replaced the Office of Naval Militia in the Navy Department by 1914. During World War I, approximately thirty thousand reserve officers and three hundred thousand reserve enlisted members served on active duty at sea and ashore.

In the period between World Wars I and II there were no

Ready Reserve units as we know them today, and no reserve officers on extended active duty. Reserve officers trained during voluntary two-week active-duty tours on combatant ships or at shore stations. Just prior to World War II some junior officers went on active duty following their graduation from NROTC, so that in the opening days of the war a few members of the reserve were serving in fleet units. After Pearl Harbor, larger numbers of reservists helped man and command the Navy's ships, submarines, and aircraft; by the end of the war four out of five naval personnel were reservists. Many reservists remained in the Navy after the war, either on extended active duty as reservists or as members of the Regular Navy. Shortly after the end of the war the Navy set up the framework for the modern-day Naval Reserve by establishing the Naval Air Reserve Training Command and the Naval Surface Reserve Training Command.

During the Korean War many reservists returned to active duty for the duration of the war. During the conflict in Vietnam the President decided not to call up the Naval Reserve, except for selected air and Seabee units, but to use the draft to obtain extra manpower. This decision resulted in the widespread perception that the Naval Reserve had become largely irrelevant to the national defense.

The Total-Force Concept. In the early 1970s, in response to a Naval Reserve force that had fallen far behind the active forces in its training and equipment readiness, the "total-force" concept was born. This plan recognized that the Naval Reserve was likely to be an important part of any response to a future national emergency, and that modern equipment and training were essential to ensure that the Naval Reserve could integrate rapidly and seamlessly into the fleet.

During the 1980s the Department of Defense introduced a "horizontal-integration" strategy, which assigned reservists to train with the active commands they would serve with in time of national emergency. During this period the Naval Reserve increased in size and received the most modern equipment, including F-14 Tomcat and F/A-18 Hornet aircraft, HH-60 Seahawk helicopters, and FFG-7-class guided-missile frigates. Horizontal integration remains a key feature of today's Naval Reserve training and mobilization strategy.

The first major test of the total-force concept came during the Desert Shield/Desert Storm operations of 1990–91. A large-scale

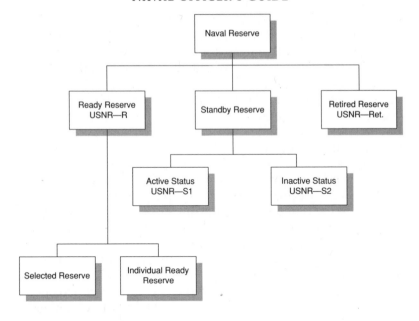

Fig. 15.1. Categories of reservists.

call-up of some twenty-two thousand medical, logistics, Seabee, and other reserve personnel demonstrated that the reserve forces could indeed be rapidly mobilized and deployed in response to a crisis situation.

Components of the Reserve

In 1997 the Naval Reserve consisted of approximately 460,000 personnel in three components: the Ready Reserve, which is the primary source of personnel for mobilization, and the Standby Reserve and Retired Reserve. The majority of reservists are in the latter two categories, which are of a lower readiness. Reservists in these categories are subject to being called for active duty only in the event of a declared war or other national emergency.

All individuals obligated to serve in the Naval Reserve are initially assigned to the Ready Reserve, and most remain in the Ready Reserve for the remainder of their service obligation. There are two groups in the Ready Reserve: the Selected Reserve, or

SELRES, and the Individual Ready Reserve, or IRR. The SELRES is that component of the Naval Reserve with the most essential wartime missions. Approximately 17,500 SELRES personnel, called Training and Administration of Reserves personnel, or TARs, are actually on active duty. These personnel maintain the readiness of the reserve component on a day-to-day basis. In addition, approximately one hundred thousand SELRES personnel, commonly called drilling reservists, are non-active-duty members who participate in monthly drill weekends and annual active-duty-for-training (ACDUTRA) periods. The IRR consists of reservists who do not have an assigned billet in the Naval Reserve SELRES organization.

Drilling reservists, the IRR, and some Standby reservists are considered to be on *active status*. This term, not to be confused with the term *active duty*, denotes personnel who are eligible to train (sometimes without pay) as well as earn points toward retirement, and who may be considered for advancement or promotion. These are also the first reservists called to active duty upon mobilization. Conversely, reservists who are not on active status may not receive drill pay, earn retirement points, or be considered for promotion.

Figure 15.1 illustrates the relationships between the various categories of the Naval Reserve.

Mission and Organization of the Naval Reserve

The mission of the Naval Reserve is to provide mission-capable units and individuals to the Navy–Marine Corps team for the full range of operations. Such operations may include war or national emergency, contingency operations, military operations other than war (MOOTW), humanitarian operations, and other operations required by national security. The Naval Reserve can provide a broad range of cost-effective, adaptable military capabilities and civilian skills to fulfill mission requirements.

The Naval Reserve is commanded by a rear admiral, with subordinate rear admirals in charge of the Naval Surface Reserve Force and the Naval Air Reserve Force. Types of Naval Reserve units include assault-craft units, beach groups/units, cargo-handling battalion units, major fleet and force staff units, Military Sealift Command units, fleet hospitals, ship and squadron augmentation units, and others.

The Naval Reserve has some distinct taskings and capabilities that are not duplicated in the active force. The Navy takes several factors into consideration when determining whether a mission is better suited to the active force or to the reserves. These factors include the demands on the personnel involved, the costs, whether the appropriate personnel mix exists in the Naval Reserve, and whether the Naval Reserve has the capability to perform the mission. The following statistics highlight some of the areas in which the Naval Reserve plays a pivotal role:

• Although fewer than 5 percent of the Navy's ships and aircraft are reserve assets, Naval Reserve personnel provide 16.3 percent of the steaming days and 13 percent of the flight hours in support of counternarcotics operations.

• The mobile inshore undersea-warfare units of the Naval Reserve constitute 100 percent of the Navy's harbor surface and subsurface surveillance forces, which have taken part in every recent major exercise and operation.

• Although Naval Reserve supply units make up only 10 percent of the total supply force, 90 percent of the Navy's expeditionary logistics support force consists of Naval Reserves. This force creates advanced bases used to move, store, and deliver war material to support in-theater operations and other vital missions.

• Naval Reserve maritime patrol aircraft provide 40 percent of the Navy's total airborne surface surveillance capability, with nine squadrons of eight aircraft each.

• Naval Reserve medical and dental personnel account for 28.5 percent of the Navy's total medical and dental assets.

• Naval Reserve helicopter squadrons provide 66 percent of the Navy's combat search-and-rescue capability. These squadrons regularly deploy for operations.

Flexible Readiness. In 1994 the Vice Chief of Naval Operations approved new flexible-readiness procedures for the Naval Reserve. Before this, reservists conducted all of their required premobilization training in peacetime, even such training as firefighting, which is most effective when conducted just prior to deployment. Under the new flexible-readiness guidelines, which recognize that transportation constraints will preclude simultaneous call-up of large numbers of reservists, the Navy made the decision to defer much of this training until actually needed. This decision not only lightened the training burden on the reserve forces but also freed more reserve units to engage in peacetime support missions.

Naval Reserve Participation and Administration

Retirement-Point Credit.   Naval Reserve officers on active status must maintain minimum participation levels, which are measured in retirement-point credits. Officers with fewer than twenty years of qualifying service must earn twenty-seven points each year, and officers with more than twenty years of qualifying service must earn fifty points each year. All officers must earn fifty points per year for that year to count as a qualifying retirement year. All members receive fifteen gratuitous points per year; they must earn any additional points. Reservists earn one point for each day of annual training or inactive-duty training. They may earn additional points for completing correspondence courses and other professional training. Members who have completed their minimum service obligations but who are not earning sufficient points to remain on active status are transferred to the inactive component of the Standby Reserve.

Transfer to the Naval Reserve from Active Duty.   Many officers who leave active duty elect to retain their commissions in the Naval Reserve. In fact, acceptance of a reserve commission is a prerequisite for acceptance of separation pay for officers who are involuntarily discharged prior to reaching retirement eligibility.

16

INTERNATIONAL ORGANIZATIONS AND FOREIGN AFFAIRS

WE ARE A STRONG NATION. BUT WE CANNOT LIVE TO OURSELVES AND REMAIN STRONG.

—General George C. Marshall

THE RESPONSIBILITY OF THE GREAT STATES IS TO SERVE AND NOT TO DOMINATE THE WORLD.

—President Harry S. Truman

Each naval officer should have an understanding of the alliances and organizations of which the United States is a member. Further, each should know the essentials of an organization or alliance that affects the national security of the United States.

The United Nations

Origin

The charter of the United Nations developed from proposals made at the Dumbarton Oaks Conference in 1944 by delegates from the United States, Great Britain, the USSR, and China.

In April 1945, fourteen hundred representatives from fifty nations met in San Francisco for a conference on international organization. The Dumbarton Oaks proposals were put before the conference, and the charter was signed after amendments were made. The required number of states ratified the charter on 24 October 1945.

Aims

The United Nations is an association of sovereign nations pledged to maintaining international peace and security and to establishing the political, economic, and social conditions necessary to that aim. The primary purpose of the United Nations is to keep the peace. Its secondary goal is to develop friendly relations among nations based upon respect for the principle of equal rights and self-determination of peoples. The United Nations seeks also to achieve international cooperation in solving economic, cultural, and humanitarian problems. It strives to promote recognition of human rights and of fundamental freedoms for all without distinction as to sex, language, or religion. Finally, the United Nations acts as a center where nations may meet to discuss their problems and try to find peaceful solutions to them.

Organization of the United Nations

The United Nations has six basic divisions, called "principal organs," as follows.

General Assembly. The General Assembly is the only organ of the United Nations that includes representatives of all 185 member countries. Decisions on ordinary matters require a simple majority; voting on certain important questions is by a two-thirds majority. The assembly holds regular sessions from mid-September through mid-December, and special or emergency sessions when necessary. The General Assembly has the right to discuss and make recommendations on all matters within the scope of the U.N. charter. It has no authority to compel action by any government, although its recommendations carry the weight of world opinion. The General Assembly votes to admit new members and appoints the U.N. Secretary-General.

Security Council. The Security Council is primarily concerned with keeping the peace. There are fifteen members of the Security Council, five of which—France, China, the Russian Federation, the United Kingdom, and the United States—are permanent members. The General Assembly elects the remaining members for two-year terms. Decisions require nine votes, although any permanent member may veto a proposal. Member states are obligated to seek peaceful resolution of disputes, and any member state may bring a dispute before the Security Council. The council seeks to resolve the dispute by peaceful means but may take measures to enforce its decisions. These measures may include imposition of sanctions on countries that threaten the peace or authorization of military action by coalitions of member states. The United Nations has used both of these measures in recent years against Iraq.

Economic and Social Council. This council coordinates the economic and social work of the United Nations and its related agencies to promote economic growth in developing countries and the observance of human rights worldwide. The General Assembly elects eighteen members each year for a three-year term, for a total of fifty-four members. The council meets for a one-month session each year, alternating between New York and Geneva.

Trusteeship Council. Powers administering territories that are not ready for self-government place the territories under the international trusteeship system. As of 1994, all trusteeships had attained self-governance or independence, and this organ is currently inactive.

International Court of Justice. Also known as the World Court, the International Court of Justice judges cases brought before it by U.N. members. All members of the United Nations automatically belong to the World Court, which has fifteen judges elected by the General Assembly and the Security Council. A judge serves for nine years, and no two judges may be nationals of the same country. The parties involved must consent to the jurisdiction of the court, but once they have consented, its decisions are binding on them. The United States withdrew its acceptance of the court's jurisdiction in 1986, following a decision on a case involving activities in Nicaragua.

Secretariat. The Secretary-General, who is the chief administrative officer of the United Nations, runs the Secretariat. The General Assembly appoints the Secretary-General on the recommendation of the Security Council. The Secretary-General appoints the staff and carries out the day-to-day work of the United Nations.

U.S. Participation in the United Nations

The United States, as the world's leading political, economic, and military power, has a strong interest in U.N. participation. The

United States can pursue many of its interests effectively through the United Nations, particularly in circumstances in which it would be impracticable or unsafe for the United States to act alone. The United Nations has been instrumental in carrying out many aims of the United States, including containing the spread of weapons of mass destruction, enforcing sanctions on nations hostile to regional peace and cooperation, and combating international terrorism and drug trafficking.

The North Atlantic Treaty Organization (NATO)

In the Atlantic and the Mediterranean, U.S. forces operate closely with NATO allies. If you are assigned to this area of the world or visit it on deployment, you should familiarize yourself with the NATO organization. The *NATO Handbook*, available on the Internet (see Sources), is a valuable source of information.

The Formation of NATO.   When World War II came to an end, the Western democracies hoped to enter an era of security and demobilized the majority of their armed forces. The emergence of postwar tensions and threatened expansion by the Soviet bloc caused the Western nations to unite for a common defense against further Soviet expansionism. In April 1949, in Washington, D.C., the foreign ministers of Belgium, Canada, Denmark, France, Iceland, Italy, Luxembourg, the Netherlands, Norway, Portugal, the United Kingdom, and the United States signed the North Atlantic Treaty to prevent aggression and, if necessary, resist attack against any alliance member. In 1952, Greece and Turkey joined the alliance, followed by the Federal Republic of Germany in 1955 and Spain in 1982.

The Treaty.   The text of the treaty is short and clear. It conforms with both the letter and the spirit of the U.N. charter. Briefly, it sets forth the following as desirable goals:

• Peaceful settlement of disputes and abstinence from force or threat of force
• Economic collaboration between signatories
• Strengthening the means of resisting aggression by individual effort and mutual assistance
• Consultation in the event that any signatory is threatened

The North Atlantic Council.   The council is the principal forum for consultation and cooperation between NATO member governments on all issues affecting their common security. Its decisions are based on consensus, and all members have an equal right to express their views. The NATO Secretary-General is chair.

Defense Planning Committee. This body deals with defense planning and other issues related to NATO's integrated military structure. It is composed of the chiefs of staff of all member countries, except Iceland, which is represented by a civilian, and France, which withdrew from the committee in 1966.

Commands. The strategic area covered by NATO is divided into two regional commands: Allied Command Europe and Allied Command Atlantic, with a regional planning group for North America. With the exceptions of Iceland and France, all member countries assign forces to the integrated command structure. The NATO defense area covers the territories of member nations in North America, in the Atlantic area north of the Tropic of Cancer, and in Europe, including Turkey. Events occurring outside this area that affect the preservation of peace and security may also be of concern to NATO.

Permanent Joint Council. The NATO-Russia Founding Act signed in 1997 established a Permanent Joint Council to serve as the principal mode of coordination between NATO and Russia. This council is composed of representatives of Russia and a member state and is chaired by the Secretary-General of NATO.

Shift in Emphasis. The threat of a full-scale Soviet attack, which provided the focus for NATO's strategy during the Cold War, no longer exists. NATO has revised its strategy in view of the changing global landscape. In recognition of the fact that the primary threats to NATO's security—such as terrorism and the proliferation of weapons of mass destruction—now require a different approach, this new strategy is centered on conflict prevention and crisis management.

Other Organizations and Agreements

Organization of American States (OAS). The Organization of American States, dating back to the First International Conference of American States in 1890, is the world's oldest regional organization. The OAS charter was signed in 1948 and entered into force in December 1951. There are currently thirty-five member states. Although Cuba remains a member, in 1962 the OAS excluded Cuba from OAS activities. The objectives of the OAS are to strengthen the peace and security of the Americas; promote democracy with due respect for the principle of nonintervention; promote and protect human rights, primarily through the Inter-American Commission on Human Rights; seek solutions to hemispheric political, juridical, and economic problems; fight drug trafficking and drug abuse; and maintain peace and security in the region.

The collective security systems of the Inter-American Treaty of Reciprocal Assistance—known as the Rio Treaty, which became part of the OAS—represented the American states' general acceptance of the principle underlying the Monroe Doctrine: an attack upon an American state by a non-American state would be an attack upon all.

North American Aerospace Defense Command (NORAD). The North American Aerospace Defense Command is a binational U.S.–Canadian organization charged with the missions of aerospace warning and aerospace control for North America. Aerospace warning includes the monitoring of man-made objects in space and the detection, validation, and warning of attacks against North America whether by aircraft, missiles, or space vehicles, utilizing mutual support arrangements with other commands. Aerospace control includes providing surveillance and control of the airspace of Canada and the United States.

A Commander in Chief (CINCNORAD) is appointed by, and responsible to, both the President of the United States and the Prime Minister of Canada. CINCNORAD, headquartered at Peterson Air Force Base, Colorado, is also the Commander in Chief of the U.S. Space Command. A command-and-control center is located a short distance away from NORAD headquarters, at Cheyenne Mountain Air Station, and three subordinate regional headquarters are located at Elmendorf Air Force Base, Alaska; Canadian Forces Base, Winnipeg, Manitoba, Canada; and Tyndall Air Force Base, Florida.

The U.S.–Republic of Korea Mutual Defense Treaty. This treaty, signed in 1953, allows the United States to station troops in South Korea.

U.S.–Japan Treaty of Mutual Cooperation and Security. This treaty, signed in 1960, provides the basis for the close relationship between the United States and Japan and their defense establishments.

ANZUS Treaty. This treaty, signed in 1951 by Australia, New Zealand, and the United States, provides for cooperation among the armed forces of those three countries. New Zealand's refusal since 1984 to permit visits by U.S. warships unless granted assurances that they are not carrying nuclear weapons has caused the United States to suspend its ANZUS security obligations to New Zealand.

Group of Seven (G-7). This organization of seven major industrial democracies was established in 1985 and meets periodically to discuss world economic issues and other mutual concerns. Members are the United States, Canada, France, Germany, Italy, Japan, and the United Kingdom.

Organization for Economic Cooperation and Development (OECD). This organization, headquartered in Paris, promotes economic and social welfare in member countries and stimulates growth in developing nations. Members are the United States, Australia, Austria, Belgium, Canada, Denmark, Finland, France, Germany, Greece, Iceland, Ireland, Italy, Japan, Luxembourg, the Netherlands, New Zealand, Norway, Portugal, Spain, Sweden, Switzerland, Turkey, and the United Kingdom.

The U.S. Department of State

Recent fundamental changes have occurred in the global landscape, including the fall of the communist bloc, new technologies, increasing population pressures, and economic and geopolitical transformations. These changes affect not only the United States' military posture but its diplomatic posture as well. Like the Department of Defense, since the end of the Cold War the Department of State is no longer primarily concerned with an immediate threat to national security. The department's current emphasis is on security, political, and economic issues, including such problems as weapons proliferation, terrorism, ethnic and religious conflict, organized crime, drug trafficking, and environmental concerns.

Mission of the Department. In order to carry out U.S. foreign policy at home and abroad, the Department of State:

• Exercises policy leadership, broad interagency coordination, and management of resource allocation for the conduct of foreign relations

• Leads representation of the United States overseas, advocates U.S. policies before foreign governments and international organizations, and supports official visits and other diplomatic missions

• Conducts negotiations, concludes agreements, and supports U.S. participation in international negotiations

• Coordinates and manages the U.S. response to international crises

• Carries out public affairs and public diplomacy

• Reports on and analyzes international issues of importance to the United States

• Assists U.S. business

• Protects and assists American citizens living or traveling abroad

• Adjudicates immigrant and nonimmigrant visas to enhance U.S. border security

• Manages those international affairs programs and operations for which the State Department has statutory responsibility

• Guarantees the diplomatic readiness of the U.S. government

Goals of U.S. Foreign Policy. The goals are to:

• Secure peace; deter aggression; prevent, defuse, and manage crises; halt the proliferation of weapons of mass destruction; and advance arms control and disarmament

• Expand exports, open markets, assist American business, foster economic growth, and promote sustainable development

• Protect American citizens abroad and safeguard the borders of the United States

• Combat international terrorism, crime, and narcotics trafficking; support the establishment and consolidation of democracies; and uphold human rights

• Provide humanitarian assistance to victims of crisis and disaster

• Improve the global environment, stabilize world population growth, and protect human health

The U.S. Foreign Service

The Foreign Service, a branch of the Department of State, is a career corps of men and women who carry out the foreign policy of our nation in day-to-day relations with other countries. Four thousand Foreign Service officers, assisted by Foreign Service specialists and civil servants, serve in 250 embassies and consulates in 170 countries. The specialty of Foreign Service officers is diplomacy, the art of conducting negotiations between nations.

The Mission of the Foreign Service.   The mission of the Foreign Service is to protect and promote the welfare and interests of the United States and the American people, to establish relations between peoples as well as between their governments, to help friendly or developing nations achieve their goals, and to represent our government before the many permanent international organizations.

Embassies.   The United States has an embassy in the capital of most countries with which diplomatic relations exist. Embassies are headed by ambassadors who, in addition to acting as personal representatives of the President to heads of the host government, are in charge of the team of agencies and attachés operating from the embassy. The ambassador also has authority over the various consuls in major ports and cities of that country. The official place of business of an ambassador is known as a chancery or chancellery. Some countries are not of sufficient size to warrant an ambassador. The diplomatic agents sent to such countries are called ministers and their posts, missions.

At posts overseas, the ambassador reports to the President through the Secretary of State, and as Chief of Mission has authority over all U.S. executive branch personnel, except for those under the command of a U.S. area military commander. The Country Team, under the leadership of the Chief of Mission, is the principal coordinating body for all U.S. government agencies represented at overseas missions. As the lead agency abroad, the State Department manages U.S. embassies, consulates, and other diplomatic posts and supports the international activities of the rest of the U.S. government.

Duties of Foreign Service Officers.   Every Foreign Service officer is in one of five functional areas of specialization, called cones:

• Administrative officers are involved in financial analysis, communications and computer technology, facilities maintenance, procurement and contracting, human resources management, and security.

- Consular officers are responsible for protecting the interests of American citizens who travel or reside abroad, adjudicating applications for nonimmigrant and immigrant visas, and monitoring migration issues of interest to the U.S. government. Consular officers play leadership roles in the local community (both official and private) to foster good will and cooperation on matters of mutual interest.

- Economic officers concentrate on matters such as money and banking, trade and commerce, communication and transportation, economic development, and government finance. In addition, they deal with environmental, scientific, and technology issues.

- Political officers' primary responsibility is to follow political events within the host country and to report significant events to the State Department. They also convey official communications from the U.S. government to host-country officials and may accompany more senior officials of the embassy as note takers when they meet with host-government officials.

- Officers who serve in the information and cultural affairs fields are not employed directly by the Department of State but instead work for the U.S. Information Agency (known abroad as the U.S. Information Service). USIA officers are charged with building bridges of communication between the United States and the host country. They practice the art of public diplomacy, as they explain to foreign audiences both the complexities of U.S. society and culture and the current administration's foreign policy agenda.

Attachés. An attaché performs a specialized function. There are, among others, attachés for labor, agriculture, and commercial activities as well as Army, Navy, and Air Force attachés. The senior military attaché is normally designated the defense attaché.

17
CAREER PLANNING

WEBSTER'S DICTIONARY DEFINES THE WORD "CAREER" AS A COURSE OR PASSAGE. YOU WOULDN'T GET UNDERWAY FOR SEA WITHOUT A NAVIGATIONAL PLAN OR CONDUCT FLIGHT OPERATIONS WITHOUT A FLIGHT PLAN, SO WHY MAKE A CAREER OF THE NAVY WITHOUT A PLAN? TAKE MY ADVICE AND SET ASIDE SOME TIME IN YOUR BUSY SCHEDULE TO PLOT A COURSE FOR SUCCESS.

—*Rear Admiral J. I. Maslowski*

YOU'VE GOT TO BE CAREFUL IF YOU DON'T KNOW WHERE YOU'RE GOING, BECAUSE YOU MIGHT NOT GET THERE.

—*Yogi Berra*

Arguably, the quality of the officer corps in the Navy has never been higher than it is today. Of course, it goes almost without saying that a strong performance record is a prerequisite for success, but in today's competitive environment being a good performer will not likely be sufficient in itself. To give yourself the best possible chance, you must aggressively manage all aspects of your career.

You should seek out the hard, operational jobs in which your outstanding performance will best stand out. A balanced career of operational, overseas, joint duty, Washington, and staff assignments will demonstrate the diversity of your talents and experiences. In determining your next career move, seek the advice of your detailer, your XO and your CO, and other senior officers whose judgment you trust. You might even want to study the biographies of senior officers in your community to find out more about their assignments and achievements as junior officers.

Your achievement of certain well-defined milestones, although no guarantee of success, will greatly enhance your promotion opportunities. Some of these are early qualification in watches and other professional accomplishments, obtaining a postgraduate degree or attending a war college, and obtaining the joint specialty officer (JSO) designation. In addition, you must carefully review and manage your official record to ensure that selection boards have a current and accurate picture of your achievements. It is safe to say that every year otherwise outstanding officers fail to select for promotion because they neglect to review their records and correct outdated or inaccurate information.

This chapter will give you an overview of the subject of career management and provide you with the tools you need to start managing your career from the time you begin your first tour.

Detailing

The Bureau of Naval Personnel (BUPERS), relocated in 1998 to Memphis, Tennessee, from the Navy Annex in Arlington, Virginia, oversees all aspects of Navy personnel policy and assignments under the direction of the Chief of Naval Personnel. Figure 17.1 shows the organization of BUPERS.

As discussed in chapter 4, two groups of officers at BUPERS, detailers and placement officers, are responsible for assigning officers to appropriate billets. Detailers are responsible for a group of officers in a particular pay grade and designator, and placement officers are responsible for a group of similar ships or commands. Detailers and placement officers have different "customers"; your detailer represents you and is primarily concerned with finding a billet that is a good match for your rank, qualifications, desires, and career needs, while a placement officer represents a command and is primarily concerned with finding the best-qualified officers to fill that command's billets. Working together, they meet the needs of individual naval officers as well as commands.

When an officer is due for rotation, the placement officer controlling the officer's current billet posts the billet with the appropriate detailer, specifying the requirements of the billet. The detailer takes into account rotation date, personal preferences as indicated on duty-preference cards, and the career-progression needs of possible candidates for the billet, and then confers with the placement officer to write a set of orders for an officer who is a good match.

Three factors, called the detailing triangle, come into play as a detailer decides where to send an officer for his or her next tour. The first factor, personal preference, is clearly the most important and visible factor to the officer being detailed. The second factor

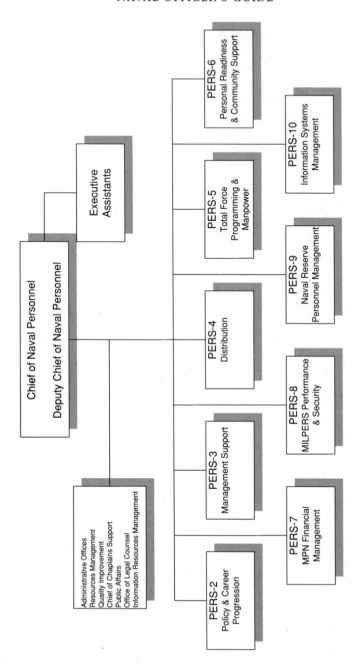

Fig. 17.1. Organization of the Bureau of Naval Personnel.

is the career interests of the officer. Detailers are well aware of the tours officers require to remain competitive with their peers, and they will not permit officers to stray too far from these requirements, regardless of their personal preferences. The third factor, often called "needs of the Navy," recognizes the sometimes harsh reality that, all other considerations aside, critical billets must be filled with the best possible candidates.

Admiral Nimitz summed it up well while talking with a group of young destroyer captains during World War II. Being asked for advice on career planning, he said:

> First, determine what career you want to follow, and plan it all the way to the top. Then ask for the best and toughest job available that suits your career path. If you present your case well to your detailer, you should get your requested job, then just continue on up the ladder as far as you can. If you don't get it, plead your case firmly and honestly. If you are turned down a second time, keep quiet, go to your assigned duty, and carry it out better than it was ever done before. If you do so, the chances are that your detailer will ask you what job you want the next time around. After all, he has to fill difficult and prestigious jobs with good men. If you have proved that you are a good man, he will need you. Remember, you are always allowed one objection. If you don't succeed, never say another word about it.

Duty-Preference Information.   Not too long after you arrive at a new duty station, you should start working with your detailer on your next set of orders. If you are coming up for a new set of orders and your detailer has no preferences on file for you, he or she may assume that you don't care where you go and detail you accordingly.

To avoid this situation, there are several ways for you to advise your detailer of your desires for your next assignment. The first is the standard paper duty-preference card. Fill it out listing your top three choices for type of command, type of billet, and geographic location, and then rank those three factors from most to least important. There is also space on the card for free-form text to describe any special circumstances or desires. The same information may now be submitted electronically, by sending your detailer e-mail. You may obtain your detailer's e-mail address at the BUPERS Website at http://www.bupers.navy.mil. You may also communicate with your detailer electronically through use of BUPERS Access, described later in this chapter. As another alternative, although it is generally preferable to put your desires in writing, you may also telephone your detailer. Detailers are difficult to get on the telephone directly, but you may leave a voice-mail message or request that he or she call back so you can speak in person at a later time.

BUPERS in Cyberspace

BUPERS Access. This direct dial-in computer bulletin board first came on line in 1991 and has been continuously updated since. BUPERS Access is a computer-based system providing the fleet with easy access to detailers, up-to-date policies, news and information, personal information on promotion boards or advancement results, orders status, status of various packages submitted to BUPERS for approval, and more. This technology allows members to use virtually any computer with a modem and telecommunications software to communicate with BUPERS Access. Services available on BUPERS Access include e-mail communication with detailers or other BUPERS departments; retention, career information, and Navy policy bulletins; NAVADMIN and NAVOP messages; advancement exam and board results; orders status information; and duty-preference submissions.

World Wide Web. The BUPERS home page at http://www.bupers.navy.mil represents a gateway to a wide array of information and links to other Navy resources on the Internet. You can access the complete text of *Perspective,* the officers' newsletter, on line, as well as other important publications such as *Link* and *All Hands,* ALNAV messages, and a growing list of instructions and other useful information. (A list of other recommended Internet sites is provided in the Sources chapter.)

E-mail. As discussed earlier in this chapter, e-mail is one of the easiest and most direct methods of communicating with your detailer. Use of e-mail instead of the telephone prevents those lengthy "on-hold" sessions waiting for your detailer to have a free minute and allows him or her to research the answers to your questions before responding.

Job Advertising and Selection System (JASS). This system, still in its testing stage, will eventually greatly expand the capability for detailers and the fleet to communicate using computer technology. When fully operational, computer detailing will allow individual officers and enlisted members to review billet vacancies and apply for available jobs electronically. Detailers may then process job applications to find the best match for each billet.

Selection Boards

Statutory vs. Administrative. Statutory boards are those governed by law, primarily Title 10 of the United States Code. These boards affect promotion, selective early retirement, and continuation of officers who have reached the maximum years of service for their rank and would otherwise be subject to statutory retirement. Statutory boards are convened by the Secretary of the Navy, and results are approved by the President, the Secretary of Defense, or the Secretary of the Navy. Membership on statutory boards is set by statute and SECNAVINST 1401.3 (which is very specific as to designator mix and pay grade of board members).

All other boards are administrative and are governed by instruction or policy rather than by law. Administrative boards are convened to decide on such matters as, for example, selection for department head, executive officer, and commanding officer, selection for postgraduate education or war college attendance, and requests for redesignation to another officer community. Administrative boards are convened and approved by either the Chief of Naval Personnel (CNP) or the Deputy CNP. The board sponsor determines membership requirements for administrative boards.

Administrative boards can be every bit as critical to an officer's career as statutory boards, as virtually all officers have career milestones, determined through administrative board action, that they must meet to maintain upward mobility. An officer's failure to select for his or her next career milestone determined by an administrative board often foreshadows failure to select for promotion during a future statutory board.

Preparation. Review your microfiche, performance summary record (PSR), and officer data card (ODC) for accuracy at least six months in advance of the board, as discussed in chapter 4. Your PSR is particularly crucial because it is used to present your record to the complete board (only one or two board members will review your entire microfiche).

In addition to your preparations, the BUPERS fitness report

master file is queried six weeks prior to the board convening for fitness report continuity. If a fitness report is missing, your command will be sent a message.

If time is short before the board's convening date and you believe that important documentation is missing from your file, you should contact your detailer for assistance and advice and send a copy of any missing documentation directly to the president of the board in accordance with guidance in the *Military Personnel Manual (MILPERSMAN)*. A command endorsement of your letter to the president of the board is not necessary. Only those officers who are eligible before a selection board may correspond with the president. The board will return without action any endorsement or letter written on your behalf that is not sent via you, as well as any correspondence received after the convening date of the board.

Take special care to ensure that your official full-length photograph is current and in the appropriate uniform and format. The photograph must be submitted within three months of your acceptance of each promotion. Before mailing your photograph, show it to your department head, XO, CO, or other officers you trust. Ask them for their opinion of the photograph. Is your posture poor, or do you appear overweight? Does your uniform or personal grooming look sloppy? Don't send in a photograph that puts you in a less than favorable light; correct the discrepancy and have a new photograph taken.

The Precept. A precept is a document, signed by the convening authority and directed to the president of the board, giving general and specific guidance to the board regarding the criteria upon which their selections should be based. The precept is the only guidance for selection provided to a board.

The mission of any selection board is to select those "best qualified." The precept provides detailed guidance on how the board should assess the relative qualifications of the individuals under consideration, and it may provide specific instructions to ensure equal consideration for minority and women officers as well as officers with nontraditional career paths. A precept may direct the board to emphasize certain particularly relevant aspects of the officers' records, such as performance of duty in a joint billet or in other positions relating to the selection.

Precepts for administrative boards may also contain additional specific guidance, including quotas or numbers of primary selectees and alternates, additional program eligibility criteria, and other information the board sponsor deems necessary.

Information Considered by the Board. Statutory boards are only allowed to consider an officer's official service record consisting of microfiche (discussed in detail in chapter 4), performance summary record, and any correspondence the officer submits to the board about his or her record. The board will not consider information submitted from any other source.

Administrative boards follow a similar procedure, except in cases that require application packages (e.g., applications for Federal Executive Fellowships or test-pilot training, lateral transfer/redesignation requests, etc.). In such cases the boards also review the application packages.

Board Procedures. Board membership is kept secret until the board convenes. To ensure a level playing field, officers under consideration by a board may not visit their detailers prior to or during board deliberations. When the board convenes, the precept is discussed and the board gets to work.

As an initial step, two board members review each individual record. One of these members annotates a copy of his or her assigned officers' PSRs and is responsible for briefing the officers' careers to the rest of the board. After this records-review phase, the board moves into a room called the "tank" (a private theater-like room) for the selection phase. The annotated PSRs are projected onto large screens in the tank, and the appropriate board members brief each officer's record.

After each record is presented, the board members, using the precept as guidance, use computer keypads located on the arms of their seats to indicate a confidence level for the selection of the candidate. Each member may vote 100 percent (if 100 percent sure that the candidate should be selected), 75 percent, 50 percent, 25 percent, or 0 percent (if certain that the candidate should *not* be selected). After all the votes have been cast, a computer in the tank combines them into an overall confidence rating, which is then displayed as a percentage on a monitor for all the board members to see.

The confidence rating of each candidate is recorded and then ranked after all the records have been reviewed. At this point the board normally votes to consider some number of top scorers to be "tentatively selected" as well as some number of the bottom-scoring candidates to be "dropped from further contention." All the candidates between the "selected" and "dropped" scores are then re-reviewed. Several tank sessions are usually required before the board comes up with the candidates they feel are best qualified.

Releasing the Results. After the board completes its deliberations and votes to confirm the tentative selections, a "select" list is provided to the Secretary of the Navy, and it is subsequently approved by the Secretary of Defense. Usually five to eight weeks after the board adjourns, a "select" ALNAV message is released, and the information also becomes available on line. Promotions to the rank of lieutenant commander and above require Senate confirmation of the selectees. Generally, only promotion lists are published in an ALNAV; individual notification is the rule for selective-early-retirement decisions, continuations, and administrative board results.

Special Board Procedures. Failure of selection (FOS) for promotion is not in itself grounds for requesting a special board. The only time a special board is granted is when the Secretary of the Navy (or other designated authority) determines that a regularly scheduled promotion selection board failed to consider an eligible officer because of an action contrary to law, because of material error of fact or material administrative error, or because the board did not have certain material information before it for consideration. Special board procedures apply to active-duty officers only.

Education Programs and Subspecialties

A postgraduate education is an absolute necessity in today's ever more competitive Navy. A master's degree demonstrates your initiative and provides you with necessary "subspecialty" skills that allow you to develop an area of expertise in addition to your primary warfare specialty.

There are many windows in your career for pursuing a master's degree and a number of ways to do it. Many postgraduate programs require some type of obligated service. If you are interested in attending a postgraduate program, you should consult with your detailer to begin the process and determine which program and what time to attend are best for you.

In almost every competitive category and grade, officers who have attended or are attending postgraduate school fare better

The Naval Postgraduate School is located in Monterey, California.

than the fleet average in selection for promotion. The following is an excerpt from a recent promotion board precept:

> Postgraduate education and specialty skills (represented by proven subspecialties) are important to our Navy and represent a key investment in our future. The Navy needs officers with formal technical and military education in a time of increasing technological sophistication. In determining an officer's fitness for promotion, selection boards should consider time spent obtaining postgraduate degrees and military education, and gaining experience in other specialized areas in a positive light. . . . [Assignment] outside the traditional career patterns that allow the Navy to use the unique skills and expertise of these officers in subspecialty areas likewise should be considered as positive.

Naval Postgraduate School (NPGS). The Navy's graduate institution, NPGS, located in Monterey, California, offers master's and doctoral degree programs in forty technical and managerial curricula that are relevant to a naval officer's career. Attending Naval Postgraduate School is contingent upon a strong professional record and past academic performance.

Academic performance is determined by use of the academic profile code (APC), computed by the NPGS admissions office. If no APC appears in block 47 on your officer data card, chances are that NPGS has not been able to compute it because you are a recent commissionee or because they do not have your transcripts. Enclosure (3) to OPNAVNOTE 1520 provides an explanation of the APC.

Civilian Universities. Many specialized curricula that are not taught at NPGS are instead offered at civilian universities, with tuition funded by NPGS. OPNAVNOTE 1520 provides a list of these curricula and schools.

Tuition Assistance (TA). This popular financial benefit pays 75 percent of off-duty college tuition, up to a maximum of $187.50 per semester-hour and $3,500 per year. You may be eligible to receive tuition assistance toward the completion of a master's degree earned during off-duty hours. To receive funds you must agree to remain on active duty for at least two years after the completion of the last course for which you used TA benefits.

Navy Campus Educational Centers. These centers, located at most large installations, provide educational counseling, testing, and referrals to service members.

Program for Afloat College Education (PACE). This program allows service members to pursue undergraduate-level college courses on board ship, either through normal classroom instruction by embarked professors or through electronic independent study.

Servicemembers Opportunity Colleges, Navy (SOCNAV). SOCNAV is a consortium of twelve hundred colleges and universities that permit Navy members to transfer credits between member institutions to complete their degree requirements.

Montgomery GI Bill. If you are eligible to participate in the Montgomery GI Bill, you may use your benefits to pursue off-duty educational opportunities. This program provides educational assistance for active-duty members (except for Naval Academy and Naval ROTC graduates) who entered the service after 30 June 1985. In return for a contribution of $100 per month for twelve consecutive months, service members are eligible to receive up to thirty-six months of educational benefits up to $416.62 per month. These benefits may be used after three years of service while still on active duty, or after separation.

Olmsted Scholarships. A small number of junior officers are selected for this program each year. Nominations are solicited annually by NAVADMIN message in the June/July time frame. The Olmsted Scholarship program offers naval officers with exceptional foreign language aptitude the opportunity to pursue two years of graduate study at a foreign university.

Subspecialty Management. The officer subspecialty system identifies officer requirements for experience and/or education in various fields and disciplines. The subspecialty system is also the basis for generating the Navy's advanced education and training program requirements. There are about 50 unrestricted line, 180 medical, and 30 other staff corps officer subspecialty codes, some of which are listed later in this chapter.

Your eligibility for subspecialty coding is based on your education and experience. You may earn a subspecialty code by completing a graduate education program or by serving in certain types of billets. Make sure that your fitness reports accurately document your subspecialty experience and that your transcripts are included in your microfiche. To save time and money, before enrolling in an off-duty graduate educational program, submit copies of the course descriptions of your chosen curriculum to NPGS to determine if the curriculum meets the Navy's requirements for subspecialty coding. Officers with graduate education not meeting the minimum educational skill requirements are assigned a generic code (0000P) indicating completion of a master's degree.

The following are some of the major subspecialty codes currently recognized by the Navy:

XX10	Public affairs
XX11	English
XX12	History
XX16	Joint
XX17	Naval technical intelligence
XX18	Regional intelligence
XX19	Operational intelligence
XX20	General political science
XX21	Middle East/Africa/South Asia
XX22	Far East/Pacific
XX23	Western hemisphere

XX24	Europe
XX28	Strategic planning
XX29	Special operations/naval special warfare
XX30	Management (general)
XX31	Financial management
XX32	Logistics management
XX33	Manpower, personnel, and training
XX35	Transportation management
XX37	Education and training management
XX41	Math
XX42	Operations analysis
XX43	Operations logistics
XX44	Undersea warfare
XX45	C^4I (command, control, communications, computers, and intelligence)
XX46	Information warfare
XX47	Geophysics
XX48	Meteorology
XX49	Operational oceanography
XX50	Naval systems engineering (general)
XX51	Naval construction engineering
XX52	Nuclear engineering
XX53	Nuclear propulsion engineering
XX54	Naval/mechanical engineering
XX55	Electrical engineering
XX60	Weapons engineering (general)
XX62	Chemistry
XX66	Combat systems science and technology
XX68	Strategic weapons (fleet ballistic missile)
XX69	Strategic naval (fleet ballistic missile)
XX70	Aeronautical systems engineering (general)
XX71	Aeronautical engineering
XX72	Avionics
XX73	Test pilot
XX75	Space systems (general)
XX76	Space systems operations
XX77	Space systems engineering
XX89	Information management
XX91	Computer technology—science
0000	Any master's (not listed)

Fellowship Programs

White House Fellowship.   The White House Fellows program was established in 1964 to provide a few motivated young Americans with the experience of direct and personal involvement in the process of governing the nation. Fellows are assigned to the White House staff, the Vice President, members of the Cabinet, and other top-level executives. In addition to their duties as special assistants, White House Fellows participate in an educational program revolving around the government's processes, personalities, and problems.

Federal Executive Fellowship (FEF).   The Navy's Federal Executive Fellowship program helps fill the Navy's requirements for senior-level officers knowledgeable in the formulation and conduct of foreign policy and in the intricacies of the decision-making process at the highest levels of government. To be eligible you must be an unrestricted or restricted line officer in the permanent pay grade of lieutenant commander or above. Graduate-level education or a subspecialty in political-military affairs or national security affairs is desired but not required.

Professional Military Education:
U.S. Service Colleges

In order to attend a war college you must have completed your bachelor's degree and be screened through a selection board. Most war college curricula are ten to twelve months in length and require an active service obligation of two years following graduation. Some award a master's degree upon successful completion, and the Navy awards subspecialty codes to the graduates of many war colleges. Additional information is available in *MILPERS-MAN* art. 6620130.

Senior War Colleges.   There are six senior war colleges (open to officers in pay grade O-5 and senior): the Air War College, Maxwell Air Force Base, Alabama; the Army War College, Carlisle Barracks, Pennsylvania; the Industrial College of the Armed Forces (ICAF), Fort McNair, Washington, D.C.; the U.S. Marine Corps "Top Level," Quantico, Virginia; the National War College, Fort McNair, Washington, D.C.; and the Naval War College, Newport, Rhode Island.

The National War College, senior college of the National Defense University, is located in Washington, D.C.

Intermediate War Colleges. Intermediate war colleges, which are open to officers in pay grade O-4 (select) and senior, are located at Air Command and Staff, Maxwell Air Force Base, Alabama; Army Command and General Staff, Fort Leavenworth, Kansas; USMC Command and Staff, Quantico, Virginia; and Naval Command and Staff, Newport, Rhode Island.

In addition to the above-listed resident programs, the Naval Command and Staff, Air Command and Staff, and Army Command and General Staff offer nonresident programs that may be pursued by means of correspondence courses or evening classes in certain areas. There are also some opportunities to attend certain foreign war colleges.

Joint Specialty Officer

Title 10, United States Code, sec. 619a, commonly referred to as the Goldwater-Nichols Act, requires that any officer appointed to flag rank must have completed a tour of duty in a joint duty assignment. Although the wording of the law is clear, the term *joint duty assignment* has been subject to some interpretation.

Officers who have attended one of the war colleges, or who have received joint-duty-assignment credit based on completion of an accredited two- to three-year joint duty tour, are assigned one of a complex array of additional qualification designator codes for joint duty. An officer who has completed both a war college education and a joint duty assignment is eligible for selection as a joint specialty officer. Only joint-duty-assignment qualification is required for promotion to flag rank, and many staff and restricted line communities are exempt from even this requirement. However, one-third of current flag billets require JSO designation.

Officer Communities

Navy officers can be broadly grouped into three categories: unrestricted line, restricted line, and staff corps. Within each broad grouping are more specific categories, called designators.

Designators. Each officer in the Navy is assigned a four-digit designator. The first three numbers of the designator correspond to the community in which the officer serves (e.g., 161 corresponds to cryptology), and the fourth indicates the officer's status: 0 for an officer in the Regular Navy, 5 for one in the active component of the Naval Reserve, and 7 for one assigned to the Training and Administration of Reserves (TAR). In the following lists of communities and designators, where two designators are given for a single community (e.g., 116X and 111X for surface warfare), the first is for officers in training and the second is for fully qualified officers.

Unrestricted Line. The distinguishing feature of an unrestricted line officer is that he or she is eligible for command at sea, meaning command of a warfighting unit. (Officers in the restricted line and staff corps are also eligible for command, but only ashore, and only within their particular specialties.) The designators of unrestricted line officers are as follows:

- Surface warfare (116X/111X). Figure 17.2 shows the notional career path for a surface-warfare officer. An officer entering this field receives his or her initial training at Surface Warfare Officers School (SWOS) in Newport, Rhode Island, before being assigned to a surface ship for duty. A subcategory of surface warfare is nuclear surface warfare (116XN/111XN). Following attendance at SWOS and completion of an initial sea tour, officers in the nuclear surface-warfare community attend Nuclear Power School before receiving follow-on orders to an engineering billet on a nuclear-powered surface combatant.

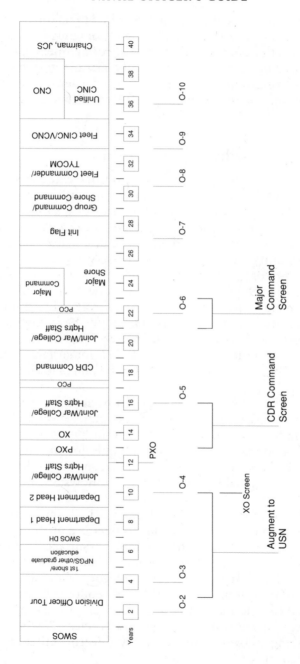

Fig. 17.2. Notional surface-warfare career path.

• Aviation warfare (pilots, 139X/131X; naval flight officers [NFOs], 137X/132X). Figure 17.3 shows the notional career path for aviation officers. All pilots and NFOs receive initial training at Naval Flight School in Pensacola, Florida, and then continue with training in specific aircraft types in fleet-readiness squadrons. Figure 17.3 shows the notional career path for an aviation-warfare officer.

• Submarine warfare (117X/112X). Submarine-warfare officers attend Nuclear Power School in Orlando, Florida, followed by prototype training before receiving their assignments to their first submarines. Figure 17.4 shows the notional career path for a submarine officer. This designator currently remains unavailable to women officers.

• Special warfare (118X/113X). Special-warfare officers serve in the areas of unconventional warfare, counterinsurgency, coastal and riverine interdictions, and tactical intelligence collection. Officers are initially assigned to Basic Underwater Demolition/ SEALs (BUDS) training in Coronado, California. This designator currently remains unavailable to women officers.

• Special operations (119X/114X). Special-operations officers perform explosive ordnance disposal (EOD) duties, operational diving and salvage, and expendable ordnance management. They receive their initial training at Diving and Salvage School in Panama City, Florida.

Restricted Line. Restricted line officers are restricted in the performance of their duties to certain specialized fields. Restricted line designators are as follows:

• Engineering duty (ED, 146X/144X). ED officers, or EDOs, specialize in ship engineering, including research, design, acquisition, construction, maintenance, and modernization of weapons and combat systems.

• Meteorology and oceanography (METOC, 180X). METOC officers are specialists in meteorologic and oceanographic mapping, charting, and geodesy.

• Aerospace engineering duty (AED, 151X). AED officers are specialists in aerospace engineering, including design, development, procurement, production, and support of air weapons systems and aircraft.

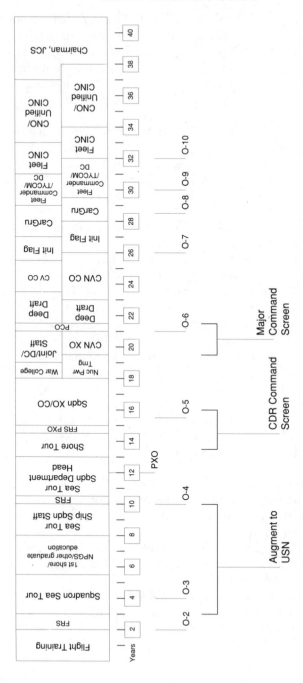

Fig. 17.3. Notional aviation-warfare career path.

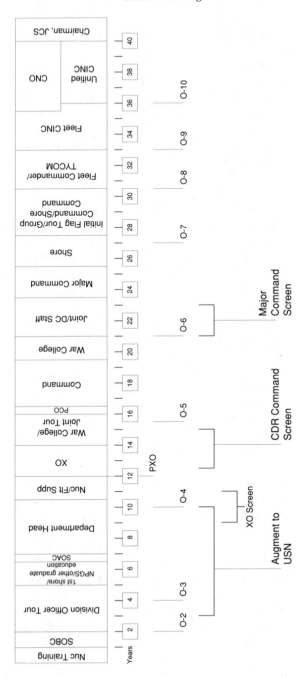

Fig. 17.4. Notional submarine-warfare career path.

• Aerospace maintenance duty (AMD, 152X). AMD officers are specialists in aviation maintenance management and related logistics support.

• Public affairs (165X). Public affairs officers are specialists in public and internal information and community relations.

• Cryptology (161X). Cryptologists are specialists in tactical cryptologic combat support and signal intelligence information.

• Intelligence (163X). Intelligence officers are specialists in counterintelligence, investigations, and information collection, analysis, and dissemination.

• Fleet support (170X). This designator was established in 1995 when the general unrestricted line officer designator was converted to restricted line. Officers in this community manage the Navy's support establishment, focusing on one of three core areas: logistics; manpower, personnel, and training (MPT); or space and electronic warfare. The 170XN designator denotes those fleet-support officers detailed to conduct nuclear reactor research and training.

Staff Corps. Staff corps officers are qualified professionals who are limited to service in their own fields of expertise. Staff corps designators are as follows:

• Supply corps (310X). Supply corps officers are specialists in business and logistics management, including such duties as financial acquisition and contracts, system inventory, transportation and physical distribution, automated data processing, integrated logistics support, petroleum management, merchandising, and food service.

• Medical corps (210X). Medical corps officers are licensed practicing physicians and osteopaths, or officers attending accredited schools of medicine or osteopathy. These officers may be general practitioners or specialists in a particular field of medicine. Medical corps officers serve aboard larger ships as well as in clinics and naval hospitals ashore.

• Medical service corps (MSC, 230X). MSC officers are health-care professionals other than physicians and nurses. This designator encompasses a wide variety of specialties, including pharmacy, hospital administration, occupational safety and health, physical therapy, and other health-care fields.

- Dental corps (220X). Dental corps officers are licensed practicing dentists. These officers serve in hospitals and dental clinics, although some large ships with dental treatment facilities have dental officers assigned.
- Nurse corps (290X). Nurse corps officers are graduates of accredited nursing schools. These officers generally rotate between shore and overseas commands; those who are specialists in particular fields may have different career paths.
- Chaplain corps (410X). Members of the chaplain corps are ordained in their particular denominations and serve afloat and ashore. The chaplain corps is responsible for the implementation of religious ministries throughout the naval service.
- Civil engineering corps (510X). Civil engineering corps officers are engineers and architects specializing in facilities management, operations, maintenance, and planning; construction and contracting; petroleum engineering; or ocean and environmental engineering.
- Judge advocate general (JAG) corps (250X). JAG officers are practicing attorneys who are responsible for administering the Navy's justice system as well as matters related to contract and business law.

Warrant Officers and Limited Duty Officers. Officers commissioned through these programs have risen through the enlisted ranks and are assigned designators and follow career paths that make use of their specific areas of expertise. Chapter 8 provides additional information on these commissioning programs.

18

SUCCESSFUL
LEADERSHIP

YOU DON'T MANAGE PEOPLE; YOU MANAGE THINGS. YOU LEAD PEOPLE.

—Rear Admiral Grace Hopper

IF YOU WANT AN ARMY TO FIGHT AND RISK DEATH, YOU'VE GOT TO GET UP THERE
AND LEAD IT. AN ARMY IS LIKE SPAGHETTI. YOU CAN'T PUSH A PIECE OF SPAGHETTI,
YOU'VE GOT TO PULL IT!

—General George S. Patton Jr.

In the program that prepared you for your commission, the instructors probably spent time discussing the traits of superior leaders. You may have read essays written by flag officers and been tasked with memorizing a list of leadership traits. Perhaps you wondered how such activities would ever turn you into a good leader.

The answer is, they won't—at least not by themselves. Classroom study plants the seeds of knowledge so that, with practice and maturity, you will be able to train yourself to become the sort of leader you admire. No training program, however well designed, can make you a leader. This is a voyage you must undertake of your own will and sustain under your own power.

A great leader won't necessarily have all of the traits that will be discussed in this chapter, but he or she will have put considerable effort into developing as many of them as possible.

Leadership Qualities

Knowledge. Your first requirement as a naval leader is to have a knowledge of yourself, your profession, and your ship or unit. Do you know your own strengths and weaknesses? Are you prepared to play to your strengths and compensate for or correct your weaknesses? Even John Paul Jones had his faults, but he led in such a way that his strengths overcame his weaknesses.

Do you know your profession? You can't maintain the respect of your people if you don't know your business. Your immediate goal should be to achieve journeyman-level proficiency in your chosen specialty, but beyond that you must also develop your knowledge of the broader aspects of naval warfare. The core competency objectives in appendix 1 will give you a place to start.

Finally, do you know your ship or unit? Knowledge of your own command, and your responsibilities in it, are prerequisites to success in any position. Once you have such a knowledge base, you will be better able to assess any new situation that arises, make a decision, and come up with a plan of action to deal with it.

Throughout your career, never be satisfied with your current level of training or qualification or knowledge. Strive for continuous self-improvement.

Integrity. One of the core values of the Navy discussed in chapter 2, integrity is the cornerstone of what naval officers do. More than simply standing up for your beliefs, the development of integrity is an active process that begins when you identify what you believe in and determine what you are willing to sacrifice for your beliefs. If you don't know what your beliefs are, decide what you want them to be, and adopt them. If you wait until you are under duress before doing this kind of introspection, you may ultimately regret the choices you make. Set aside some time early in your career to give some thought to your values, because the decisions you make will lie at the heart of your performance as a leader.

Loyalty. Many different kinds of loyalty will be demanded of you. Your paramount loyalty, of course, lies with the oath you have taken to defend the United States and the Constitution, but you also will, and should, feel loyalty to the U.S. Navy, to your ship or unit, to your superiors in command, to your subordinates, to your shipmates, and, of course, to your family and friends.

Seniors in the Navy rightfully demand a high degree of personal loyalty from their subordinates. The so-called acid test of loyalty is the ability to pass on the order of a superior, perhaps an unpopular order with which you don't agree, and make it appear to your subordinates as if the order originated with you. Equally important as loyalty up the chain of command to your superiors is loyalty down the chain of command to your subordinates. Look after your people, their interests, their welfare, and their careers. Such loyalty will help your subordinates build their own loyalty to you.

There will be occasions when your different loyalties will pull you in opposing directions, when you find that you cannot be loyal to a shipmate, a superior, or a friend without sacrificing your loyalty to the United States. If that is the case, your choice is clear.

Maturity. More than simply the state of being fully grown, maturity entails a sense of responsibility, of willingness to take "ownership" of a problem and see the solution through to its completion. An immature individual tends to believe that a problem, whatever it is, will always be taken care of by someone else. This kind of attitude can be absolute poison in an organization in which individuals must rely on each other to take care of problems without being told.

Displays of temper and incidents of ridicule and verbal abuse of subordinates are signs of immaturity. This type of behavior, although it has never been condoned in the Navy, does occur, and it has been drawing increased scrutiny in recent years. There have been several well-publicized instances in which COs have been relieved of their commands for such conduct, and many lesser known instances in which it cut short the otherwise promising careers of junior officers.

Will. In war, it is insufficient to simply "try" to win; the only alternative to winning a battle is losing it. To have will means to not give up in the face of overwhelming obstacles, to find a way around them, over them, or through them to achieve your goal. Will means not undertaking a mission with the thought that you will do your best; it means never allowing yourself any thought but that you will succeed.

Followership. You cannot successfully lead without in turn being a successful follower of your own leaders. Your ability to do this will reinforce the followership skills of your own subordinates.

Self-Discipline. Learn to set realistic goals and hold yourself to them. From your boss's perspective, discipline is probably the most highly prized quality you can have. You cannot impose discipline on your subordinates without first imposing it on yourself.

A lieutenant practices leadership under stressful conditions as she tends to a wounded Marine. She is participating in a medical casualty response exercise on board the amphibious assault ship USS *Tarawa*. PH2 McNeeley

Confidence. In an emergency situation, your subordinates will be looking to you to be cool and confident. If you seem frightened or indecisive, or if you lack self-confidence or appear not to trust your own judgment, you will put yourself and your people at unnecessary risk. Mental rehearsals will help you learn to maintain your composure in stressful situations, as will repetition and drill.

You can't expect to have confidence in your ability to perform as a naval officer right away; true confidence comes at least in part from knowledge and experience. Hone and practice your skills, and learn from your own mistakes as well as the mistakes of others until you are comfortable with your expertise and have learned to rely on your own judgment.

Flexibility. The need for flexibility is often mistakenly used as an excuse not to make plans, but this is the wrong approach. In order to be flexible you must not only make plans but also make backup plans, and backup plans for your backup plans. Don't become too accustomed to the status quo, and be ready to adapt without complaint when the situation changes without notice.

Endurance. Serving in the Navy can be hard work and is often both physically and mentally stressful. The sometimes extreme demands of this profession are one reason the Navy places so much emphasis on the requirement that you maintain yourself in good physical condition. You can't effectively lead your people if you are exhausted and stressed out.

Decisiveness. There is a feeling among some officers that decisiveness means voicing an instant and unchanging opinion on every subject. A better name for this is stupidity.

Decisiveness means the ability to commit yourself, and your subordinates, to a course of action. Once you have announced a decision and set a plan in motion, you risk sabotaging your success every time you have to change your plans. Although you should not hesitate to reverse your decision when necessary, you should bear in mind the costs of making this change and do so only with good reason.

In peacetime you may have the luxury of taking some time to make up your mind on a possible course of action. If the matter is not urgent, and if the situation is sufficiently complex to warrant it, spend time gathering information and consulting with others before you make your final decision. Don't announce your decision until it is necessary for you to do so; this permits you to keep evaluating new information with an open mind.

Initiative. Initiative has several allied qualities: imagination, aggressiveness, and the ability to look and think ahead. Don't wait for your superiors to tell you what needs to be done. A wise old seaman once said, "Initiative is the ability to do the right thing without being told."

Justice. Endeavor to treat your subordinates with absolute fairness. Personal prejudice—against race, gender, ethnic origin, personal appearance, or other similarly irrelevant factors—has no legitimate place in a leader's decision making.

Compassion. While you must insist on loyalty, discipline, performance, and dedication, you must remember that the men and women who work for you are not always motivated by the same things that motivate you. Make an effort to find out what motivates your subordinates, and keep it in mind in your dealings with them.

Be considerate of your subordinates' feelings. Remember the adage "Praise in public, criticize in private." It is equally important to be considerate of the feelings of your superiors and peers.

Forcefulness. The meek may someday inherit the earth, but in the interim they are unlikely to succeed as naval officers. To do your job effectively, you will have to learn to stand up to your peers, to recalcitrant subordinates, and occasionally to your superiors.

Positive Attitude. Your attitude is incredibly contagious. If you radiate negativity, the people who work for you will radiate negativity as well, and they won't perform at their best. Be enthusiastic, and demonstrate your enthusiasm to your people at every opportunity.

Communication Skills. It is not critical for you as a junior officer to be known as a great speaker or writer. However, you must be reasonably competent in both written and oral communications, or your lack of skill will adversely affect your performance and the performance of your people. Chapter 9 discusses oral and written communications in detail.

Personal Behavior. It is not enough to *be* ethical and moral; as a leader and a role model you must also be *perceived* as ethical and moral. Strive to set an example for your subordinates. Set the highest standard you possibly can; the standard to which you hold yourself will determine the standard you can set for your subordinates.

Courage. Courage comes in two forms, physical and moral. Physical courage means overcoming your fears to carry out your duties in a dangerous situation. Moral courage can be even more difficult; it means having the courage of your convictions, "calling them as you see them," admitting your own mistakes and speaking up when you feel that a senior is about to make an error. Moral courage includes the ability to counsel subordinates honestly on their weaknesses, one of the hardest and most painful tasks of any leader.

Leadership Continuum Training

Although there is no substitute for leadership learned through on-the-job training, the Navy recognizes that these lessons should be augmented by formal classroom leadership training.

The Leadership Continuum provides mandatory leadership training at each milestone in a Navy leader's career, from second-class petty officer to commanding officer. Enlisted personnel attend training upon advancement to E-5, E-6, and chief petty officer, and upon selection to serve as command master chief or chief of the boat. Sailors must successfully complete the appropriate leadership course prior to recommendation for advancement to the next pay grade. Officers attend leadership training en route to tours as division officers, department heads, executive officers, and commanding officers.

19

COMMAND

YOU SHOULD ENTER THE NAVY FOR ONE PURPOSE, TO COMMAND SHIPS, SUBMARINES AND AIRCRAFT. ONCE YOU GET SUCH A COMMAND ENJOY EVERY MINUTE OF IT.

—*Fleet Admiral Chester Nimitz*

THE CAPTAIN OF A SHIP, LIKE THE CAPTAIN OF A STATE, IS GIVEN HONOR AND PRIVILEGES AND TRUST BEYOND OTHER MEN. BUT LET HIM SET THE WRONG COURSE, LET HIM TOUCH GROUND, LET HIM BRING DISASTER TO HIS SHIP OR TO HIS MEN, AND HE MUST ANSWER FOR WHAT HE HAS DONE. NO MATTER WHAT, HE CANNOT ESCAPE.

—Wall Street Journal, *14 May 1952*

Navy Regulations art. 0801 states, "The responsibility of the commanding officer for his or her command is absolute. . . . The authority of the commanding officer is commensurate with his or her responsibility."

Preparation for Command

You will often hear that command is, and should be, the aspiration of every naval officer. Up to the point when you assume your first command, you will spend your entire career preparing for it. It isn't too early to start your preparations now. The Naval Institute publication *Command at Sea* contains more detailed information on preparations for, and the responsibilities of, command.

General Preparation. As you progress in your career, you should make an effort to learn all you can about the different aspects of your ships or units. You should pursue your professional education with vigor, through reading, seminars, and classes, and by asking questions of your seniors and engaging your peers in discussion.

Observe your seniors and how they do their jobs. Study the careers of officers you admire and who have held the kinds of positions you aspire to hold. Find out all you can about what made these officers successful; base your own goals on their achievements, and emulate their personal qualities as much as possible. Maintain a familiarity with the notional career path for your designator, as discussed in chapter 17, as well as any new opportunities announced in message traffic and the BUPERS publication *Perspective.*

Shiphandling. Every ship CO, regardless of his or her background, must be an outstanding shiphandler. The CO must be able to train the ship's junior officers in all aspects of shiphandling and, when necessary in an emergency, must be prepared to make rapid decisions or even to relieve the conning officer.

Like any other skill, shiphandling is an art that must be practiced. As a junior officer, take every possible opportunity to rehearse making approaches on other ships for underway replenishment, coming into an anchorage, conducting shipboard recovery during man-overboard drills, and other similar shiphandling evolutions. Many junior officers shy away from these opportunities because they are afraid of being embarrassed by their lack of skill. All novice shiphandlers make mistakes, but if you allow yourself to be discouraged by such fears, your skills will never improve. It is far better to perform poorly in a man-overboard drill, or in many man-overboard drills, than to perform poorly when a real sailor is lost over the side. If you are always the first junior officer on the bridge when you hear a training opportunity announced, you will make a favorable impression on your CO, and your skills will develop rapidly.

If your duties permit, when you aren't actively engaged in conning the ship you should study the actions of the officer who is. Continually ask yourself what orders you would be giving to the helm and lee helm in the same situation, and attempt to project, from the conning officer's orders, how the ship will respond. You can learn nearly as much by observing the actions of a skilled boat coxswain as you can from observing a skilled officer of the deck (OOD). Because different classes of ships can handle quite differently, you should also ask your chain of command to allow you to spend time under way on other types of ships to broaden your experience.

Watchstanding. It is natural to look on your watchstanding requirements as a chore to be gotten through, but your watches are also your most valuable opportunities for learning your profession. When you become qualified as OOD under way, it means

This tactical action officer and his assistant prepare to assume the watch aboard the aircraft carrier USS *Theodore Roosevelt.* PH3 Jason Morris

that your CO has the confidence in your judgment to allow you to make decisions in his or her absence. This is not only an enormous responsibility but also an opportunity to practice, to some small degree, the experience of command. Similarly, when you become qualified to stand command duty officer (CDO) in port, you will be completely responsible for the ship in your CO's absence. Treat these watches as rehearsals for your future command.

Training and Qualification for Command. As you progress through the ranks, selection boards will periodically review your record to determine your fitness for the next career milestone: department head, XO, CO. Start early to find out what it takes to ensure that your record will compare favorably with those of your peers. Always ask your detailer to give you the most challenging assignments possible; provided that you perform well, these are the jobs that will make you stand out in your peer group. Prior to the time you will be considered for command, make sure you have completed whatever your designator requires for command qualification. This process is at least partially intended to separate those who are committed to their desire to command from those who are not.

It is critically important that COs possess comprehensive knowledge of all aspects of their commands. If you are a surface-warfare officer, it is well worth your while, regardless of your billet, to spend sufficient time standing watches in engineering as a junior officer to complete your engineering officer of the watch (EOOW) qualification, and similarly to complete your tactical action officer (TAO) qualification at the earliest opportunity. Regardless of your community, you should seek out opportunities to add to your qualifications and to hone those you already have.

Mental Preparation. In addition to the qualities of successful leaders discussed in chapter 18, successful commanding officers share certain values that have been ingrained in the Navy's culture for hundreds of years. If you hope to follow in their footsteps you should work to develop these values in yourself.

A CO's reputation is based in large part on the appearance and military smartness of the crew and ship, because the CO's own example is what sets the standards for his or her subordinates. You should become familiar with the rules of military etiquette and practice them diligently. In addition, make sure that your appearance, grooming, and personal conduct are always above reproach, and demand no less from your subordinates.

Not solely a health and safety issue, cleanliness is as much a part of the Navy's culture as nearly any other visible quality. Cleanliness in work spaces, living spaces, and the exterior of the ship or unit represents visible evidence of a crew that takes pride in its command. Begin early to cultivate this habit in yourself, both by demanding the highest standards in your own spaces and by enforcing these standards throughout the command when you are standing watch as CDO.

Although commanding officers are not averse to risk, nor could they be, they are willing to work hard and ensure the same of their subordinates in order to minimize *unnecessary* risk. Examples of this are repetitive drills and exercises to keep a crew's readiness at its peak, and making extensive preparations for heavy weather whenever the possibility of a storm exists. It is far better to take precautions that later turn out to have been unnecessary than to find out too late that you should have made more extensive preparations.

You probably were exposed to the importance of "attention to detail" during your preparation for commissioning. Attention to detail means never leaving anything to chance or assuming that someone else will take care of it. An officer who exhibits this characteristic will ensure that his or her organization works through an entire inspection checklist before the inspection team ever steps aboard, to preclude the possibility of unpleasant surprises.

The abbreviation UNODIR, when used in official communication to a superior in command, means that a CO intends to take a particular action "unless otherwise directed." Superiors encourage this kind of boldness in their subordinate officers, which relieves them of some of the burdens of routine decision making yet allows them to exercise "command by negation" when they disagree with the proposed action. You will find throughout your career that your COs use UNODIR whenever possible in their communications with superiors.

Similarly, a good CO will help subordinates develop good judgment by telling them *what* to do without telling them *how* to do it. In the short run this makes the CO's job harder, as there is a good chance that inexperienced subordinates will make mistakes that could have been avoided had the CO offered additional "rudder orders." In the long run, however, the subordinates will learn more, develop more initiative and confidence in their own judgment, and be better prepared to respond in an emergency.

Assumption of Command

Relieving Command.   Prior to reporting aboard, you will attend any necessary pipeline schools designated in your orders. Once reporting aboard, turnover can take as little as a few days or as long as a month. One to two weeks is normal. You will have to be flexible in arranging your turnover schedule, as the schedule of the ship or other deployable unit will likely be relatively fixed, and you owe the officer you will be relieving the courtesy of accommodating his or her scheduling needs.

Navy Regulations art. 08070 provides guidance on turnover procedures, and your type commander will likely have a separate, more detailed list of procedures. *Navy Regulations* requires, at a minimum, the following of the departing commanding officer:

- Inspect the command in company with the relieving officer.
- In the case of a ship or other operational command, exercise the crew at general quarters and general drills, unless impracticable.
- Advise the relieving officer of any known defects or peculiarities in the command, particularly with regard to safety, operational readiness, training, habitability, or material conditions.
- Deliver to the relieving officer all unexecuted orders, all regulations and orders in force, and all official correspondence and information concerning the command and its personnel.
- Deliver to the relieving officer all documents required to be held by the CO, and inventory the postal account (if the command has a post office).
- Deliver to the relieving officer all magazine keys and other keys in his or her possession.
- Inventory all communications security material.
- Submit fitness reports on all assigned officers, and sign all logs, records, and other documents prior to the date of relief.
- Call the crew to muster for the change-of-command ceremony. (Shore commands may modify this procedure.)

In addition to these required turnover items, if time permits you should review the ship's bills, conduct a supply inventory, review the results of recent inspections and subsequent corrective actions on any discrepancies, determine the status of any equipment that is reported as out of commission, and attend to other similar matters. It is customary for the departing CO to refrain from offering personal opinions of the members of the wardroom, so that the relieving CO has an open mind on the matter.

The departing CO prepares a letter listing any unsatisfactory conditions in the command at the time of turnover—particularly those dealing with safety, inoperative machinery or armament, significant lack of spare parts, ordnance, or supplies, notable personnel deficiencies or training shortfalls, fiscal integrity, or command performance—and proposing a plan of corrective actions. The relieving officer endorses this letter, noting any areas of disagreement and allowing the departing CO the opportunity to respond.

The departing CO has the primary responsibility for making arrangements for the change-of-command ceremony, although the relieving CO will be asked to provide a list of his or her personal guests. If a reception is held following the ceremony, the new and old COs share the expenses.

Organization and Administration

The *Standard Organization and Regulations Manual (SORM)* describes the basic principles of ship organization as well as the duties of officers and enlisted personnel. Your type commander and immediate superior in command (ISIC) may provide additional guidance. You or your XO will need to stay in frequent contact with your officer and enlisted placement officers to anticipate arrivals and detachments and to deal with other detailing contingencies that may arise.

Command Excellence

In a 1985 study published in the Navy booklet *Command Excellence* (see Sources), hundreds of officers and enlisted members at twenty-one commands were interviewed in order to identify those qualities that distinguish the outstanding CO from the merely average CO. The study identified the following twelve characteristics of an outstanding CO:

- Targets key issues. Outstanding COs recognize that no commander, and no crew, can do everything that someone else wants done. Instead, these COs learned to set priorities to accomplish their most important tasks first.
- Gets crew support for command philosophy. Whether transcribed into a formal document or not, successful COs have a command philosophy, and they communicate this philosophy to their wardrooms and crews both formally and through personal example.
- Develops the XO. The successful CO recognizes his or her responsibility to prepare the XO for command.
- Staffs to optimize performance. Although few commanders have the luxury of being able to choose their own crews, those who are most successful make an effort to put the best person in each position to take advantage of his or her talents.
- Gets out and about. The successful CO doesn't hide in his or her stateroom but practices what some have called MBWA ("management by walking around"). This keeps the CO in touch with the individual members of the command on a daily basis.
- Builds esprit de corps. The morale, pride, and teamwork of a command are the intangibles that make the difference between an outstanding command and an ordinary one. The best COs pro-

ject a "can-do" positive attitude, work to overcome conflicts among the crew, and praise and reward good performance.

- Keeps his or her cool. An outstanding CO is not a "screamer" and doesn't react emotionally or impulsively.
- Develops a strong wardroom. The best wardrooms are cohesive, cooperative, and supportive of each other. A CO can do much to foster this environment by encouraging teamwork among members of the wardroom and taking a personal interest in the career development of each individual officer.
- Values the chiefs' quarters. Outstanding COs recognize that the range of expertise and experience in the chiefs' mess is one of a command's most valuable assets, and they treat the chiefs accordingly.
- Ensures that training is effective. The best COs believe the old Chinese proverb "The more you sweat in peace, the less you bleed in war." These COs stress frequent, realistic, and thorough training.
- Builds positive external relationships. Outstanding COs understand the importance of establishing and maintaining strong relationships with external organizations such as the staff, shipyards and contractors, placement officers, base commanders, and others. Strong ties help the command to better accomplish its mission.
- Influences successfully. An outstanding CO is able to persuade the crew to do an unpleasant job enthusiastically rather than grudgingly.

Setting Command Policy

By the time you achieve your first command, you will have had ample opportunity to formulate your own command philosophy through the study of leadership and daily observations of your seniors' practices. Before you arrive at your new command, you should plan to spend time formalizing this philosophy into a command policy statement that you can share with your new wardroom and crew. They will be eager to find out what you expect of them, and their learning curve will be considerably steeper if you provide them with written guidance than if they have to figure out by trial and error what you expect. Once you have determined your command policy, you should consider holding an all-officers meeting and a series of "captain's calls" to put the word out to your wardroom and crew personally.

The following are some considerations you may want to include in your command policy.

Safety. There is no higher priority in peacetime operations than the safety and well-being of the ship and crew. Make clear to the crew that this is your highest priority, and that you expect it to be theirs as well.

Standards. What are your standards for excellence? However self-evident you may feel your standards are, it is still a good idea to put them in writing.

Priorities and Goals. Make sure every member of your crew is aware of what your top priorities are and what goals you have set for them.

Command Policies. Different COs have different philosophies about such mundane but important matters as leave and liberty, discipline, habitability, appropriate civilian attire, watchstanding, and qualifications. Particularly if your policies differ from those of your predecessor, make them known.

Support for Navy Policies. Your crew will be looking to you to endorse the Navy's policies on such issues as equal opportunity, drug- and alcohol-abuse prevention, sexual-harassment prevention, smoking cessation, and physical readiness. If you fail to do this, they might conclude that these issues are not important to you.

20

SEPARATION AND RETIREMENT

MY SWORD I GIVE HIM THAT SHALL SUCCEED ME IN MY PILGRIMAGE, AND MY COURAGE AND SKILL TO HIM THAT CAN GET IT. MY MARKS AND SCARS I CARRY WITH ME, TO BE A WITNESS FOR ME, THAT I HAVE FOUGHT HIS BATTLES WHO WILL NOW BE MY REWARDER.

—*John Bunyan*

SO SAFE ON SHORE THE PENSIONED SAILOR LIES,
AND ALL THE MALICE OF THE STORM DEFIES.

—*William Somerville*

Sooner or later, whether you decide to separate at the end of your initial obligated service or reluctantly retire after a distinguished thirty-year career, you will face the prospect of leaving the Navy. It is never too early to start planning for this eventuality, and this chapter is intended to help you in this effort.

Preseparation Plan

Like any complex undertaking, your successful transition to civilian life requires a plan. The following suggestions for developing a transition plan come from the publication *Preseparation Guide* (NAVPERS 15616).

Six Months Prior to Separation. Develop a detailed road map for your transition to civilian life. Assess and document your skills, training, and talents, and determine how best to market yourself in the civilian employment force. Discuss future career options and plans for relocation with your family. Research career fields that interest you, using resources available in your base transition assistance office or family service center. Determine whether you need to obtain additional training or academic credentials. Develop a plan to conduct your job search in a systematic way, by attending a transition class, job fair, or résumé-writing workshop.

Four Months Prior to Separation. Begin putting your career goals in more concrete form. Write a résumé, and begin networking with friends, acquaintances, and former shipmates to seek out employment in your chosen field. Develop a financial plan to see you through a period of unemployment, and research transitional health-care options, relocation assistance, and educational benefits for which you may be eligible. Make arrangements to terminate your government housing or lease, and decide whether you will affiliate with the Naval Reserve upon separation (you will be required to affiliate with the reserve in certain circumstances discussed later in this chapter).

Three Months Prior to Separation. Attend a Transition Assistance Program (TAP) workshop in your area. Begin your automated job search through the Defense Outplacement Referral Service (DORS) and DoD Transition Bulletin Board (TBB). (Information on these services is available at the transition assistance office.) Mail résumés to prospective employers. Schedule your final dental examination and separation or retirement physical, and take advantage of free legal service assistance to update your will.

One Month Prior to Separation. Schedule job interviews and visit the area to which you plan to move. Make final decisions on your need for interim health care and life insurance. Finalize arrangements to store or move your household goods to your new location.

Separation

Officers who are not eligible for retirement may separate from the Navy. Such separation may be voluntary or involuntary.

Voluntary Separation. Officers who have fulfilled their initial obligated service may request separation from the Navy. Officers may also request early separation in special circumstances including pregnancy and hardship. Subject to the needs of the Navy, separations are normally approved when the officer has completed minimum time on station for the particular type of assignment and has fulfilled any service obligations due to receipt of educational benefits, special pay, or other circumstances. When requesting separation, submit your letter of unqualified resignation nine to twelve months in advance of the date you desire to separate.

Involuntary Separation. Officers in the Naval Reserve may be involuntarily separated for twice failing to select for promotion, or be involuntarily released from active duty (IRAD) because of demobilization or drawdown. Officers in the Regular Navy may generally be involuntarily separated only for twice failing to select for promotion. In addition, administrative separations "in the best interest of the service" may be awarded to officers under certain circumstances, and courts-martial may award punitive dismissals for violations of the Uniform Code of Military Justice.

Separation Pay. Officers who are involuntarily separated from the Navy may be entitled to separation pay if they meet the following criteria:

• Officers must be retention-eligible, and not separated because of substandard performance or dereliction of duty. Officers who are separated because of failure to select for promotion, as well as reserve officers involuntarily released from active duty, meet this requirement.

• The separation must be truly involuntary, and not initiated by the officer or caused by the officer's own conduct.

• Officers must have served at least six years of active duty.

• Officers must agree to serve in the Ready Reserve for a minimum of three years in addition to any existing obligation. (This agreement does not obligate the reserve to accept the officer for service.)

The amount of separation-pay entitlement is equal to 10 percent of the officer's years of service (each full month of service is counted as one-twelfth of one year), times 12, times the amount of the officer's monthly basic pay at the time of separation.

Officers separated under certain adverse circumstances are entitled to one-half of the normal amount of separation pay.

Naval Reserve Affiliation. Officers who separate from the Navy prior to completing eight years of active service, and officers who receive separation pay, are required to affiliate with the Naval Reserve upon separation. Such officers may voluntarily affiliate with the Selected Reserve or be involuntarily assigned to the Individual Ready Reserve. Other separating officers may also request to affiliate with the Selected Reserve. Chapter 15 provides descriptions of these reserve categories.

Retirement

Eligibility. Officers are eligible to retire upon completion of twenty years of active service. You should plan to submit your request for retirement six to nine months prior to your desired retirement date if it coincides with the projected rotation date (PRD) of your tour, and nine to twelve months in advance if your desired retirement date is prior to your PRD.

Retirement Pay. There are three formulas for computing nondisability retirement pay:

• The "final basic pay" plan applies to members who first entered military service prior to 8 September 1980. Multiply your basic monthly pay at the time of retirement by 2.5 percent for each whole year of service (each whole additional month counts as one-twelfth of one year). The amount of retirement pay under this formula may not exceed 75 percent of basic pay.

• The "high 3" plan applies to members who first entered military service between 8 September 1980 and 31 July 1986. Compute pay using the same formula as for the "final basic pay" plan, except use the average basic pay for your three highest-earning years rather than your final basic pay.

• For members who first entered military service on or after 1 August 1986, calculate retired pay based on the average basic pay for your three highest-earnings years, times 2.5 percent for each year of creditable service, minus one percentage point for each year less than thirty years of service.

Military retired pay is usually cost-of-living- (COLA-) adjusted annually.

Loss of Citizenship. Loss of U.S. citizenship generally results in the loss of retired pay. As payment of retired pay is contingent on a member maintaining his or her military status, the Comptroller General has held that loss of citizenship is "inconsistent" with a continuation of that status.

Veterans' Benefits

Eligibility for most Veterans Administration (VA) benefits is based upon the type of discharge from active service. Honorable and general discharges qualify a veteran for most VA benefits, and punitive discharges issued by courts-martial bar most VA benefits. Certain types of benefits and medical care require wartime service. Your service discharge form (DD 214), which documents your service dates and type of discharge, will be an important document when seeking any type of VA benefit.

Educational Benefits. The VA administers benefits under the Montgomery GI Bill, discussed in chapter 17. In addition, the VA administers a vocational rehabilitation program for disabled veterans and their dependents and surviving spouses.

Home Loan Guaranties. The VA guarantees loans made to service members and veterans for the purchase or refinancing of homes. The VA guarantees part of the total loan, which permits the purchaser to obtain a mortgage with a competitive interest rate, in some circumstances with no down payment. Applicants must have a good credit rating, have an income sufficient to support mortgage payments, and agree to live in the property.

Life Insurance. The VA oversees Servicemen's Group Life Insurance (SGLI), discussed in chapter 4. This type of insurance is available only to active-duty members. Within 120 days of separation or retirement, you may convert SGLI to Veterans' Group Life Insurance (VGLI), which is renewable five-year term coverage. In addition to VGLI, the VA offers Service Disabled Insurance to veterans with service-connected disabilities and Veterans' Mortgage Life Insurance to veterans granted specially adapted housing grants.

Veterans Assistance. The Veterans Assistance Service provides information, advice, and assistance to veterans and their dependents and beneficiaries. In addition, the Veterans Assistance Service cooperates with the Department of Labor and other federal, state, and local agencies in developing employment opportunities for veterans, and referral for assistance in resolving socioeconomic, housing, and other related problems.

Disability Compensation. The VA pays monetary benefits to veterans who are disabled by injury or disease that was incurred or aggravated during active military service. Benefits, based on the level of disability and the number of dependents, are set by Congress and not subject to federal or state income tax. Disability compensation is also affected by eligibility for military retirement pay and by receipt of disability severance pay and separation incentive payments. Veterans whose service-connected disabilities are rated at 30 percent or more are entitled to additional allowances for dependents, based on the number of dependents and the degree of disability.

Hospital and Outpatient Care. There are two categories of eligibility for VA hospital and outpatient care. Category 1 includes veterans in need of care for a service-connected condition or disability, veterans who are former prisoners of war or who were exposed to certain kinds of radiation or chemical hazards, and veterans whose annual income and net worth falls below an annually determined "means test" threshold. Within category 1, the VA will also pay for medical services for the treatment of service-connected disabilities and related conditions for veterans abroad. Category 2 includes all other veterans. In order to receive treatment, category 2 veterans must agree to make co-payments.

VA medical benefits are separate and distinct from CHAMPUS/TRICARE medical benefits (discussed in chapter 4). Retirees and their dependents are eligible to participate in the CHAMPUS/TRICARE programs. Transitional medical coverage programs for separatees are described later in this chapter.

Other Benefits

Leave and Travel. Retirees and members who are being involuntarily separated are entitled to up to twenty days of permissive temporary duty for job hunting, house hunting, or other relocation activities, subject to the needs of their commands. Up to thirty days may be authorized for those relocating from overseas.

Terminal Leave. Subject to the approval of their commands, all separatees and retirees may detach from their commands in sufficient time to use the remainder of their accrued leave prior to separation from active duty. If early detachment is not authorized, members may sell back up to sixty days of accrued leave.

Storage and Relocation of Household Goods. All separatees are entitled to store household goods for up to six months following separation, and to move their possessions to their homes of record or to other locations a shorter distance away. Retirees and involuntary separatees are entitled to store household goods for up to one year and to move their possessions to any location in the United States or to an overseas home of record.

Government Housing Extensions. Under certain circumstances, separatees may request to remain in their government quarters for up to 180 days following separation. When granted such an extension, the former member is charged rent equal to the appropriate amount of local basic allowance for housing (BAH).

Transitional Health Care for Separatees. Involuntary separatees are eligible for up to 120 days of transitional health-care coverage under CHAMPUS. This coverage is intended to prevent separatees and their families from experiencing gaps in their health-care coverage before beginning coverage with new employers. Following termination of this coverage, these members may purchase up to eighteen months of additional health-care coverage under the Continued Health Care Benefit Plan (CHCBP). CHCBP is also available to voluntary separatees.

Survivor Benefit Plan (SBP). Under SBP, a retiree contributes 6.5 percent of retired pay each month to provide a surviving spouse or children an annuity equal to 55 percent of retired pay. At age sixty-two, a surviving spouse's annuity is reduced from 55 percent to 35 percent. Enrollment in SBP is automatic, unless the retiree and the spouse elect in writing not to participate, or to participate to a lesser extent. An election into the plan is irrevocable except by death or divorce. A retiree who had no eligible spouse when first eligible to enroll in SBP, or who subsequently divorced and married a different spouse, may elect during the first year of marriage to cover the new spouse.

Postservice Employment Regulations

Seeking Postservice Employment. Various laws restrict the employment activities of former military members. There are additional restrictions on regular retired officers and for officers who retired above certain pay grades or who were involved in procurement activities. These restrictions are based upon the need to prevent activity that conflicts with the interests of the United States and to preserve the public's confidence in government integrity.

Before beginning negotiations with a prospective employer, you should consult with a Navy ethics counselor (a designated JAG corps officer) to assist you in determining the restrictions that apply to your situation. If a potential violation exists, you should disqualify yourself from taking any action on behalf of the government that could affect your prospective employer. The standards of conduct prohibit not only actual violations of the rules but also any act that could create the appearance of using public office for private gain or for giving preferential treatment, or that could result in a conflict of interest or loss of impartiality.

The Procurement Integrity Act imposes additional restrictions on federal employees who are involved in procurement. This act bars employees who were involved in large procurements from employment with the private employers concerned for a period of one year.

Working during Terminal Leave. With several exceptions, if there is no bar to your employment with a specific employer, you may begin working for that employer while on terminal leave. If you intend to work for a defense contractor, you should obtain written permission prior to doing so. In addition, because military officers are prohibited by law from serving in a "civil office" with a state or local government, you may not perform duties of such office while on terminal leave. Surprisingly, if you take a federal civil service job, you may legally receive both military and civil service compensation at the same time.

Employment with Foreign Governments and Foreign Principals. The U.S. Constitution prohibits any person holding any office of profit or trust under the federal government from accepting any present, emolument, office, or title of any kind from any king, prince, or foreign state without the consent of Congress. Congress has authorized certain exceptions for retired military members; if you wish to accept such employment you should submit a written request, detailing the particulars, to the Bureau of Naval Personnel, Office of Legal Counsel.

Dual Compensation Prohibition. Two provisions in current law reduce the retired or retainer pay of retired or former military members who are employed in federal civil service positions. The current law, the Dual Compensation Act of 1964 (as amended), generally applies to all former members who leave active duty after 11 January 1979.

The first reduction provision applies only to retired regular officers who are employed in federal civilian positions. This provision provides that such officers are entitled to receive the full pay of the civilian positions, but their retired pay will be reduced to an annual rate equal to a base amount of the retired or retainer pay plus one-half of the remainder, if any. The base amount ($10,104.46 as of 1997) is adjusted periodically to reflect changes in the Consumer Price Index. This provision does not apply to officers retired for disability resulting from either injury or disease received in the line of duty.

The second reduction provision provides that any former member who is employed in a federal civilian position shall have his or her retired or retainer pay reduced if the annual rate of basic pay for the civilian position, when combined with the former member's annual rate of retired or retainer pay, exceeds the rate of basic pay then currently paid for level V of the Executive Schedule.

Waivers to these two provisions are available in certain limited circumstances, for positions for which there is exceptional difficulty in recruiting or retaining a qualified employee, or for temporary employment in an emergency situation.

APPENDIX 1

PROFESSIONAL CORE COMPETENCIES (PCC) MANUAL FOR OFFICER ACCESSION PROGRAMS, APRIL 1996

Letter of Promulgation

All naval officer accession programs are designed to produce officers with a basic knowledge of the naval profession and to enhance moral, mental, and physical development. The goal is to instill in each graduate the highest ideals of duty, honor, and loyalty and prepare them to assume the highest responsibilities of military service and command.

This manual provides the professional core competencies for developing course objectives for the following officer accession programs:

United States Naval Academy
Naval Reserve Officers Training Corps
Officer Candidate School
Officer Indoctrination School
Chaplain Basic Course
Direct Commission Officer School
U.S. and State Merchant Marine Academies

These competencies establish the Chief of Naval Operations–approved professional training requirements for each officer accession program as noted. These competencies are the minimum which should be attained for the various accession programs and are based on fleet requirements. This manual does not limit the depth or breadth to which these competencies are covered. Source programs are encouraged to expand these competencies as their time and resources permit.

The composite of all classroom and practical instruction provides the basis for the sense of dedication and commitment to the naval service and established personal standards of excellence which will remain with the graduate throughout the individual's professional career. Program emphasis is directed toward providing a foundation for future training, education, and professional growth.

This manual is approved for implementation upon receipt. *Professional Core Competencies (PCC) Manual (2-93)* is hereby cancelled and superseded.

REVIEWED AND APPROVED
T. W. Wright
Vice Admiral, U.S. Navy
Director of Naval Training (CNO N7)

Definition of Measurement Terms

I. Know—Recall facts, bring to mind and recognize the appropriate material.

Examples: Know the objectives of damage control aboard ship.

Know the safety procedures used to provide the fullest measure of safe small-boat operations.

II. Comprehend—Interpret principles and concepts and relate them to new situations.

Examples: Comprehend the mission of the U.S. Navy and Marine Corps.

Comprehend the concept of internal forces (e.g., stress, strain, shear).

III. Apply—Utilize knowledge and comprehension of specific facts in new relationships with other facts, theories, and principles.

Examples: Apply correct plotting procedures when navigating in pilot waters.

Apply correct procedures to determine times of sunrise and sunset.

IV. Demonstrate—Show evidence of ability in performing a task.

Examples: Demonstrate third-class swimming skills and fundamental water survival skills.

Demonstrate the correct procedure used in radio-telephone communications.

Executive Summary

This professional core competencies (PCC) manual is organized to expand on major domains of knowledge accumulation which a naval officer should have acquired by the time of graduation from an accession program. Not all of the major competency statements apply to all naval officer accession programs. For example, Marine corps officer accessions are exempt from much of the entire section relating to shipkeeping, seamanship, and navigation. In addition, some accession programs are exempt from specific subordinate competency elements or related series of elements. In these cases, a statement of exemption applies, as well, to subordinate elements of the statements, if any.

An inclusive summary of each major competency area follows:

I. Academic Preparation—For USNA and NROTC, this statement outlines the requirement for an accredited baccalaureate degree which incorporates certain specified courses. The choice of academic major is free except where governed otherwise by institutional requirements. Academic preparation for the other officer accession programs will be governed by the applicable requirements and instructions of the specific program and designator.

II. Leadership and Management—This competency area covers the specific basic levels of knowledge of moral and ethical behavior, organizational design, goal setting, decision making, and objective attainment needed to function as a leader and manager. Theories of leadership, motivation, and group dynamics are prominently included.

III. Naval Orientation and Naval Science—This section covers a broad spectrum of competencies required of a newly commissioned naval officer, including: customs and traditions, organization of the Armed Forces and the Navy Department, missions of ships and aircraft, capabilities of weapon systems, warfare doctrines, communications, division officer administration, UCMJ and legal aspects, and many other subjects.

IV. Role of Sea Power in National Policies and Strategies—This section addresses the newly commissioned officer's requirement for understanding the role of naval forces in national policy formulation and strategies. Specific competency statements address historical evolution of sea power, U.S. Navy and Marine Corps history, naval missions, and the impact of third world development and terrorism. The current U.S. maritime strategy is included. Additionally, evolution of land warfare and more specific coverage of amphibious-warfare development is included for Marine Option NROTC accessions.

V. Technical Foundations—Competencies in this section require the newly commissioned officer to be able to comprehend quantitative mathematical and scientific problem-solving techniques in relation to basic application of Navy material systems. Competency statements by implication require solution of basic problems related to the principles and theories covered. Coverage includes: thermodynamic laws, propulsion systems, electrical power generation/distribution, electromagnetic wave theory and application, sound in water, ship design/stability, and fluid/aerodynamics.

VI. Shipkeeping, Navigation and Seamanship—The competency statements in this section address the traditional nautical science base. Specific areas include: seamanship, small boats, damage control, shiphandling, relative motion, formations, rules of the road, laws of the sea, and navigation.

VII. Personal and Personnel Excellence and Fitness and Navy/Marine Corps Fitness and Wellness Programs—This section contains competency requirements for demonstration of physical fitness and swimming readiness on the part of newly commissioned officers. It also covers the officer leadership role in current Navy and Marine Corps fitness and wellness programs such as tobacco use prevention/cessation, weight control, stress management, suicide prevention, drug and alcohol abuse, and drug detection programs.

Appendix A. U.S. Marine Corps Programs—This appendix covers lab topics and requirements particular to the Marine Option package.

Appendix B. Officer Candidate School Technical Foundations—This appendix covers the technical foundation competencies specific to OCS.

Appendix C. Officer Indoctrination School—This section covers the specific competency requirement of the particular professional concerns of the officers attending this accession program.

Appendix D. Chaplain Basic Course—This appendix covers the specific professional foundations for the prospective Navy/Marine Corps Chaplain.

Appendix E. Direct Commission Officer Indoctrination Course—This section covers professional foundations for prospective DCO reserve officers and PCCs which are exempted and/or require further individual training during follow-on reserve drill-periods.

I. Academic Preparation

For USNA and NROTC only. All other officer accession programs will meet requirements per applicable instructions.

A. Demonstrate a proficiency of the English language through usage, both spoken and written.

    1. Satisfactorily complete a minimum of two semesters, or equivalent, of English grammar and composition, as part of the bachelor's degree program.

B. Know the major developments in the United States and world history with comprehension of the evolution of the political, military, and diplomatic history of the United States in the background of the modern world.

1. Satisfactorily complete one semester, or equivalent, in the area of modern United States or European political/military history, national security policy, modern western diplomatic history, or equivalent, as part of the degree program.

C. Apply sound working knowledge and ability to solve quantitative problems in a logical manner employing advanced mathematics and physical science theories.

1. Navy option NROTC College Program midshipmen shall complete two semesters, or equivalent, of mathematics at the level of college algebra or advanced trigonometry and, in addition, be required to complete two semesters, or equivalent, of physical science courses.

2. Navy option NROTC Scholarship midshipmen and all USNA midshipmen shall be required to complete, in lieu of the courses above, a minimum of two semesters, or equivalent, of calculus and two semesters, or equivalent, of calculus-based physics.

D. Know modern basic computer systems including hardware and software.

II. Leadership and Management

The Newly commissioned officer must understand and be able to apply leadership principles necessary to accomplish the Navy's mission through people.

A. Comprehend the interrelationship between authority, responsibility, and accountability within a task-oriented organization.

B. Apply leadership and management skills to prioritize among competing demands.

1. Demonstrate ability to establish meaningful goals and objectives.

2. Apply techniques of prioritization and time management to resources and personnel.

C. Apply leadership skills to achieve mission objectives through groups.

1. Comprehend the difference between informal and formal groups.

2. Comprehend the contribution of the formal group organi-

zation and standard procedures to mission accomplishment.

3. Apply leadership and management skills to design work groups based on task requirements, group capability, and available resources.

4. Apply techniques and skills to measure organizational effectiveness by establishing qualitative and quantitative performance standards.

D. Comprehend the importance of planning and follow-up to mission accomplishment.

1. Comprehend the importance of planning and forecasting.

2. Comprehend the relationship between goal setting and feedback and apply this understanding to establishment of control systems.

3. Know the important reasons for development of and constant reevaluation of alternatives in decision making.

4. Comprehend major reasons why change is resisted in organizations.

5. Comprehend specific techniques that may be used to bring about changes in organizations.

E. Demonstrate, in officer leadership situations, an understanding of the influence of the following on a leader's ability to achieve organization's goals:

1. Use of authority

2. Degree of delegation and decentralization

3. The officer-enlisted professional relationship

4. Chain of command

5. Morale and esprit de corps

F. Comprehend the moral and ethical responsibilities of the military leader.

1. Comprehend the leader's moral and ethical responsibilities to the organization and society.

2. Comprehend the relationship of integrity, moral courage, and ethical behavior to authority, responsibility, and accountability.

3. Comprehend the standards of conduct for government officials.

4. Comprehend the current Navy and Marine Corps regulations, policies, and programs regarding equal opportunity.

5. Comprehend the provisions of official policies regarding prevention of sexual harassment, fraternization, and hazing.

6. Comprehend the Navy and Marine Corps policies regarding single parenting and pregnancy.

G. Know the types of, and importance of, communication within the military.

1. Comprehend the communications process.

2. Comprehend the major causes of communication breakdowns.

3. Demonstrate characteristics of effective oral and written communication.

H. Demonstrate an understanding of basic counseling skills.

1. Comprehend the importance of feedback to mission effectiveness.

2. Comprehend various motivational techniques which may be useful in leadership situations.

3. Apply counseling skills to performance evaluation debriefings, discipline infractions, career guidance, and personal problems.

I. Comprehend the following personal qualities and be able to relate them to a leader's effectiveness:

1. Loyalty

2. Honor

3. Integrity

4. Courage (moral and physical)

J. Comprehend the major principle of the Code of Conduct and be able to apply it to a leader's role in a prisoner of war situation.

K. Know the basic principles of Total Quality Leadership (TQL).

L. Comprehend the relationship of Core Values to the role and responsibilities of a naval leader.

III. Naval Orientation and Naval Science

The newly commissioned officer must have extensive knowledge of the special requirements, tasks, and unique characteristics of the Naval Services which make leadership and management in them different from that required in other formal organizations.

A. Know the missions and basic organization of the major components of the U.S. Armed Forces, including:

1. Know the current organization of the Department of the Navy and the relationship of this organization to the Na-

tional Security Council, the Department of Defense, the Joint Chiefs of Staff, and the unified and specified commands.

2. Comprehend the missions of the United States Navy and Marine Corps.

3. Know the major missions of the U.S. Army, U.S. Air Force, and U.S. Coast Guard.

4. Know the operational and administrative chains of command within the Department of the Navy.

5. Know each warfare specialty, restricted line specialty, and staff corps community and how each contributes to the missions of the U.S. Navy.

B. Know the customs and traditions of the Navy and Marine Corps and relate them to current usage.

1. Know the definition of custom and its origin.

2. Know the definition of tradition and its origin.

3. Know the legal effect of custom in the Naval Services.

4. Demonstrate the following:

(a) Wear the uniform in accordance with appropriate regulations.

(b) Correctly demonstrate military courtesy, etiquette, and greetings.

(c) Demonstrate proper shipboard protocol with respect to quarterdeck procedures, wardroom etiquette, boarding and disembarking, honors to passing ships, and boat etiquette.

(d) Know basic flag etiquette and proper display of basic Navy flags and pennants.

(e) Conduct military ceremonial functions including parade formation, platoon drill, and officer's sword manual in accordance with the appropriate manual. (OIS and Chaplain Basic are exempt from the officer sword manual portion of this competency.)

(f) Exercise a military unit in basic evolutions.

(g) Present a military unit for inspection.

5. Know the Navy and Marine Corps rank and rate/grade structures and insignia and relate them to their equivalents in the Army and Air Force.

6. Know relevant Navy and Marine Corps unrestricted and restricted line career paths and opportunities, including the requirement for joint duty.

7. Comprehend the role of commissioned officers as members of the U.S. Armed Forces and know the obligations and responsibilities assumed by taking the oath of office and accepting a commission, including the constitutional requirement for civilian control.

C. Comprehend the UCMJ, practice of military law, and applications of regulations as they may involve a junior officer in the performance of duties.

1. Comprehend the purpose, scope, and constitutional basis of Navy Regulations and the Uniform Code of Military Justice and relate these regulations to personal conduct in the military service.

2. Comprehend junior officer responsibilities relative to the military justice system, including familiarization with:

    (a) Essential publications relating to military justice
    (b) Search and seizure (except Chaplain Basic)
    (c) Apprehension and restraint (except Chaplain Basic)
    (d) Nonjudicial punishment
    (e) Investigations
    (f) Courts-martial
    (g) Administrative discharges

3. Comprehend Secretary of the Navy–published standards of conduct required of all naval personnel.

4. Be familiar with the International Law of Armed Conflict, including rules of engagement, conduct of hostilities, rights of individuals, obligations of engaged parties, and the Code of Conduct for members of the U.S. Armed Forces.

D. Know shipboard command relationships and organization for both operational and administrative environments as prescribed by the SORM.

1. Know the shipboard administrative organization including the primary duties of Commanding Officer, Executive Officer, department heads, and division officers.

2. Know the organization of the shipboard battle, and peacetime routine watch teams, in port, at anchor, and under way.

3. Know the requirements for, and be able to demonstrate, a proper watch relief and the requirements, procedures, and format for keeping the deck log. (Exempt Chaplain Basic.)

E. Know basic administrative responsibilities of an officer, including correspondence procedures, maintenance management, personnel management, security, and safety procedures and programs. (NROTC USMC option exempt from E3, E4[a], E5, and E8.)

1. Know financial, medical, and recreational benefits available to military personnel.

2. Know the basic elements of personal finances, including pay, taxes, death benefits, insurance, savings, investments, and wills.

3. Know the principles and administration of the PQS system.

4. Know the personnel administrative actions in dealing with actions with regard to officer and enlisted service records, performance evaluations, and advancement recommendations for:

(a) Navy:

(1) Know the role of the enlisted performance evaluation with regard to advancement and detailing and demonstrate an ability to complete the evaluation form.

(2) Comprehend the role of officer fitness reports with regard to promotion and officer detailing and demonstrate an ability to complete a fitness report form.

(3) Know the general requirements for enlisted advancement, including time in rate, required courses, practical factors, and examinations.

(4) Know the purpose and basic operation of a selection board.

(5) Know the purpose for and typical contents of a division officer's notebook. (Exempt Chaplain Basic.)

(6) Know the principal programs for achieving a commission, including those available to enlisted personnel.

(7) Know of the requirement for submission of the Officer Duty Preference Form and comprehend its use in the officer assignment process.

(b) Marines:

(1) Comprehend the role of proficiency and conduct marks with regard to enlisted advancement.

(2) Comprehend the role of officer/enlisted fitness reports with regard to promotions and assignments.

(3) Know the principal programs for achieving an offi-

cer's commission in the U.S. Marine Corps, including those available to enlisted personnel.

(4) Comprehend the general procedures for officer MOS selection, assignments, promotions, and professional military education.

5. Know the purpose of the Navy Maintenance Material Management (3-M) System and its PMS and MDS subsystems, including the duties of division officer and work center supervisor. (Exempt Chaplain Basic.)

6. Know the requirements and procedures for proper handling and disclosure of classified material, consequences for inadvertent disclosure, and consequences for violation of the espionage laws, including:

(a) Maintaining security over classified material, including security for avoiding technology transfer

(b) Disclosure (clearance and need to know)

(c) The basic security classifications and the handling requirements for each

7. Know the governing documents for Navy correspondence.

8. Be familiar with the Navy Directives System.

9. Perform the proper handling and firing of U.S. service small arms using current safety procedures. (Exempt OIS and Chaplain Basic.)

F. Know the basic characteristics and capabilities of the major weapons systems and platforms of the U.S. naval forces. (Exempt Chaplain Basic.)

1. Know the designations, characteristics, capabilities, and missions of ships, aircraft, and weapon systems of the U.S. Navy and the Marine Corps.

2. Know the mission of the U.S. Merchant Marine relative to national security, including its integration with the combat fleet.

3. Know the broad tactical implications of the multi-threat environment.

4. Know the role of active and passive electronic warfare and their employment in the fleet.

5. Know the significance of intelligence in the application of naval warfare.

G. Know the basic air, surface, and subsurface assets which potential adversaries can employ to prevent accomplishment of the sea-control and power-projection missions of the United States Naval Services. (Exempt Chaplain Basic and Merchant Marine.)

H. Know the concept of naval command and control within the armed forces. (Exempt Chaplain Basic.) (NROTC USMC options exempt from this section, except H1, H2, and H6.)

1. Know the chain of operational command from the National Command Authority to the platform commander.

2. Know and be able to discuss the Composite Warfare Commander (CWC) concept and the organization of a typical ship CIC, and understand their interrelationship in formation maneuvering and in accomplishing the ship's warfare mission.

3. Know how each of the following doctrines contributes to the basic sea-control and power-projection missions of the naval service:

(a) Antiair warfare
(b) Antisubmarine warfare
(c) Submarine warfare
(d) Surface warfare
(e) Mine warfare
(f) Strike warfare
(g) Amphibious warfare
(h) Electronic warfare
(i) Mobile logistics support
(j) Special warfare
(k) Expeditionary warfare
(l) C^4I warfare (command, control, communications, computers, intelligence)

4. Know the basic information found in Naval Tactical Publications (NTP), Naval Warfare Publications (NWP), and Allied Tactical Publications (ATP) systems.

5. Know the basic concepts of the Detect-to-Engage sequence.

I. Know the basic forms of naval communications.

1. Know proper radio-telephone terminology; demonstrate proper procedure by simulating a radio-telephone communication. (OIS will "know" vice "demonstrate" proper procedure by simulating a radio-telephone communication.)

2. Know the proper procedures and correct formats for naval messages.

3. Know various methods of visual communications, including flags and pennants, flashing light, and semaphore, and demonstrate procedures for their proper use as outlined below (exempt Chaplain Basic):

(a) Demonstrate a knowledge of international signal flags and allied tactical flag hoist procedures through simulated messages. (OIS will "know" vice "demonstrate" standard flag meaning.) (Exempt Chaplain Basic.)

(b) Know the use of ATP-I Volume II and the International Code of Signals (HO-102). (Exempt OIS and Chaplain Basic.)

4. Be familiar with procedures for effecting communications security, including the common causes of security compromise and safeguards to prevent unauthorized disclosure.

5. Know various systems for internal shipboard communications and demonstrate proper sound-powered phone procedures. (Exempt OIS and Chaplain Basic.)

J. Comprehend the requirement for operations security for military forces, including the following elements (exempt Chaplain Basic):

1. Comprehend the OPSEC process.

(a) Understand the need for OPSEC including recognition of the OPSEC threat.

(b) Understand the concept of Essential Elements of Friendly Information (EEFI).

(c) Know the protective measures used in OPSEC.

IV. Role of Sea Power in National Policies and Strategies

Through a study of history, the newly commissioned officer must comprehend the part naval forces play in the current national policies and diplomatic and military strategies of the United States.

A. Know the significant events of U.S. naval history.

1. Know the significant milestones in the history of the evolution of the U.S. Navy and Marine Corps, including the prominent leaders and their contributions.

2. Know the role U.S. naval forces played in the national

strategies and policies of the United States in peacetime expansion and war through the present time.

B. Comprehend the historical evolution of sea power and its effects on world history.

1. Comprehend the importance of power projection by seaborne forces and be able to cite historical examples.

2. Know the significant historical developments in the technical evolution of naval weapons systems and platforms.

3. Comprehend the contributions of 19th/early 20th century naval strategists and relate their concepts to current situations.

4. Know the major historical facts in relation to sea power in the global wars 1914–1918 and 1939–1945, including the developments in submarine, amphibious, and air warfare at sea.

C. Know the fundamental national interests of the U.S. and potential adversaries.

1. Know the significant historical events of the Cold War period.

2. Comprehend the concepts of limited and total war.

3. Comprehend the national interests, policies, and overall military strategy of the U.S. and how these policies and strategies are formulated in the U.S. political system.

4. Comprehend the role of the military forces of the United States within the Constitutional framework and the effect of the National Security Act of 1947 and the Goldwater-Nichols Department of Defense Reorganization Act of 1986.

5. Know the current U.S. maritime strategy for employment of naval forces.

D. Know the effect the evolution of third world countries and the development of international terrorist movements have had on the interests, policies, and strategies of the U.S.

1. Comprehend the policies and related military actions of the U.S. in developing countries since 1945 and know examples of successes and failures of these policies and actions.

E. Comprehend the evolution of the means and methods of warfare, particularly land warfare, including the following areas (NROTC USMC option only):

1. Know the preeminent leaders and military organizations of history and the reasons for their success.
2. Know the interrelationship between technological progress and military change in rendering obsolete previous successful strategies, policies, doctrines, and tactics.
3. Comprehend the evolution of the influence of economic, psychological, moral, political, and technological factors.
F. Comprehend the evolution of amphibious warfare. Include the following areas (NROTC USMC option only):
    1. Know the significant events of history relating to amphibious operations. Comprehend their impact on the evolution of amphibious warfare doctrine.
    2. Comprehend the problems and advantages relative to employment of amphibious forces in the modern era, including the impact of nuclear warfare on amphibious tactics and amphibious doctrine.

V. Technical Foundations

The newly commissioned officer must be able to apply quantitative mathematical and scientific problem-solving techniques in basic situations of Navy material systems.

NROTC USMC option, OIS, and Chaplain Basic exempted. See Appendix B for OCS requirements. Merchant Marine PCCs attained by academic/professional licensing curriculum and experience credentialing.

A. Comprehend the basic physical principles of open and closed thermodynamic systems.
    1. Comprehend the various forms of energy, including potential, kinetic, thermal, and mechanical, and the process of energy conversion.
    2. Comprehend the "laws of thermodynamics" and types of thermodynamic cycles.
    3. Comprehend the concepts of "work" and "efficiency" and determine levels of output and efficiency in theoretical situations.
B. Apply understanding of the "laws of thermodynamics" and concepts of work, power, and efficiency to various shipboard propulsion systems.
    1. Comprehend the basic operation, key components, and

safety considerations within major propulsion systems, including the following:

    (a) Gas turbine engines (single and split shaft) and associated propulsion systems, elements, and secondary support systems

    (b) Conventional steam propulsion plants

        (1) Apply the laws of thermodynamics to determine the changes in state/energy which water undergoes in the basic steam cycle and comprehend the purpose of the various components and their effect on these energy and state changes.

        (2) Know the purpose of routine feed water chemistry control aboard ship. (Exempt OCS.)

    (c) Internal combustion engines and associated propulsion systems

    (d) Know the features of various fuel oil systems and how they provide fuel to the thermodynamic cycle in each of the applicable systems above.

C. Comprehend the basic operation, principal components, and safety considerations related to key shipboard auxiliary systems and apply the concept of efficiency to such systems.

    1. Comprehend the theory of operation of distilling plants.

    2. Comprehend the theory of refrigeration and air-conditioning systems.

D. Comprehend the theory of operation and key components of shipboard main propulsion power transmission from power source to propellers, including the effects of cavitation.

E. Comprehend and be able to apply basic physical principles of electrical theory to shipboard power generation and distribution systems.

    1. Comprehend basic electrical theory including Ohm's law and its derivations; compare AC and DC electrical power and their uses and transmission.

    2. Comprehend generator theory to determine frequency and voltage in an AC generator and comprehend fundamentals of generator construction and control mechanisms, including prime movers and power ratings.

    3. Comprehend the functions of the various elements in electrical distribution systems.

    4. Comprehend the following with respect to shipboard electric power distribution systems:

(a) Parameters which must be matched in paralleling generators

(b) Measures to counter a ship's magnetic field

(c) Identification of vital and nonvital systems

(d) Functions of the main switchboard

(e) Difference between ship's service and emergency power distribution systems

(f) Casualty power system

F. Comprehend the basic application of electronics systems, communications theory and electromagnetic wave theory to maritime and naval application in radars, communications, and radio-navigation systems.

1. Know the theory of operation and key components used with naval electronics and communications systems, including:

(a) Amplifiers

(b) Antennas

(c) Power amplifiers

(d) Oscillators

(e) Filters

(f) Wave guides

2. Know the fundamental means of imparting information to radio waves and comprehend the uses, advantages, and disadvantages of various means.

3. Know the use of computers and digital electronics in naval and maritime communications.

4. Know wave theory, including relationship between frequency and wave length.

5. Know refraction, polarization, and propagation as related to electromagnetic waves.

6. Know the definition of the effects of ground plane, free space, re-radiation, sky waves, space waves, ground waves, and tropospheric waves.

7. Know the characteristics, advantages, and disadvantages of various communication frequency ranges.

8. Be able to apply radar theory, and comprehend basic operation, major components, and parameters.

9. Know radio theory, basic operation, major components, and parameters.

10. Know basic electromagnetic interference factors in ship and weapon design.

G. Comprehend the physical properties associated with sound travel in water and the application of these properties to sensing and detection systems.

1. Comprehend sound propagation, including Snells' law, effects of temperature, pressure and salinity, sound velocity profiles, sound ray traces, sound channels, and convergence zones.

2. Comprehend sound propagation loss, including spreading and absorption.

3. Comprehend concepts of self and ambient noises.

4. Apply the active and passive sonar equations.

5. Comprehend basic transducer and hydrophone theory.

6. Comprehend the differences between active and passive sonar systems; contrast advantages and disadvantages of each.

7. Comprehend the basic properties of ocean currents.

H. Know the factors and criteria of ship design for seaworthiness, structural integrity, and operational employment.

1. Know the design priorities used in construction of various warship types.

2. Comprehend the factors involved in machinery plant layout and design.

3. Know basic ship hull and structural component nomenclature.

4. Know the effects of stress, strain, and shear forces on hull design and know considerations involved in selection of materials for ship construction and basics of structural design.

5. Comprehend how ship stability and stability redundancy are designed into a ship before construction, including allowance for future modifications.

6. Comprehend the factors involved in ship stability and be able to apply them in determination of stability conditions.

(a) Comprehend hydrostatics, buoyancy, and Archimedes' principle.

(b) Comprehend static equilibrium and the relationship of center of gravity and buoyancy to righting arms and stability.

(1) Comprehend positive, neutral, and negative stability conditions.

(2) Comprehend the effect of movements of centers of buoyancy and gravity on stability.

(3) Know the use of stability curves/nomograms.

(4) Know the effect of free communication and free surface on stability characteristics.

I. Comprehend basic principles of fluid dynamics and be able to apply them in shipboard situations.

1. Know Bernoulli's principle, kinetic versus potential energy in terms of fluid flow, and the concept of pressure "heads."

2. Comprehend Pascal's principle and basic hydraulics.

3. Know the definition of *boundary layers.*

4. Know the concepts of lift and drag, atmospheric properties and effect, subsonic and supersonic flow characteristics, and high-speed aerodynamics.

5. Know aerodynamic and hydrodynamic controls.

J. Comprehend and be able to apply the basic geometry of the fire-control problem and applicable principles of internal and external ballistics, propulsion, launching, and guidance.

1. Comprehend the basic concepts of relative motion, bearing rate, and speed across and in the line of sight.

2. Know the basic factors of the fire-control problem.

3. Comprehend the factors affecting solution of the fire-control problem.

K. Comprehend countermeasure principles, including basic principles of electronic warfare.

L. Comprehend the basic application of space and electronic warfare in naval operations.

1. Know the military space roles, including the role of space systems in strategic and tactical command-and-control architectures.

2. Know the military opportunities and applications in space.

(a) Know the fundamentals and limitations of space-based navigation and comprehend the operation of the global positioning system and the uses of precise positioning and time.

(b) Know principles of space-based communications.

(c) Know the basics of space-based remote sensing and applications to space-based surveillance opportunities.

3. Know how to utilize space assets and information for mission planning.

VI. Shipkeeping, Navigation, and Seamanship

The newly commissioned officer must have knowledge of requirements unique to organizational leadership, management, and task accomplishment in a maritime environment.
OIS and Chaplain Basic exempt entire section. NROTC USMC option exempt entire section except A2 and B. Merchant Marine PCCs attained by academic/professional licensing curriculum and experience credentialing.

A. Know terms and nomenclature of shipboard deck seamanship equipment and fittings and the fundamentals of their usage.

1. Know the use and safety precautions associated with the following groupings of shipboard equipment:

(a) Ground tackle, anchoring, and mooring equipment and fixtures

(b) Boat-lifting and handling equipment

(c) Weight-handling equipment

(d) Fiber and synthetic lines and wire ropes

2. Know responsibilities and safety precautions relative to small-boat operations.

B. Know the basics of shipboard safety and comprehend the reasons for extraordinary attention to safety and preparedness.

1. Know Navy safety programs and precautions, including ordnance, electrical, workplace, NAVOSH, and environmental programs.

2. Know the requirements for shipboard damage-control training and preparedness.

(a) Know the typical shipboard damage-control organization and responsibilities of key personnel assigned.

(b) Know how shipboard watertight integrity is obtained through installed shipboard features to increase material conditions of readiness.

(c) Know the procedures, objectives, and priorities in combating progressive deterioration from fire and underwater hull damage.

(1) Know classes of fire and agents, equipment, and procedures used to extinguish them.

(2) Demonstrate the use of equipment, materials, and procedures for countering progressive flooding and structural deterioration.

3. Know standard procedures to be implemented prior to, during, and after CBR attack.

4. Demonstrate donning, doffing, and proper operation of oxygen breathing apparatus (OBA), Supplementary Emergency Escape Device (SEEDs), standard Navy gas mask, and emergency escape breathing device (EEBD).

C. Know the basic terms, equipment, procedures, and safety precautions used for replenishment at sea (UNREP).

D. Comprehend the theory and practice of navigation at sea.

1. Know the theory and the information that can be obtained from the practice of celestial navigation at sea. (OCS exempt.)

(a) Know the motions of celestial bodies and relate these motions to coordinate systems.

(b) Comprehend the longitude/time relationship, and time conversion, zone time determination, and motions of the sun as the basis of time.

(c) Know the correct procedures to determine the times of sunrise and sunset.

2. Comprehend the theory and practice of marine navigation by GPS/NAVSSI and other electronic methods.

(a) Know the theory and basic principles of radar navigation.

(b) Know the theory and basic operating principles of the GPS/NAVSSI, including the importance of correcting for differences between the GPS/NAVSSI and navigation chart datum.

(c) Know the basic principles of inertial navigation, and bottom contour navigation.

3. Apply the fundamentals of the practice of marine navigation at sea.

(a) Comprehend the uses of navigational datums and the various chart projections. Know chart symbology, particularly those symbols pertaining to hazards and dangers.

(b) Know how to select the proper charts (both paper and electronic) and how to determine chart accuracy and reliability.

(c) Apply correct plotting procedures when navigating in pilot water.

(1) Apply the six rules of deduced reckoning in keeping a plot of ship movements.

(2) Comprehend the definitions of the terms *track, speed of advance, speed over ground, PIM, EP, LOP, relative bearing,* and *course made good.*

(3) Plot and interpret turn and danger bearings.

(4) Plot and interpret simultaneous and running fixes.

(5) Know the variables to compute visibility of lights.

(d) Know the advantages, disadvantages, and applications of gyro and magnetic compasses.

(1) Apply terrestrial navigation methods to determine compass error.

(2) Apply magnetic variation and deviation or gyro error to convert from compass to true course or bearing and vice versa.

(e) Know the capabilities and limitations of various instruments used in piloting to determine direction, speed, distance, and depth of water.

(f) Know the essential publications and records used in navigation and comprehend their value in all applications.

(g) Know the characteristics and application of various aids to navigation in piloting and comprehend their importance in safe navigation, including:

(1) Buoyage systems—IALA

(2) Lights/day markers

(3) Sound signals

(4) Radar beacons/markers

(h) Apply correct procedures in planning and plotting approaches to harbors and anchorages.

(i) Comprehend tidal action and know tide classifications and reference planes.

E. Know environmental weather factors affecting naval operations. (Exempt OCS.)

1. Know the principles of basic weather phenomena, including fronts and subtropical and tropical storms.

2. Know the relationship between wind and current in wind-driven current systems.

3. Know the sources of environmental predictions, including pilot charts and weather broadcasts.

4. Know the earth's major wind and current systems.

5. Know how wind velocity relates to storm warnings and comprehend the effect of wind velocity on sea state.

6. Know the characteristics of the approach of tropical storms and hurricane/typhoon evasion techniques.

F. Know controllable and noncontrollable forces in shiphandling.

1. Know the effects of controllable forces in shiphandling such as engines, rudders, propellers, lines, anchors, and tugs.

2. Know the effects of noncontrollable forces in shiphandling such as wind, current, and depth of water, etc.

3. Know the terms associated with tactical data and comprehend how tactical data tables may be employed in planning shiphandling evolutions.

4. Demonstrate procedures and standard terminology in giving engine, rudder, and line-handling commands.

5. Demonstrate the techniques for using binoculars, stadimeter, radar, and bearing circles when involved in shiphandling situations.

6. Demonstrate the operation of sail craft to attain qualification as skipper "B" or offshore crewman using current CNET/USNA standards. (Exempt OCS, OIS, Chaplain Basic.)

G. Comprehend relative motion and demonstrate capability to solve problems associated with relative motion.

1. Comprehend the theory of relative motion as graphically displayed by the geographic and relative plot.

2. Comprehend the significance of bearing drift and apply bearing drift to determine relative motion. Comprehend the following related terms: *relative bearing* and *target angle.*

3. Know the terminology and relationship of the speed triangle and the relative plot associated with the maneuvering board.

4. Demonstrate the use of the maneuvering board to accurately:

(a) Determine the CPA and time of CPA of an approaching vessel.

(b) Determine the course and speed of a maneuvering ship.

(c) Determine course, speeds, and time for proceeding to a new station or to intercept another vessel.

(d) Determine true wind direction and velocity.

(e) Determine course and speed to produce desired wind.

5. Know the principal rules for maneuvering in formation and the use of ATP-1 (C) Volume I.

H. Know inland and international laws and systems of regulations which govern conduct of vessels in national waters and on the high seas.

1. Know major aspects of the U.S. position on International Law of the Sea regarding territorial seas, contiguous zones, high seas, and rights of innocent passage. (Exempt OCS, OIS, Chaplain Basic.)

2. Know the U.S. Inland Rules of the Road and the international regulations for preventing collisions at sea, to include:

(a) The purpose and scope of the rules, including application

(b) Terms and definitions used in the rules

(c) Steering rules for vessels in sight of each other, including sound signals

(d) Lights and day shapes for frequently encountered vessel classes

(e) Use of radar and conduct of vessels in reduced visibility, including sound signals

(f) Definition of situations falling under "special circumstances"

3. Know the purpose and maneuvering rules associated with Traffic Separation schemes established by International Maritime Consultative Organization (IMCO) agreement.

VII. Personal and Personnel Excellence and Fitness and Navy/Marine Corps Fitness and Wellness Programs

The newly commissioned officer must demonstrate a high level of personal physical fitness and be able to apply leadership skills in implementing Navy or Marine Corps personal excellence and wellness programs.

A. Demonstrate personal physical fitness by conforming to

Navy or Marine Corps physical-fitness testing standards. (Exempt OIS and Chaplain Basic.)

B. Present a fit military appearance by conforming to applicable Navy or Marine Corps directives concerning percent body fat and/or height-weight standards.

C. Demonstrate fundamental swimming skills through successful completion of Class 3 swimmer qualifications, as well as fundamental survival skills.

D. Comprehend current Navy or Marine Corps regulations, policies, and programs relative to the following wellness issues:

   1. Substance- and alcohol-abuse prevention and detection, including urinalysis testing programs, treatment, and consequences

   2. Physical fitness, nutrition, and weight control

   3. Tobacco use cessation/prevention

   4. Stress management

   5. Suicide prevention

   6. HIV/AIDS awareness, prevention, and testing programs

   7. Safe driving

   8. Athletics, recreational, and home safety

E. Know current methods and techniques of first aid, self aid, and CPR for adults.

Appendix A—U.S. Marine Corps Programs

To familiarize the NROTC Marine Corps Option student and USNA midshipman desiring U.S.M.C. commission with the missions and structure of the Marine Corps and to prepare the student for the Marine Option 1/C cruise.

A. Be familiar with the organization structure of the USMC as outlined in the current edition of the *Marine Officer's Guide.*

B. Be familiar with the missions, status, and development of the Marine Corps as a separate service as outlined in the current edition of the *Marine Officer's Guide.*

C. Be familiar with the essential subjects contained in the *Marine Battle Skills Training Handbook* series (based on MCO 1510.89 and MCO 1510.90).

D. Preparation for Officer Candidate School:

   1. Know, and be able to command in, the basic movements

of close order drill, including the manual of arms with the M-16.

2. Be familiar with the assembly, disassembly, care, cleaning, and functioning of the M-16.

3. Be familiar with the basic fire team offensive tactics.

4. Be familiar with basic map reading and the use of a compass.

5. Be familiar with Marine Corps history, interior guard, and basic general military subjects.

6. Be in appropriate level of physical conditioning that emphasizes total body fitness.

E. Successfully complete Marine Option 1/C cruise.

F. Understand the requirements for, and be able to perform at the requisite level of, physical conditioning necessary for Marine Officers.

G. Conduct adventure training, emphasizing skills to enhance individual confidence and survivability on the battlefield. This training should be ground-combat-oriented.

Appendix B—Officer Candidate School, Technical Foundations

To address *minimum acceptable* technical foundations to prepare candidates for follow-on training and fleet service within the current capabilities of a thirteen-week program. Most applicable to surface and submarine designators.

A. Know the basic physical principles of open and closed thermodynamic systems.

1. Know the various forms of energy, including potential, kinetic, thermal, and mechanical, and the process of energy conversion.

2. Know the "laws of thermodynamics" and types of thermodynamic cycles.

B. Know the concepts of work, power, and efficiency [as applied] to various shipboard propulsion systems.

1. Know the basic operation, key components, and safety considerations within major propulsion systems, including the following:

(a) Gas turbines (single and split shaft) and associated propulsion systems, elements, and secondary support systems

(b) Conventional steam propulsion plants
   (1) Determine the changes in state/energy which water undergoes in the basic steam cycle and know the purpose of the various components and their effect on these energy and state changes.
(c) Internal combustion engines and associated propulsion systems

C. Know the basic operation, principal components, and safety considerations related to key shipboard auxiliary systems.
   1. Know the theory of operation of distilling plants.
   2. Know the theory of refrigeration and air-conditioning systems.

D. Know the operation and key components of shipboard main propulsion power transmission from power source to propellers, including the effects of cavitation.

E. Know the basic physical principles of electrical theory as related to shipboard power generation and distribution systems.
   1. Know fundamentals of generator construction and control mechanism, including prime movers and power ratings.
   2. Know the factors that affect frequency and voltage output of an AC generator.
   3. Know the functions of the various elements in electrical distribution systems.
   4. Know the following with respect to shipboard electric power distribution systems:
      (a) Parameters which must be matched in paralleling generators
      (b) Measures to counter a ship's magnetic field
      (c) Identification of vital and nonvital systems
      (d) Functions of the main switchboard
      (e) Difference between ship's service and emergency power distribution systems
      (f) Casualty power system

F. Know the basic application of electronics systems, communications theory, and electromagnetic wave theory to maritime and naval application in radar, communications, and radio-navigation systems.
   1. Know the fundamental means of imparting information

to radio waves and comprehend the uses, advantages, and disadvantages of various means.

2. Comprehend refraction, polarization, and propagation as related to electromagnetic waves.

3. Know the definition and effects of reflection, refraction, diffraction, attenuation, and sky waves.

4. Know the characteristics, advantages, and disadvantages of various frequency ranges.

5. Know basic radar theory, operation, and components.

G. Know the physical properties associated with sound travel in water and the application of these properties to sensing and detection systems.

1. Comprehend sound propagation, including effects of temperature, pressure and salinity, sound velocity profiles, sound ray traces, sound channels, and convergence zones.

2. Comprehend sound propagation loss, including spreading and absorption.

3. Comprehend concepts of self and ambient noise.

4. Comprehend basic transducer and hydrophone theory.

5. Comprehend the differences between active and passive sonar systems; contrast advantages and disadvantages of each.

6. Comprehend the basics of ocean currents.

H. Comprehend the factors and criteria of ship design for seaworthiness, structural integrity, and operational employment.

1. Comprehend the design priorities used in construction of various warship types.

2. Know basic ship hull and structural component nomenclature.

I. Apply basic principles of fluid dynamics to shipboard situations.

1. Know Pascal's principle and basic hydraulics.

2. Know the components of a basic hydraulic system.

J. Comprehend the basic geometry of the fire-control problem and applicable principles of propulsion, launching, and guidance.

1. Know the basic concepts of relative motion, bearing rate, and speed across and in the line of sight.

2. Know factors affecting solution of the fire-control problem.

K. Know countermeasure principles including basic principles of electronic warfare.

Appendix C—Officer Indoctrination School

To provide the new staff corps officer with a basic knowledge of where the specific community fits within the military structure and how current regulations and policies affect their profession.

A. Know the specific duties, responsibilities, career path, and operational capabilities within the individual's respective corps.

B. Know how the specific duties, responsibilities, career path, and operational capabilities of a specific corps relate to the other communities in the Department of the Navy.

C. Know the specific corps duties and responsibilities which place the individual in a "special status" in relation to DoD and DoN policies.

Appendix D—Chaplain Basic Course

To provide the new Navy/Marine Corps chaplain with a basic knowledge and guiding principles for adapting ministerial duties to the military environment.

A. Adapt general ministerial duties to the USN/USMC/USCG environment in accordance with applicable instructions and the practices and standards of the student's endorsing religious body.

1. Identify Chaplain Corps charter and features of ministry within the military which are unique when compared to civilian ministry.

2. Know responsibilities of working in a pluralistic environment and the sensitivities required when operating with personnel and chaplains of various faith groups.

3. Know the major concepts of institutional ministry and the role of the military chaplain concerning worship services, lay readers, religious education programs, weddings, ceremonies, funerals, counseling, transitioning skills, and relational skills with young adults.

4. Know the functions and responsibilities for major claimant and senior chaplains, supervisory chaplains, chaplain coordinators, and the Chief of Chaplains.

5. Know the role of the chaplain and the general principles of providing ministry in the following assignments:

(a) Naval hospital

(b) Surface unit
(c) USN/USMC brig
(d) Joint commands
(e) USNR organization
(f) Command chapel
(g) USMC unit
(h) USCG unit
(i) Service academy
(j) Subsurface unit
(k) Air unit
(l) Merchant marine

6. Know the organization and operating procedures of Joint Staff and Joint Service arena.

7. Know the chaplain's responsibilities as a department head and principal adviser to the Commanding Officer in moral, spiritual, and ethical matters.

8. Know the Commanding Officer's responsibility for moral, spiritual, and personal well-being of the unit and the chain of command as it relates to the chaplain's ministry.

9. Know the primary and collateral duties appropriate and prohibited for chaplains.

10. Know the responsibility of the chaplain in respect to privileged communication, counseling, the Privacy Act, and military law.

11. Know the administrative procedures for the maintenance of the Chaplain's Office, to include administration of the Religious Offering Fund.

12. Know the procedures for counseling and referring USN/USMC/USCG personnel and family members for counseling to civilian, special, or religious agencies and other military chaplains.

13. Know the policies and referral procedures for the Navy Marine Corps Relief Society, American Red Cross, Family Service Center, Family Advocacy Program, CREDO, CAAC, Ombudsman, Champus, and other federal, state, and local agencies.

14. Know the policies, procedures, and the chaplain's role with regard to processing requests for conscientious objectors, humanitarian reassignment, and hardship discharge.

15. Know the chaplain's role in the Casualty Assistance Calls Officer (CACO) Program.

16. Know the role of the chaplain in pastoral care of USN/USMC/USCG personnel and family members of diverse religious and ethnic traditions.

17. Know the policies and status of chaplains in regard to the Geneva Convention of 1949 and the chaplain's assigned place of duty in a combat environment.

18. Know the role and responsibility of a chaplain in a combat environment in regard to ministry and Code of Conduct issues.

19. Demonstrate how to plan, program, and budget a USN/USMC/USCG Command Religious Program through oral and written presentations.

20. Demonstrate safety knowledge and procedures when approaching, being lifted, and riding in a helicopter.

21. Demonstrate the safe utilization of basic firefighting equipment.

Appendix E—Direct Commission Officer Indoctrination Course

To provide the new reserve officer with a basic knowledge of the naval profession and an understanding of where their communities fit within the military structure and how current regulations and policies affect their profession.

The following specific items are exempted from the DCO course of instruction:

Section III	PARAs	B. 4 (d) (e)
		D.2
		D.3
		E.5
		F. 3
		H except H.1 and 3
		I except I.2 and I.4
Section V	All	
Section VI	All except PARAs	B.1
		B.2 C(1)
		H.1
Section VII	PARAs	D.7
		D.8
		E

Those PCCs required for mobilization will be included in follow-on study during reserve training.

Appendix F—U.S. and State Merchant Marine Academies

To provide the new Naval Reserve Merchant Marine Individual Ready Reserve Group (MMIRRG) officer with a basic knowledge of their community relationship with the total force structure as well as regulations and policies affecting preparation for their professional development.

1. The student will know merchant ship communications procedures for convoy operations and independent sailing.
2. The student will know the significant events in the history of the United States merchant marine.
3. The student will know the importance of the United States merchant marine to the economy and national security of the United States.
4. The student will know the current legal position of the United States merchant marine and the current policies pursued by the federal government to ensure that merchant shipping is available to the government in the event of war or national emergency.
5. The student will know the basic procedures for defending merchant ships from common wartime threats, including aircraft, surface vessels, submarines, mines, divers, cruise missiles, and chemical/biological/nuclear (CBR) weapons.
6. The student will be familiar with and apply the procedures for merchant ships in convoy operations, including preparations, activation of naval control of shipping, sailing conferences, harbor entry/exit procedures, communications, and tactical maneuvering.
7. The student will know the wartime shipping organization, including:
    a. The structure and responsibilities of the Civil Direction of Shipping organization (CDSORG), the Naval Control of Shipping Organization (NCSORG), and the Military Sealift Command (MSC)
    b. The merchant marine mobilization process

8. The student will know how merchant ships can function as military auxiliaries, including:

a. Which merchant ships are useful for what types of military operations

b. The principles of strategic sealift and Joint Logistics over the Shore (JLOTS) and how merchant ships would be used in such operations

c. How merchant ships are used in direct support of naval forces and the plans for modifying them as needed for underway replenishment (UNREP) tasks

9. The student will comprehend the opportunities and obligations of a second career in the Merchant Marine Reserve.

APPENDIX 2

PROFESSIONAL READING LIST

This professional reading list is drawn from the 1992 *Navy Policy Book*. The list is divided into three categories: basic, intermediate, and advanced.

Basic

Edward L. Beach	*Run Silent, Run Deep*
_____	*The United States Navy:* *A Two Hundred Year History*
Tom Clancy	*The Hunt for Red October*
_____	*Red Storm Rising*
Steven Coonts	*Flight of the Intruder*
Stephen Crane	*The Red Badge of Courage*
Stephen M. Hawking	*A Brief History of Time:* *From the Big Bang to Black Holes*
John F. Lehman	*Command of the Seas:* *A Personal Story*
Richard McKenna	*The Sand Pebbles*
William Manchester	*American Caesar:* *Douglas MacArthur, 1880–1964*
James A. Michener	*The Source*
Nicholas Monsarrat	*The Cruel Sea*
Samuel E. Morison	*The Two-Ocean War: A Short* *History of the United States* *Navy in the Second World War*
Thomas J. Peters	*In Search of Excellence*

Erich M. Remarque	*All Quiet on the Western Front*
Al Santoli, ed.	*Everything We Had: An Oral History of the Vietnam War*
Michael Shaara	*The Killer Angels*
Hedrick Smith	*The Russians*
James B. and Sybil Stockdale	*In Love and War*
Tom Wolfe	*The Right Stuff*
Herman Wouk	*The Caine Mutiny*
———	*War and Remembrance*
———	*The Winds of War*
Elmo Zumwalt	*On Watch*

Intermediate

John Barron	*The KGB Today: The Hidden Land*
Ruth Benedict	*The Chrysanthemum and the Sword: Patterns of Japanese Culture*
Thomas Buell	*Master of Seapower: A Biography of Fleet Admiral Ernest J. King*
———	*The Quiet Warrior*
Blair Clay	*Silent Victory: The U.S Submarine War against Japan*
W. Edwards Deming	*Out of the Crisis*
William Ebenstein and Edwin Fogelman	*Today's Isms: Communism, Fascism, Capitalism, Socialism*
David Eisenhower	*Eisenhower at War, 1943–1945*
John L. Gaddis	*The U.S. and the Origins of the Cold War*
Ernest K. Gann	*Fate Is the Hunter*
Colin S. Gray	*The Maritime Strategy, Geopolitics, and the Defense of the West*
Eric J. Grove	*The Future of Sea Power*
Masaaki Imai	*Kaizen: The Key to Japan's Competitive Success*
Paul Johnson	*Modern Times: The World from the Twenties to the Eighties*
Stanley Karnow	*Vietnam: A History*
John Keegan	*The Face of Battle*
———	*The Mask of Command*

——	*The Price of Admiralty*
——	*The Second World War*
Victor H. Krulak	*First to Fight: An Inside View of the U.S. Marine Corps*
Eric Larrabee	*Commander in Chief: Franklin Delano Roosevelt, His Lieutenants, and Their War*
Carnes Lord	*The Presidency and the Management of National Security*
Edward N. Luttwak	*The Pentagon and the Art of War*
William Manchester	*The Last Lion, Winston Spencer Churchill: Alone, 1932–40*
——	*The Last Lion, Winston Spencer Churchill: Visions of Glory, 1874–1932*
Paul Nitze	*From Hiroshima to Glasnost*
Peter Paret, ed.	*Makers of Modern Strategy: From Machiavelli to the Nuclear Age*
E. B. Potter	*Admiral Arleigh Burke: A Biography*
——	*Bull Halsey: A Biography*
——	*Nimitz*
E. B. Potter and Chester Nimitz	*Sea Power: A Navy History*
Gordon W. Prange	*At Dawn We Slept: The Untold Story of Pearl Harbor*
——	*Miracle at Midway*
Neil Sheehan	*A Bright Shining Lie: John Paul Vann and America in Vietnam*
Perry M. Smith	*Assignment—Pentagon*
Ronald H. Spector	*Eagle against the Sun: An American War with Japan*
Harold and Margaret Sprout	*The Rise of American Naval Forces, 1776–1918*
Barbara W. Tuchman	*The Guns of August*
Adam B. Ulam	*The Rivals: America and Russia since World War II*
Dan Van Der Vat	*The Atlantic Campaign: World War II's Great Struggle at Sea*
David Walder	*Nelson: The Biography*

Mary Walton	*The Deming Management System*
Russell F. Weigley	*The American Way of War*
Philip Ziegler	*Mountbatten*

Advanced

Bernard Brodie	*War and Politics*
Carl von Clausewitz	*On War*
Julian S. Corbett	*Some Principles of Maritime Strategy*
Thomas L. Friedman	*From Beirut to Jerusalem*
Alexander George	*Deterrence in American Foreign Policy: Theory and Practice*
James L. George	*The U.S. Navy: The View from the Mid-1990s*
Colin S. Gray	*The Geopolitics of Superpowers*
Colin S. Gray and Roger Barnett	*Seapower and Strategy*
Thomas C. Home	*Power and Change: The Administrative History of the Office of the CNO*
Wayne P. Hughes	*Fleet Tactics: Theory and Practice*
Samuel P. Huntington	*The Soldier and the State: The Theory and Politics of Civil-Military Relations*
Henry Kissinger	*The White House Years*
Edward N. Luttwak	*Strategy: The Logic of War and Peace*
Alfred T. Mahan	*The Influence of Sea Power upon History, 1660–1783*
John Newhouse	*Cold Dawn: The Story of SALT*
Michael A. Palmer	*Origins of the Maritime Strategy: American Naval Strategy in the First Postwar Decade*
Robert L. Pfaltzgraff Jr. and Richard H. Shultz Jr.	*U.S. Defense Policy in an Era of Constrained Resources*
Jean-François Revel	*How Democracies Perish*
James R. Schlesinger	*America at Century's End*
U. S. Grant Sharp	*Strategy for Defeat: Vietnam in Retrospect*
Alexis de Tocqueville	*Democracy in America*

Sun Tzu	*The Art of War*
Kenneth N. Waltz	*Man, the State, and War:*
	A Theoretical Analysis
F. W. Winterbotham	*The Ultra Secret*
Joseph C. Wylie	*Military Strategy: A Naval Theory*
	of Power Control

APPENDIX 3
MILITARY JUSTICE

JUSTICE AND POWER MUST BE BROUGHT TOGETHER, SO WHATEVER IS JUST MAY BE
POWERFUL, AND WHATEVER IS POWERFUL MAY BE JUST.

—*Blaise Pascal*

JUSTICE IS THE FIRST VIRTUE OF THOSE WHO COMMAND, AND STOPS THE COMPLAINTS
OF THOSE WHO OBEY.

—*Denis Diderot*

You should be familiar with the fundamentals of military law and
naval discipline. As a junior officer, you are likely to be called to
serve as the investigating officer for a crime, mishap, or complaint; to serve as a witness at a court-martial or a nonjudicial
punishment hearing; to conduct a summary court-martial or
serve as a member of a special or general court-martial; or to serve
as a member of an administrative discharge board. Each of these
duties carries with it the responsibility to act honorably and
fairly, to consider carefully the particulars of the case as well as
the applicable military law, and to act with respect for the rights
of individual service members as well as for the good of the naval
service.

Sources of Military Law

Until relatively recent times, the administration of justice in the
Navy was largely the sole prerogative of the CO, according to the
law and customs of the sea. The sea is a cruel place, and ship's
captains have traditionally had the power of life or death over the
members of their crew. More recently, this power has been somewhat tempered by the standardization of laws and regulations de-

signed to prevent the mistreatment and arbitrary punishment of military personnel.

Constitution. Art. 1, sec. 8, of the Constitution states that "Congress shall have the power . . . to make rules for the government and regulation of the land and naval forces." The Constitution is printed in its entirety in appendix 1 to the *Manual for Courts-Martial,* described below.

Uniform Code of Military Justice (UCMJ). The UCMJ is the fundamental military law that applies to all members in every branch of the armed services. The code is printed in its entirety in appendix 2 to the *Manual for Courts-Martial.*

Manual for Courts-Martial (MCM). The *MCM* explains the UCMJ and prescribes regulations that carry out the basic rules of the code for all branches of the service.

Manual of the Judge Advocate General (JAG Manual, or JAG-MAN). The *JAG Manual* applies only to the Navy and Marine Corps. It implements the UCMJ and other regulations outlined in the *MCM* within the Department of the Navy and contains regulations pertaining to administrative law.

Criminal Justice

Punitive Articles and Specifications. A crime is a violation of the penal law. Arts. 78–134 of the UCMJ define military crimes. Each crime is defined in terms of a group of facts or elements, each of which must exist for the crime to have taken place.

Part IV of the *MCM* describes the elements of each article of the UCMJ. Each section provides the text of a UCMJ article, the elements of the crime described in that article, and a short explanation of the elements. In addition, each section identifies the permissible maximum punishment for the crime and provides a sample showing the language that should be used to charge an individual with the crime.

Alternatives of the Commander. When faced with a crew member who has apparently committed a crime, the CO either may take no action or may initiate any of the following:

- Administrative actions
- Nonjudicial punishment (NJP)
- Court-martial

Each of these is described in greater detail later in this chapter.

Jurisdiction

In order for an offense to be disposed of under the military justice system, both the accused and the crime must be under military jurisdiction. In addition, certain other procedural requirements must be met.

Jurisdiction over the Accused. The accused is subject to military jurisdiction if he or she is an active-duty service member or a cadet, midshipman, or reserve member performing active duty; certain categories of reservists not on active duty and certain civilians are also subject to military jurisdiction.

Jurisdiction over the Offense. An offense is subject to military jurisdiction if it is related in some way to the individual's military service. An offense occurring on board a naval vessel or at a shore installation would always be considered service-connected, although an offense that takes place off base may not be, depending on the circumstances. Almost every involvement of military members with the use, possession, and distribution of drugs is considered service-connected.

Statute of Limitations. The statute of limitations described in art. 43 of the UCMJ requires that the trial of most types of offenses begin within five years. Exceptions to this rule are any offense punishable by death, unauthorized absence, or missing a movement of a ship during wartime. For periods of unauthorized absence, the statute-of-limitations clock begins to run when the period of absence ends.

Former Jeopardy. This concept, often referred to in crime novels as "double jeopardy," means that an accused cannot be tried twice for the same offense. A previous trial that did not result in an acquittal is not considered a "complete" trial for purposes of former jeopardy and is not a bar to a second trial. A trial by a state or foreign country, whatever the outcome, is also not a bar to a trial by court-martial, which is conducted under federal law.

Former Punishment. An individual who has received nonjudicial punishment for a particular minor offense may not then be tried at court-martial for the same offense. The word *minor* is key; if the offense is not minor, or if it turns out to be more serious than it appeared at the time the NJP hearing was held, the imposition of nonjudicial punishment will not serve as a bar to trial by court-martial.

Procedural Rules

Apprehension. Apprehension is the act of taking a person into custody. Officers, noncommissioned officers, petty officers, masters-at-arms, military police, and Naval Criminal Investigative Service/Criminal Investigation Division (of DoD) agents have the authority to apprehend anyone who is subject to the UCMJ. However, enlisted personnel may apprehend commissioned officers only when actually performing law enforcement duties or when so directed by a commissioned officer.

Apprehension may entail voluntary submission by the person apprehended, or it may require the use of physical force. The individual performing the apprehension is required to make the situation clear by first saying, "I am placing you in custody" (or something similar), then identifying himself or herself to the person being apprehended and stating a reason for the apprehension. There are limitations on the authority to apprehend service members off base or in private dwellings.

All apprehensions must be based on probable cause. That is, facts and circumstances must exist that would lead a reasonable person to conclude that an offense has been or is being committed, and that the person to be apprehended committed or is in the process of committing the offense.

Restraint. Once a suspect is apprehended, the appropriate authority may impose restraint. Restraint may be moral rather than physical, as when a suspect is ordered to remain within the limits of a particular command. Restraint may also, of course, be physical. A suspect may be placed in restraint pending disciplinary action if the appropriate authority, acting in a neutral and detached manner, has a reasonable belief that an offense has been committed, that the person to be restrained committed it, and that restraint is warranted under the circumstances. Restraint is considered to be warranted when the individual is a flight risk or when there is reasonable grounds to believe that he or she will engage in future acts of serious misconduct if not restrained.

Searches and Seizures. The Fourth Amendment to the Bill of Rights, which protects the people against unreasonable searches and seizures, also applies to military personnel. Evidence obtained by an unlawful search may not be admissible in a court-martial proceeding. Inspections in which the primary purpose is not to seek evidence of a crime (e.g., a health and welfare inspection of a berthing area or an inventory of a supply storeroom) are not considered searches, and evidence that turns up during such inspections is always admissible in a trial by court-martial. The products of searches, which are conducted specifically to seek evidence of crimes, are also admissible provided that the searches are legally conducted.

Legal searches may be divided into two categories: those that require probable cause and those that do not. Probable cause is not required for border searches, searches of persons and vehicles entering or leaving naval installations or ships, searches of government property, or searches for which the cognizant individual gives consent. In addition, a frisk for weapons incident to a lawful stop by a law enforcement official, a search incident to an apprehension by such an official, searches of confinement facilities, and searches under emergency situations do not require a finding of probable cause. All other kinds of searches are subject to the probable-cause requirement, meaning that the CO with jurisdiction over the person or place to be searched must determine that a reasonable person would conclude that a crime was committed, and that a search would be likely to produce evidence of this crime. A CO may not delegate this authority.

Investigations

Initiation of Charges. Any civilian or service member may initiate charges against another service member, either orally or in writing. Once charges have been initiated and the CO or designated command representative determines that the situation warrants further investigation, the command appoints an investigating officer.

Conduct of the Investigation. If the offense is a minor one, a preliminary inquiry officer (PIO)—normally the division officer of the accused—conducts the investigation. This officer interviews witnesses, examines any physical or documentary evidence, and advises the accused of his or her rights before taking an oral or written statement. After concluding the investigation, the PIO forwards a report up the chain of command that includes a brief summary of the evidence, comments on the performance and prior disciplinary record of the accused, and a recommendation for the disposition of the offense.

For more serious offenses that are subject to referral to court-martial, a so-called article 32 investigation (described in UCMJ art. 32) is initiated. A pretrial investigating officer (PTIO) in pay grade O-4 or above, or a JAG officer, is appointed to investigate the charges. The PTIO's function is similar to that of the PIO as described above, except that the procedures for conducting the investigation are considerably more formal. After concluding the investigation, the PTIO forwards a written report to the court-martial convening authority to take action as appropriate.

Administrative Actions

Administrative actions include such activities as use of the Navy's informal resolution system for minor misconduct; oral performance counseling; written counseling in the form of a non-punitive letter of caution or letter of instruction; extra military instruction (EMI, discussed in chapter 7); denial of privileges; appropriate comments or downgraded marks in fitness reports or evaluations; adjustment or withdrawal of security clearances (in cases where an individual's conduct brings into question his or her trustworthiness); withholding or withdrawal of advancement or promotion recommendations; reassignment or delay of reassignment; detachment for cause (DFC); or administrative separation from the Navy.

In the case of the withholding of privileges, an individual with the power to grant a privilege (such as special liberty, the wearing of civilian clothing, or on-base driving) also has the power to revoke that privilege. Although privileges may be withheld, rights such as compensation, medical care, quarters, food, and normal liberty may not be administratively withheld.

Normal liberty may only be withheld administratively by the use of EMI, the extension of working hours as necessary to accomplish mission requirements, limited authorized health and safety reasons, and the overseas liberty risk program. The once-common use of so-called voluntary restraint ("hack") is not authorized.

Administrative actions are not legally considered punishment and are not intended to serve in lieu of punishment; punishment may be awarded only "at NJP" (by means of an NJP proceeding) or by a court-martial. Administrative actions may be taken in addition to or instead of disciplinary action as circumstances warrant. Such action does not preclude further disciplinary action, and in many cases both disciplinary action and appropriate administrative actions are taken.

Nonjudicial Punishment (NJP)

Authority to Impose NJP. The authority to impose NJP rests with the commander, CO, or officer in charge (OIC) of a unit, and it may normally be delegated only in the case of a flag officer to a principal assistant who acts as NJP authority for the unit. For the purposes of this appendix, the person with the authority to administer NJP at a unit is called the CO.

The CO has NJP authority over all military personnel who are members of the command at the time the punishment is imposed, regardless of whether such authority existed at the time the crime occurred. This authority extends to all personnel temporarily assigned to the command and members of embarked staffs and units.

Types of Offenses. The CO has broad discretion to decide whether to handle an offense administratively, to pursue NJP, or to refer it to a court-martial. In general, NJP is used for "minor" offenses that could not result in a dishonorable discharge or in confinement for more then one year if tried at a court-martial.

Executive Officer's Inquiry (XOI). Most commands precede NJP with an informal hearing called the executive officer's inquiry. The XO reviews the report of the PIO and may personally examine the evidence and interview witnesses, the chain of command, and the accused before making a determination whether to forward the case to the CO for NJP. Some commands utilize a disciplinary review board (DRB) consisting of the command master chief and other senior enlisted members who review the evidence and make recommendations for disposition of the case prior to, or instead of, XOI.

Refusal of NJP. Enlisted personnel who are not attached to or embarked in a vessel may refuse NJP and request court-martial, as may all officers. The right to refuse NJP expires when punishment is imposed. The accused has the right to be present at the NJP hearing. Although he or she may request to waive the right to a personal appearance, the CO may require appearance. An NJP hearing may not be held on someone who is an unauthorized absentee or is otherwise in absentia.

Rights at NJP. The accused has the right to remain silent, to have a personal representative (not necessarily an attorney), to examine the evidence against him or her, to present matters in defense or in mitigation and extenuation, and to call any reasonably available witnesses (although civilian witnesses may not be subpoenaed to appear at an NJP hearing). The accused does not have the right to consult with an attorney, and military attorneys are not appointed to represent service members at NJP, although those who have the right to refuse NJP must be afforded the opportunity to consult with an attorney specifically about that right. The accused may hire a civilian lawyer at his or her own expense, but this lawyer enjoys no special status at NJP beyond that of any other personal representative. The accused has the right to a public hearing but may request a "closed mast." If the CO grants the request for a closed mast, at least one other witness, such as the command master chief, generally remains present.

As the name indicates, NJP is not a judicial proceeding, and imposition of punishment is not considered a finding of guilt or a conviction. Military rules of evidence do not apply at NJP; the CO's standard for imposing punishment is a preponderance of the evidence rather than proof beyond a reasonable doubt. However, COs generally do not pursue NJP in cases in which the evidence would not be sufficient for a court-martial conviction.

At NJP, the CO may take one of the following actions:

• Dismiss the offense, with or without warning, and/or take administrative measures
• Impose authorized punishment
• Refer the matter to a court-martial
• Postpone the matter, such as when waiting for additional evidence to become available

The punishments for enlisted personnel at NJP vary, depending on the pay grade of the CO imposing the punishment. A CO in the pay grade of 0–4 or above is authorized to impose punishments that include:

• Punitive reprimand or admonition
• Restriction to the limits of the ship (or, for a shore command, to prescribed limits of the command) for up to sixty days;

or correctional custody for up to thirty days; or, if attached to or embarked in a vessel, confinement on bread and water for up to three days

- Extra duties of no more than two hours per day for up to forty-five days
- Reduction in rate one pay grade
- Forfeiture of up to one-half of one month's pay for up to two months

These punishments are more severe than those that may be imposed by COs below pay grade O-4 or by OICs of any rank. There are also varying limits to the punishments that may be imposed on officers, again depending on the pay grade of the CO imposing the punishment.

The entire punishment may be set aside, or the unexecuted portion of it may be remitted, by the officer imposing NJP, by his or her successor in command, by the service member's next CO (if the member is transferred), or by a higher appellate authority. Such actions must normally be taken within four months of the date of the imposition of punishment, and they may be undertaken only to correct a clear injustice. In addition, these same authorities may mitigate the punishment, by reducing it in quantity or severity, or suspend the punishment for up to six months. Suspension is normally contingent on another action being performed by the individual, such as completion of a rehabilitation course or restitution to a victim of theft or vandalism. Someone who violates the terms of suspension or UCMJ may have his or her initial sentence vacated by any authority competent to impose punishment.

A service member may appeal any punishment awarded at NJP to the area coordinator or flag officer with general court-martial authority. There are only two grounds for appeal: that the punishment was unjust (the evidence did not indicate that the accused committed the offense), or that the punishment was disproportionate (excessively harsh or unfair) in relation to the offense. Appeals must be filed in writing via the officer imposing the punishment within five calendar days, although extensions may be requested and granted. An individual appealing NJP may request a stay of any restriction, extra duty, or confinement on bread and water pending the outcome of the appeal.

Courts-Martial

Courts-martial are used to try more serious offenses than those normally disposed of at nonjudicial punishment, although less serious offenses may also be referred to court-martial when a service member refuses NJP. The standard of proof for conviction at a court-martial is "beyond a reasonable doubt."

Summary Court-Martial (SCM). The function of a summary court-martial is to exercise justice promptly for relatively minor offenses. Any CO may convene an SCM. Any person subject to the UCMJ, except officers, cadets, and midshipmen, may be tried by summary court-martial. A summary court-martial is composed of one commissioned officer in pay grade O-3 or above in the same armed force as the accused. All personnel have the right to consult with counsel prior to the court-martial, but not to be represented by counsel. Personnel may refuse trial by summary court-martial, in which case the offense will likely be referred to a higher court-martial.

The maximum punishment that may be awarded at an SCM is confinement at hard labor for thirty days (for those in pay grade E-4 and below); reduction in rate to pay grade E-1 (for those in pay grade E-4 and below), or reduction in rate one pay grade (for those above pay grade E-4); and forfeiture of two-thirds pay for one month.

Special Court-Martial (SPCM). A special court-martial is convened for noncapital or capital crimes for which the mandatory sentence for the crime does not exceed the maximum punishment that such a court may impose. A CO or anyone senior to the CO in the chain of command may convene an SPCM. The court consists of at least three members; any commissioned or warrant officers are eligible to serve on the court-martial. If the accused so requests, enlisted members may serve on the court-martial. A two-thirds majority is required to convict. The accused may also request a trial by military judge alone.

A service member appearing before an SPCM has the right to be represented by counsel, which may be either a military lawyer or a civilian lawyer retained at the expense of the accused. A trial counsel represents the government.

The maximum punishment that an SPCM may impose on an enlisted member is either (1) a bad-conduct discharge, confinement at hard labor for six months, forfeiture of two-thirds pay per month for six months, and a reduction in rate to pay grade E-1, or (2) the maximum punishment for that particular offense, whichever is less. Officers are subject to lesser punishments.

General Court-Martial (GCM). The convening authority for a general court-martial is generally a flag officer or other senior officer serving as an area coordinator. A general court-martial is convened for capital crimes and serious noncapital crimes. The court consists of at least five members; as in the special court-martial, the court may include any commissioned or warrant officers or, if the accused so requests, enlisted members. In most circumstances a two-thirds majority is required to convict; imposition of more than ten years at hard labor requires a three-fourths majority; and imposition of the death penalty must be unanimous. In noncapital cases an accused may request a trial by military judge alone.

A service member appearing before a GCM has the right to be represented by counsel, either a military lawyer or a civilian lawyer retained at his or her own expense. A trial counsel represents the government.

The maximum punishment that may be imposed on an officer or enlisted member by a GCM is the maximum punishment for the particular offense. This may be death, dishonorable discharge, confinement at hard labor for life, total forfeiture of pay, or reduction in rate to pay grade E-1.

Administrative Law

Administrative Fact-Finding Body. An administrative fact-finding body, which may be as small as one individual, is constituted under the *Manual of the Judge Advocate General* to collect and record information on a particular incident. Such investigations are commonly referred to as *JAG Manual* investigations. Common situations in which such an investigation would be initiated are accidents resulting in serious injury, death, or significant damage to or loss of government property. An administrative fact-finding body is not judicial; its findings and opinions do not represent legal judgments. The findings may, however, be used as the basis for a convening authority's decision to pursue a trial by court-martial. *JAG Manual* investigations may be informal fact-finding bodies, formal fact-finding bodies, or courts of inquiry, depending on the seriousness of the incidents under investigation.

Line of Duty/Misconduct Investigations. Whenever a service member is seriously injured or contracts a serious disease, a specific type of *JAG Manual* investigation, called a line of duty/misconduct investigation, must be conducted. This investigation reviews the circumstances of the injury or illness and makes specific recommendations on whether the injury/illness occurred in the line of duty and whether it was due to the individual's own misconduct.

"Line of duty" is not synonymous with "on duty" or "while performing official duties" but rather indicates the service member's good standing at the time of the incident. Injuries or illnesses that occur while the individual is not an unauthorized absentee, and that do not occur as a result of his or her own misconduct, are presumed to have occurred in the line of duty.

"Misconduct" is wrongful conduct. An illness or injury is considered to be due to the service member's own misconduct when it results from gross negligence, reckless disregard of the consequences, or commission of a crime. A finding of misconduct always results in a finding of "not in the line of duty."

Although a similar investigation is done when an injury or illness results in death, opinions as to line of duty and misconduct are not expressed in the investigation report. In such cases the Veterans Administration makes this determination.

Administrative Discharges. There are four types of administrative discharge that may be awarded to enlisted personnel:

• Honorable: An honorable discharge is awarded when the service member has performed honorable and proper military service.

• General under honorable conditions: This type of discharge is awarded to those whose military records are satisfactory but less than what is required for an honorable discharge.

• Other-than-honorable (OTH): The most negative administrative discharge, an OTH discharge is awarded to those whose performance in the military has not been satisfactory. The long-term effects of an OTH discharge on an individual's VA benefits and future employability in the civilian sector are nearly as severe as the effects of a punitive discharge.

• Entry-level separation: An entry-level separation may be awarded to members within the first 180 days of service. This type of separation is neutral in nature and is intended as a means of separating individuals who are truly not suited for the service.

Bad-conduct discharges and dishonorable discharges are not administrative and may only be awarded as the result of a trial by court-martial.

Enlisted members may be involuntarily separated from the Navy for a variety of reasons that include (but are not limited to) misconduct, unsatisfactory performance, homosexuality, and drug abuse. When the reason for the separation could result in an other-than-honorable discharge, or when the individual has six or more years of military service, he or she is permitted the opportunity to appear before an administrative discharge board. This board, consisting of three or more commissioned officers, warrant officers, or enlisted members in pay grade E-7 and senior, evaluates the circumstances and makes a determination on whether the misconduct (or other reason for discharge) occurred, and whether to retain or discharge the individual. If the board determines that the individual should be discharged, it also recommends the characterization of discharge.

The findings of the board are forwarded through the chain of command to the Chief of Naval Personnel for final disposition. If the board recommended separation, the Chief of Naval Personnel may retain the individual or separate him or her with a more favorable type of discharge. If the board recommended retention, the Chief of Naval Personnel may overrule the retention recommendation only with the approval of the Secretary of the Navy. In such cases, OTH discharges may not be awarded.

GLOSSARY

Above zone. An officer being considered by a selection board who, because of having been previously passed over, is more senior than the officers who are **in zone.** *See also* **below zone.**

A-gang. Auxiliaries division of the engineering department.

Airedale. Slang term for a member of the aviation community.

Allotment. A selected amount of a member's take-home pay that is designated to be automatically withheld for a certain purpose. Allotments may be designated to be sent to certain charitable organizations or bank accounts, or to be used as loan repayments.

Allowance. A component of military compensation that is not taxable (e.g., BAH, BAS, etc.).

Attention on deck. A response given by a junior when a senior officer enters the room.

Augmentation. The process by which active-duty Naval Reserve officers become officers in the Regular Navy. Generally requires attainment of the appropriate warfare qualification, submission of an augmentation request letter, and selection by a transfer/redesignation board.

Aye, aye. A response to an order signifying that the order was heard, was understood, and will be carried out.

BAH. Basic allowance for housing. A component of compensation to help offset the cost of off-base housing. Varies by pay grade and location.

BAS. Basic allowance for subsistence. A component of compensation to help defray food costs for service members who are not required to take their meals "in kind."

Base pay. The primary component of military compensation. Increases with pay grade (rank) and length of service. *See also* **fogey.**

Below zone. An officer being considered by a selection board who is junior to the officers **in zone.** If selected, this officer would be an early selectee. *See also* **above zone.**

Bilge. The rounded interior of the hull. When used as a verb, a slang term indicating utter failure.

Binnacle list. Sick list.

Black shoe. Slang term for a member of the surface or submarine community. Refers to the black shoes traditionally worn by nonaviators.

Blue water. Literally, "deep water," but more traditionally, "away from land."

Boat. A small vessel that may be hoisted aboard a ship. Also used to refer to a submarine.

Boomer. Slang term for a ballistic-missile submarine.

Boondoggle. Slang term for a temporary assignment viewed as largely recreational in nature.

Bravo Zulu. Phonetic pronunciation of BZ, from the NATO signal codes, signifying "Well done."

Bridge. The location on board ship from which the conning officer gives orders to the helm.

Brown shoe. Slang term for a member of the aviation community. Refers to the brown shoes traditionally worn by aviators.

Brown water. Shallow, inland water.

Bubblehead. Slang term for submariner.

Bull ensign. Senior ensign in a command. Traditionally wears oversized ensign insignia.

Bullnose. A chock placed right over the stem of the ship.

BUPERS. Bureau of Naval Personnel. Formerly known as NMPC, Navy Military Personnel Command.

Captain's mast. Nonjudicial disciplinary procedure, a.k.a. NJP.

Carry on. An order to resume or continue previous activity, given by a senior after juniors have come to attention.

Cheng. Chief engineer.

Chit. A form used to request leave, liberty, or other special requests.

CMAA. Chief master at arms. The enlisted member serving as the head of a command's law enforcement organization.

CMC. Command master chief. Senior enlisted person in the command. *Cf.* **COB,** for submarines.

CO. Commanding officer. The captain or skipper of a vessel.

COB. Chief of the boat. Senior enlisted person on board a submarine.

CONUS. Continental United States.

Crow. Slang term for the rate insignia of a petty officer (E-4 and above), so called because of the eagle surmounting the rate chevrons.

Cumshaw. Unauthorized, unofficial procurement of needed material outside the supply system, usually involving barter.

DC. Damage control.

DCA. Damage-control assistant. The officer responsible, under the chief engineer, for damage control and stability of a ship.

DDS. Direct deposit system. A mandatory process of directly depositing a member's paycheck to his or her bank account.

Dead horse. A pay advance (usually one to two months' base pay) taken in conjunction with a **PCS** move, generally paid back over the following twelve months. The equivalent of an interest-free loan.

Designated striker. A sailor in pay grades E-1 though E-3 who has a rating.

Designator. The four-digit code (e.g., 1165, 1700) assigned to an officer to designate his or her community/warfare specialty.

DFAS. Defense Finance and Accounting Service. Managers of the military pay system.

Dink. Slang term for delinquent watch qualifications.

DITY. Do it yourself. Refers to a type of **PCS** move in which the service member moves some or all of his or her own household goods and is reimbursed by the government some percentage of what a commercial mover would have charged.

Dog watch. A shortened watch period. Generally, breaking up the four-hour 1600–2000 watch into two two-hour watches, 1600–1800 and 1800–2000, so that personnel on watch can eat the evening meal. This practice also provides an odd number of watches to rotate sections through the daily watches.

Dolphins. Slang term for the warfare insignia of submariners.

Due course. A "due course" officer is one who has been promoted **in zone** (as opposed to **above zone** or **below zone**).

Duty-preference card. A.k.a. "dream sheet." Form used to advise detailers of members' duty-assignment preferences.

EAOS. End of active obligated service. The end of an enlistment or extension to an enlistment. Term is applicable only to enlisted members; all officers have "indefinite" EAOSs, even if they are obligated for a certain amount of continued service.

8 o'clock reports. Equipment status reports made, usually at 2130, by all department heads to the XO, who then takes them to the CO. *Cf.* **12 o'clock reports.**

EMI. Extra military instruction. Additional duties assigned to improve a sailor's performance of duties or military knowledge. Not legally considered a form of punishment.

Ensign. The national colors, or the most junior commissioned officer rank.

EOOW. Engineer officer of the watch.

Field day. To clean a ship's spaces thoroughly.

First lieutenant. Deck division officer or department head aboard a surface ship.

FITREP. Fitness report. Performance assessment issued to officers and senior enlisted members. (Similar form for junior enlisted members is called an enlisted evaluation.)

Flag officer. Admiral (pay grade O-7 and senior).

Fogey. Slang term for an increase in base pay as a result of longevity (time in service).

FOS. Fail of select (for promotion).

Gedunk. Slang term for junk food/candy, or a place to buy it.

George. Slang term for the junior ensign in a command.

Goat locker. Slang term for chiefs' mess.

Gouge. Slang term for valuable information. The naval equivalent of *scoop.*

GQ. General quarters. The call for all hands to man battle stations.

Green water. The littoral, or coastal areas. Intermediate between open ocean (blue water) and inland (brown water).

Gundecking. Intentional falsification, generally in reference to maintenance records.

Hack. Informal (and not legally sanctioned) confinement to quarters or to the ship.

Head. Naval term for bathroom.

Hollywood shower. An excessively long shower that wastes water. *Cf.* **Navy shower.**

In zone. That group of officers, delineated by date of rank, who are to be considered by a promotion selection board. Most officers selected are those who are "in zone." *Cf.* **above zone** and **below zone.**

IRAD. Involuntary release from active duty. Can apply to a Naval Reserve officer or an enlisted person who is sent home involuntarily, usually as a result of a drawdown.

ISIC. Immediate superior in command. The officer who is next senior in the chain of command to a unit's CO.

Jack. A triangular replica of the blue star-studded field of the national ensign. It is flown at the bow by ships at anchor or moored to a pier from 0800 to sunset.

Jacob's ladder. A portable ladder used to board a ship.

Joint duty. Specifically designated duty with a "joint" (i.e., multiservice) command, staff, or mission. Joint duty credit is generally required for selection to flag rank.

Leave. All service members earn thirty days of paid leave each year (two and a half days per month) and (under most circumstances) may carry up to sixty days of leave on the books. Up to sixty days of unused leave may be sold back (exchanged for an equivalent number of days' base pay) in the course of a career; officers may generally do this only at separation or retirement, and enlisted members may do it at the end of any enlistment period.

LES. Leave and earnings statement. Monthly statement of a member's pay and allowance entitlements, taxes withheld, and leave balance.

Liberty. Authorized absence from an enlisted member's duty station. The correct equivalent term for officers is *shore leave*.

Line. Naval term for rope.

Lose the bubble. Originally, to assume such an extreme up- or down-angle in a submarine that the bubble of the inclinometer is no longer visible. In common slang usage, to lose situational awareness or to panic.

Lucky bag. Lost and found administered by the chief master at arms.

Main control. The engineering space from which the **EOOW** controls operations of the engineering plant.

Main space. The engine room.

Manning the rails. The practice of stationing sailors along the rails of a ship when rendering honors or entering port, or upon returning to home port at the end of a deployment.

Mess. A space where meals are served (e.g., the chiefs' mess).

Midwatch. A watch stood from midnight until 0400.

MPA. Main propulsion assistant.

Mustang. An officer who started out as an enlisted member and rose through the ranks.

MWR. Morale, welfare, and recreation.

Navy shower. A shower that utilizes appropriate water conservation measures. The procedure is to turn on the water to get wet, turn it off while soaping up, then turn it on to rinse. *Cf.* **Hollywood shower.**

NEC codes. Navy enlisted classification codes. Numerical codes used to designate special skills and qualifications of enlisted personnel.

NFO. Naval flight officer.

NJP. Nonjudicial punishment, a.k.a. captain's mast.

Nuc or **nuke.** Slang term for nuclear-trained officer or enlisted member.

OBE. Overcome by events, meaning that a previous concern or question is no longer applicable because of changed circumstances.

ODC. Officer data card. A summary sheet containing information on an officer's training, qualifications, billets held, designator and promotion history, and other key information.

Oh dark thirty. Slang term meaning "the middle of the night."

OOD. Officer of the deck.

Oscar. The dummy used for man-overboard drills, so named for the international signal flag hoisted for "man overboard."

OUTUS. Outside the continental United States (includes Alaska and Hawaii). *Cf.* CONUS.

Padeye. A recessed tie-down point or anchor point on a bulkhead or deck.

Pay. A component of military compensation that is taxable (e.g., base pay, sea pay, special duty assignment pay, etc.).

Pay grade. Alphanumeric designation corresponding to the relative seniority of a member of the service. *O* designates an officer, *W* a warrant officer, and *E* an enlisted member. For example, O-1 is an ensign, W-2 is a chief warrant officer two, and E-1 is a recruit.

PCS. Permanent change of station. Used in reference to orders that permanently move a service member from one duty station to another.

PEBD. Pay entry base date. The date (usually the day a member begins active-duty service) from which all **fogeys** are calculated.

Per diem. Daily allowance to cover cost of meals, lodging, and certain other authorized expenses incurred while in a **TAD** or travel status.

Pilothouse. The location aboard ship in which the helmsman stands watch.

Police. To inspect and clean up.

POV. Privately owned vehicle.

PQS. Personnel Qualification System. A method of formalizing and tracking the qualification process of personnel toward watch station certification.

PRD. Projected rotation date. The date (generally month and year) a service member's tour at a given duty station is anticipated to end.

Proceed time. Additional time, not charged as leave, allowed for **PCS** transfers to or from certain types of duty.

PSD. Personnel support detachment. A shore-based organization that handles service records and pay for a group of commands in the geographic area.

Quarterdeck. The ceremonial area of a ship where the **OOD** stands watch in port.

Rack. Slang term for bunk.

Rate. Combination of enlisted rating and pay grade. For example, a service member in the YN rating with a pay grade of E-5 has the rate YN2.

Rating. Enlisted occupational specialty—e.g., YN (yeoman), MM (machinist's mate), etc.

Ring knocker. Slang term for a graduate of the U.S. Naval Academy.

Scuttle. A watertight opening set in a hatch or bulkhead. Used as a verb, the intentional sinking of a ship to prevent its capture.

Sea daddy. Slang term for a mentor who takes a less experienced crew member under his or her wing.

Sea lawyer. Slang term for a sailor who has or professes to have significant knowledge of military laws and regulations and attempts to use this knowledge for personal benefit.

SERB. Selective early retirement board. Reviews the records of senior, retirement-eligible officers or enlisted personnel for involuntary early retirement.

SGLI. Servicemen's Group Life Insurance. A type of term life insurance available to service members, which is charged at a flat rate of 8 cents per month per $1,000 coverage, to a maximum of $200,000 coverage.

Shift colors. When a ship moors or anchors, the ensign is broken on the stern, and the jack is broken on the bow, simultaneously with the ensign being hauled down from the mainmast. "Shift colors" occurs when the first line is made fast to the pier or the anchor touches the bottom. When a ship gets under way, the process is reversed as soon as the last line is let go from the pier or the anchor breaks free of the bottom.

Shore leave. The correct term for the officer equivalent of liberty.

Small boy. Slang term for a small combatant, such as a frigate or destroyer.

Smoking lamp. From the days of sail, a lamp from which personnel could light their pipes or cigars. In contemporary usage, the sentence "The smoking lamp is lighted" (never "lit") signifies that smoking is permitted.

Snipe. Slang term for an engineer.

Subspecialty code. A code assigned to an officer to document specific advanced education or significant experience in a particular recognized area.

TAD. Temporary additional duty. Describes duty under orders issued by a permanent duty station for a relatively brief assignment in another location.

TAR. Training and Administration of Reserves. Active-duty personnel whose mission is to provide for the readiness of the Navy's reserve forces.

TEMDUINS. Temporary duty under instruction. Assignment to a training facility while en route to a permanent duty station.

Turn to. Commence work.

12 o'clock reports. Reports on various administrative matters, including fuel and water, magazine temperature, position, and other reports, provided to the **OOD** by the appropriate officers for delivery to the CO just prior to 1200. *Cf.* **8 o'clock reports.**

Two-blocked. Having reached the maximum limit of something. The term originated from the use of block and tackle for hoisting. When the two blocks touch, lifting can proceed no farther.

UA. Unauthorized absence. The naval equivalent of the Army's AWOL (absent without leave).

UIC. Unit identification code. A five-digit numerical code used to identify a particular command or an individual component of a large command.

UNREP. Underway replenishment. The transfer of supplies, fuel, munitions, and personnel from one ship to another while at sea.

VERTREP. Vertical replenishment. The transfer of supplies, munitions, or personnel via helicopter.

Very well. A response given by a senior to a junior in response to a report. Never said by a junior to a senior.

Wardroom. The space aboard ship where officers take their meals, relax, and socialize. Also used as a collective term for a command's officers.

XO. Executive officer. Second in command.

Zulu time. Greenwich Mean Time (GMT).

SOURCES

Works Consulted

In preparing this book the authors have consulted various instructions, directives, and general messages published by the Department of Defense, the Department of the Navy, OPNAV, BUPERS, and other Navy commands, as well as the following specific sources.

U.S. Government Publications

The Armed Forces Officer. DoD GEN-36A, 1988.

Career Information Team Pre-Separation Brief. Commander, Naval Reserve Recruiting Command, 1995.

Command Excellence: What It Takes to Be the Best. Naval Military Personnel Command, 1985.

The Commander's Quick Reference Manual for Legal Issues. Naval Justice School, 1997.

Educational Programs in the Department of Defense. Department of Defense, 1996.

Federal Benefits for Veterans and Dependents, 1997 Edition. Department of Veterans Affairs, 1997.

Forward . . . from the Sea. Department of the Navy, 1994.

From the Sea. Department of the Navy, 1992.

Instructor Guide, Introduction to Naval Science. Chief of Naval Education and Training P1550/5, Rev. 4-96.

It's Your Move. NAVSUP Publication 380, 1991.

Joint Warfare of the U.S. Armed Forces. Joint Publication 1, 1991.

Law for the Junior Officer. U.S. Naval Academy, NL-400, 1987.

Manual for Courts-Martial. Joint Service Committee on Military Justice, 1995.

National Military Strategy. Joint Chiefs of Staff, 1995.

Naval Command and Control. Naval Doctrine Publication 6, 1995.

Naval Orientation. NAVEDTRA 12966, 1991.

Naval Warfare. Naval Doctrine Publication 1, 1994.

Navy Policy Book. Chief of Naval Operations, May 1992.

Organization of the United States Army. Department of the Army Pamphlet 10-1, 1994.

Origin of Naval Terminology. U.S. Government Printing Office, 1976.

Preseparation Guide. DA PAM 635-4; NAVMC 2916; AFJMAN 36-2128; NAVPERS 15616, 1994.

Reference Guide to Post-Government Service Employment Activities of Department of the Navy Personnel. Department of the Navy, Office of the Judge Advocate General, NAVSO P-1778, Rev. 3-97.

Standard Organization and Regulations Manual, U.S. Navy (SORM). Office of the Chief of Naval Operations, OP-NAVINST 3120.32, Apr. 1994.

Student Guide for Command Leadership Course. CIN P-1B-0004, Chief of Naval Education and Training, 1997.

Summary of Educational Benefits. VA Pamphlet 22-90-2, 1996.

U.S. Navy Regulations. U.S. Government Printing Office, 504-691/0, 1990.

Useful Information for Newly Commissioned Officers. NAVEDTRA 12967, 1992.

Veterans Benefits . . . Don't Leave the Service without Them! Department of Veterans Affairs, 1993.

Internet Sites

Air Force home page:
www.af.mil

Army home page:
www.army.mil

Bureau of Naval Personnel home page:
www.bupers.navy.mil
(includes text of *Perspective* and file of NAVADMIN messages)

Chief of Naval Education and Training home page:
www.cnet.navy.mil

Coast Guard home page:
www.uscg.mil

Code of Federal Regulations:
www.access.gpo.gov/nara/cfr/cfr-table-search.html

Cyberspace Association of U.S. Submariners:
www.subnet.com

Defense Finance and Accounting Service:
www.dfas.mil
(includes pay and allowance tables)

Defense Link:
www.defenselink.mil
(includes text of *DoD Organization and Functions Guidebook*)

Defense Technical Information Center:
www.dtic.mil
(includes JCS home page)

Department of Veterans Affairs:
www.va.gov

Marine Corps home page:
www.usmc.mil

Military Spouses' Career Network:
w3.nai.net/~military/

NATO Handbook:
www.nato.int/docu/handbook/home.htm

NATO home page:
www.nato.int

Naval Academy home page:
www.nadn.navy.mil

Naval Historical Center:
www.history.navy.mil

Naval Reserve home page:
www.ncts.navy.mil/navresfor/
(includes text of *Merchant Marine Reserve Handbook* and *One Navy Force . . . a Guide to the Naval Reserve*)

Navy Electronics Directives System (NEDS):
neds.nebt.daps.mil
(includes downloadable text of all SECNAV and OPNAV unclassified directives)

Navy Office of General Counsel ethics information page:
www.ogc.secnav.hq.navy.mil/ogcwww/ethics.html

Navy Public Affairs Library:
www.chinfo.navy.mil/navpalib/.www/subject.html
(including links to *All Hands*, Navy fact files, and other Navy commands)

NORAD home page:
131.15.144.52/norad/noradfs.htm

OAS home page:
www.oas.org

Per Diem, Travel, and Transportation Allowance Committee
(PDTATAC):
www.dtic.mil/perdiem/
(includes text of *Joint Federal Travel Regulations* at
www.perdiem.osd.mil)

Personnel Support Activity, San Diego:
www.psasd.navy.mil

State Department pages:
www.state.gov

Surface Navy Association:
www.cais.net/sna/

United Nations home page:
www.un.org

United States Code:
www.law.cornell.edu/uscode/

United States Naval Institute:
www.usni.org

Washington Headquarters Services Directives and
Records Branch:
web7.whs.osd.mil/corres.htm
(downloadable text of unclassified DoD directives)

Further Reading

U.S. Government Publications

The Department of the Navy Social Usage and Protocol Handbook. OPNAVINST 1710.7, 1979.

Joint Vision 2010. Chairman, Joint Chiefs of Staff (Gen. John M. Shalikashvili), 1996.

Navy Military Personnel Manual. Chief of Naval Personnel, NAVPERS 15560 (current edition is 15560C), Aug. 1991.

United States Naval Uniform Regulations. Chief of Naval Personnel, NAVPERS15665 (current edition is 15665I), Aug. 1995.

Other Publications

Beardon, Bill. *Bluejacket's Manual.* 21st ed. Annapolis, Md.: Naval Institute Press, 1990.

Mack, William P., Vice Adm., and Lt. Cdr. Royal W. Connell. *Naval Ceremonies, Customs, and Traditions.* 5th ed. Annapolis, Md.: Naval Institute Press, 1980.

Mack, William P., Vice Adm., and Cdr. Albert H. Konetzni. *Command at Sea.* 4th ed. Annapolis, Md.: Naval Institute Press, 1982.

Shenk, Robert. *Naval Institute Guide to Naval Writing.* 2d ed. Annapolis, Md.: Naval Institute Press, 1997.

Stavridis, James, Cdr. *Division Officer's Guide.* 10th ed. Annapolis, Md.: Naval Institute Press, 1995.

———. *Watch Officer's Guide.* 13th ed. Annapolis, Md.: Naval Institute Press, 1992.

Swartz, Oretha D. *Service Etiquette.* 4th ed. Annapolis, Md.: Naval Institute Press, 1988.

INDEX

ABOUT THE AUTHORS

Vice Admiral William P. Mack retired in 1975 after forty-two years of service. He served in battleships, destroyers, and amphibians and culminated his sea service with command of the Seventh Fleet during the height of the 1972 North Vietnamese offensive. Ashore he served in a number of personnel billets and as a naval aide to the secretary of the navy, deputy assistant secretary of defense for personnel, and finally as superintendent of the Naval Academy. He has written several books on naval subjects and three novels.

Captain Harry A. Seymour Jr. is a 1965 graduate of the Naval Academy and completed many assignments, including two tours at his alma mater and two at-sea commands, before he retired in 1989. He currently serves as the vice president of the Naval Academy Fund for the Alumni Association.

Commander Lesa A. McComas is an active duty surface warfare officer currently serving as associate professor of naval science at the University of California at Berkeley.